Allegories of One's Own Mind

Allegories of One's Own Mind

Melancholy in Victorian Poetry

David G. Riede

The Ohio State University Press
Columbus

Copyright © 2005 by The Ohio State University.
All rights reserved.

Library of Congress Cataloging-in-Publication Data
Riede, David G.
Allegories of one's own mind : melancholy in Victorian poetry / David G. Riede.
p. cm.
Includes bibliographical references and index.
ISBN 0–8142–1008–2 (cloth : alk. paper)—ISBN 0–8142–9085–X (cd)
1. English poetry—19th century—History and criticism. 2. Melancholy in literature. I. Title.
PR595.M34.R54 2005
821.'809353—dc22

2005005578

Cover design by Dan O'Dair
Type set in Adobe Garamond

The paper used in this publication meets the minimum requirements of the American National Standard for Information Sciences—Permanence of Paper for Printed Library Materials. ANSI Z39.48–1992.

9 8 7 6 5 4 3 2 1

For Natalie

Contents

Acknowledgments — ix

CHAPTER 1
Melancholy and Victorian Poetry — 1

CHAPTER 2
Tennyson's Hollow Oes and Aes — 41

CHAPTER 3
Elizabeth Barrett and the Emotion of the Trapped — 91

CHAPTER 4
"Filthy Rags of Speech": Browning's Melancholy Optimism — 134

CHAPTER 5
Edward Fitzgerald: Melancholy, Orientalism, Aestheticism — 188

Notes — 203

Works Cited — 211

Index — 221

Acknowledgments

This book has been an unconscionably long time in production, partly because "melancholy" remains a notoriously difficult term to define with any precision and partly, no doubt, because, like Lou Gehrig's disease, it tends to reproduce its symptoms in its students—all of its symptoms, it seems, except genius. A crucial Victorian symptom, I argue, is "multitudinousness," an anomic lack of focus producing kaleidoscopic, disordered representation. I am grateful to a number of colleagues and critics who struggled through the multitudinous earlier versions of this book, or parts of it, for helping me to find and articulate foci to organize a structured argument, to the extent that I have done so. I am particularly indebted in this regard to Audrey Jaffe, John Maynard, Walter Davis, Herbert Tucker, Maneck Daruwala, Marlene Longenecker, and Jean Gregorek. For helping to dissipate other symptoms of melancholy, I am grateful not only to these helpful readers, critics, and friends, but also to the support of numerous others, including especially Jim Battersby, Lisa Kiser, Clare Simmons, Mark Conroy, and the many geniuses at O'Reilly's. I am grateful also for research support from the Department of English and the College of Humanities at Ohio State, and for the support of Heather Lee Miller at The Ohio State University Press. Part ii of chapter 2 is a slightly revised version of an earlier article, "Tennyson's Poetics of Melancholy and the Imperial Imagination," reprinted with permission from *SEL Studies in English Literature 1500–1900* 40 (Autumn 2000), and I am grateful to be able to use it here. Finally, I am boundlessly grateful to Natalie Tyler for limitless intellectual and emotional support.

CHAPTER ONE

Melancholy and Victorian Poetry

I. Victorian Melancholy

In many respects the transition from the Romantic to the Victorian poetic tradition is nearly seamless: the early poetry of Tennyson, Robert Browning, and Elizabeth Barrett Browning so closely apprentices them to the second generation of Romantic poets that this first generation of Victorian poets, who began to publish well before Victoria's ascension, can reasonably be regarded as a third generation of Romantics. Similarly, the clear apprenticeship of Arnold to Wordsworth suggests a smooth continuation of early Romanticism into the mid-Victorian period. In one highly significant respect, however, the Romantic and Victorian periods are sharply divided, at least to the extent that Victorians continued to identify Romanticism with Wordsworthian formulations of the poetic character and with Coleridge's theological/philosophical poetics of "joy," the healthy mind's imaginative echo of the "eternal I AM," both God's creative Word and "Nature's holy plan."[1] The Victorians, yet more eager for poetry to supply the need for an authoritative cultural discourse, were much less confident about the sources of poetic authority and tended to see their age as suffering from a disabling post-Wordsworthian melancholy akin to the mood Coleridge had already described in "Dejection: An Ode" at a time when the creative power of "joy" was denied to him:

> A grief without a pang, void, dark, and drear,
> A stifled, drowsy, unimpassioned grief,
> Which finds no natural outlet, no relief,
> In word, or sigh, or tear—(ll.21–25)

Coleridge's dejection anticipated the more poetically productive melancholy of the first generation of post-Wordsworthian poets: the titanic suffering of Byron's gloomy heroes, the bleak skepticism of Shelley, and the luxuriant melancholy of Keats, but it more accurately anticipated the later dejection of the Victorians, who often saw melancholy as we now see depression, as a mute or incoherent mood that imprisons the sufferer within himself and the precise antithesis of poetic creativity. Ironically, however, as we will see, the rejection or policing of melancholy actually intensifies melancholy as it divides the mind more emphatically against itself and, more, the Victorian melancholy of melancholy turns out to be poetically productive rather than disabling.

In denying melancholy, such influential Victorian writers as Thomas Carlyle and Matthew Arnold evidently "protest too much" and indirectly, but emphatically, reveal the continuation of the discourse of melancholy in their work. Carlyle, in particular, counseled his generation to "close thy Byron" (*Works*, 1: 153), described Shelley "filling the earth with inarticulate wail, like the infinite, inarticulate grief and weeping of forsaken infants" (28: 31), and lamented the "diseased self-conscious state of literature" (28: 24) as a symptom of the age's degradation. At about the same time, John Stuart Mill was urging the young Robert Browning away from diseased self-conscious Romanticism by describing his Shelleyan *Pauline* as morbidly introspective to the point of insanity. By mid-century Matthew Arnold, returning to the healthier early Romantic emphasis on "joy" that he found in Schiller, was to reject the titanic, Byronic lamentation of his own *Empedocles on Etna* as morbid and unfitted for poetic representation, a "continuous state of mental distress [that] is prolonged, unrelieved by incident, hope, or resistance, in which there is everything to be endured, nothing to be done" (*Works*, 1: 1).

The urgency of Arnold's protest against melancholy, however, is symptomatic of the inevitability of melancholy in modern literature. He cited Schiller as his exponent of joy, no doubt because his usual exponents of healthy, strong-minded poetry, Goethe and Wordsworth, could not be drawn on in this context. Wordsworth, as Arnold acknowledged in "Stanzas in Memory of the Author of Obermann," attained serenity and joy only because his "eyes avert their ken / From half of human fate" (ll.53–54), and Goethe, as the author of *Faust*, was guilty of creating a prototype of just the kind of poetry Arnold was rejecting. For that matter, even Schiller could only be used here if Arnold averted his eyes from the argument of *On the Naïve and Sentimental in Literature* that "senses and reason" are now "separated in their function" and the poet no longer "gives the impression of an undivided sensuous unit and of a harmonious whole." The cultivated poet "can only express himself as a *moral* unit, i.e., as someone striving for unity" (39) and is necessarily melancholy because the "ideal is an infinite one to which he never attains" (40). The civilized poet must ever strive for the unattainable—a notion that we will see recapitulated in the melancholy of Carlyle, Ruskin, and Browning. For Schiller, "Our feeling for nature is like that of the sick man for health" (38). Nevertheless, with the supposed authority of Schiller, Arnold suppressed *Empedocles on Etna* in his "Preface" to *Poems* of 1853 and wrote the best known of all Victorian complaints about the difficulties of the modern poet:

> Into the feelings of a man so situated there entered much that we are accustomed to consider as exclusively modern. . . . What those who are familiar only with the great monuments of early Greek genius suppose to be its exclusive characteristics, have disappeared; the calm, the cheerfulness, the disinterested objectivity have disappeared; the dialogue of the mind with itself has commenced; modern problems have presented themselves; we hear already the doubts, we witness the discouragement, of Hamlet and Faust. (*Works*, 1: 1)

Rather oddly, Arnold seems to have dated the beginning of the melancholy, modern age from the time of Empedocles in the fifth century B.C., but the references to Hamlet and Faust indicate that he is really thinking back to the origins of the modern subject in the Renaissance and, implicitly, no doubt, to the more recent extravagance of that subject's representation in the overreaching of Goethe's Faust and Byron's Harold, Manfred, and other protagonists.[2] Arnold's reaction against the melancholy of such late Romanticism was most forceful in the age's most famous self-representation, "Stanzas from the Grande Chartreuse," in which he explicitly rejected the melancholy of Byron's "bleeding heart" (1.136) and Shelley's "Lovely wail" (1.140). For good or ill, the melancholy of post-Romantic literature was so pervasive as to be an "outworn theme" (1.100), as also seemed self-evident to Arthur Henry Hallam, whose early review of Tennyson's poetry referred to the "melancholy, which so evidently characterizes the spirit of modern poetry" (190). As Carlyle, Arnold, and Hallam clearly demonstrate, even the warnings against melancholy continue to keep the literary and philosophic discourse of melancholy at the center of literary history in the Victorian age.

It is probably because the Victorians often and emphatically described melancholy as we now describe depression rather than within the ancient discourse associating melancholy with "great men"[3] that Victorian melancholia has been generally neglected in literary history, as in Juliana Schiesari's excellent study of melancholy and gender. As Schiesari shows, such prominent postmodern theorists as Jacques Lacan, Jean-François Lyotard, and Julia Kristeva positioned "themselves as various kinds of melancholics" in the wake of "contemporary poststructuralist, postmodern, postMarxist, postFreudian, even postfeminist discourses" (2). In a discussion that only accidentally illuminates post-Romantic Victorian melancholy, Schiesari compares "Renaissance and postmodern melancholias" and suggests that

> we are dealing not with two different periods of dramatized loss but rather with the historical boundaries of a great age of melancholia (in Foucault's terms: an epistemic formation), whose edges are coterminous with the historic rise and demise of "the subject" as the organizing principle of knowledge and power. The prominence of the discourse of melancholia at the edges of that historical block does not point so much to a disjunction or repetition as it does to the continuity of a tradition, inaugurated by the Renaissance, refined by the Enlightenment, flaunted by Romanticism, fetishized by the Decadents and theorized by Freud. (2–3)

The omission of the high Victorian age from this catalogue of melancholic periods is not entirely surprising, if only because, due to insufficient recognition of James Thomson's *The City of Dreadful Night* (1867), the Victorians seem to have produced no literary monument to melancholia comparable to Burton's *Anatomy*, Shakespeare's *Hamlet*, Milton's "Penseroso," or Keats's "Ode."

In addition, from the scientific outlook of the Victorians, the association of melancholy with genius would look merely superstitious. Like Ebenezer Scrooge's visions, the conceptions of a disordered mind would characteristically be attributed to a malfunction of the body, a "slight disorder of the stomach . . . an undigested bit of beef, a blot of mustard, a crumb of cheese, a fragment of an underdone potato," perhaps. As William James disparagingly summed up the "medical materialism" (13) of the Victorian age, "there is not a single one of our states of mind, high or low, healthy or unhealthy, that has not some organic process as its condition" (14).[4]

Even when psychologists were inclined to speculate on the relationship of mental states to genius, they remained so attracted to the promised pleasures of the healthy imagination that they tended to associate not melancholy but exaltation with genius. One of the "medical materialists" referred to by James, the eminent psychologist Henry Maudsley, for example, attempted to associate a psychological state with "genius," but like other Victorians he looked to "genius" as a source of quasi-religious consolation in a world increasingly barren of such solace. His speculations consequently endorsed "exaltation" and he anticipated Freud's later analysis of the "true source of religious sentiments" in a "sensation of 'eternity,' a feeling as of something limitless, unbounded, as it were, 'oceanic'" (21: 64). But though he anticipated Freud in this respect, his own account of the (illusory) sources of religion and poetic feeling in a "transport of being" or "extravagant elation" (12) is in the tradition of a Wordsworthian "feeling" that can be

> claimed to represent its fundamental root in and union with the nature it issues from and always remains part of; so that where elemental instincts come into play the domain of intellect can be prescribed to end and the domain of religion to begin. Necessarily a somewhat vague and vacuous region—a spacious feeling of an infinite within as of an infinite without—but for that reason all the more delectable. (10)

Maudsley's account helps to explain why Victorians bereft of the doctrine and creeds of the Christian past found "healing power" (Arnold, "Memorial Verses,"1.63) in Wordsworth's transports of feeling in harmony with nature: in the feeling of religion, if not the creed.[5] In an age looking for spiritual solace from poetry, the Wordsworthian and Coleridgean intuition of a divine order of things glimpsed in experience of the oceanic depths of self made it difficult to formulate an idea of poetic genius associated with melancholy rather than joy. Maudsley, for example, was willing to associate genius with a very possibly pathological sense of beatitude (13–15), but he saw melancholy as mute or incoherent depression: a "feeling of deepest dejection and desolate misery with appalling loss of a sense of realities—a vast, vague, ineffable woe—notably overwhelms the victim of profound melancholia" (13). Though not published until 1908, Maudsley's *Heredity, Variation and Genius, with an Essay on Shakespeare* demonstrates a widespread Victorian hope that a consoling poetic discourse might take on the cultural work for which traditional religion was disabled by the intellectual enterprises of the day, especially the "higher criticism" of the Bible and the encroaching studies of philology, geology, astronomy, and evolution.

A reminder that early-twentieth-century works often reflect the earlier Victorian culture that engendered them, Maudsley's work encourages us to look at the work of his far greater contemporary, Freud, whose celebrated "Mourning and Melancholia" was written in 1917 but "can be shown to derive seamlessly from earlier work on melancholia and loss in the letters to his friend Wilhelm Fliess, written in 1902" (Radden, "Love and Loss," 223). Freud's immensely influential theorization of melancholia, then, may reasonably be taken as a product of the nineteenth-century culture that underlay the foundations of his thought. "Mourning and Melancholia" is recognizably akin to the work of Carlyle and Arnold in the age's literary discourse, but it also reflects the larger cultural history behind the Victorian age's characteristic nostalgia and especially its cult of mourning. Freud distinguishes mourning, the response to the loss of a specific object of love, from melancholy, which he sees as a pathology involving an impoverished sense of self, a lost sense of wholeness of being. Unlike mourning, melancholy does not necessarily result from the loss of a loved person, but rather from the loss of an internalized ego-ideal (14: 246). Freud's analysis, rooted in his prior study of narcissism, posits the internalization of loved ideals into a separate part of the ego, the conscience (later evolving in his thought as the superego) and argues that this division of the self leads to a situation in which "one part of the ego sets itself over against the other, judges it critically, and, as it were, takes it as its object" (14: 247). For Freud, melancholy consists of the loss of a loved person or ideal and the "*identification* of the ego with the abandoned object": "the shadow of the object fell upon the ego and the latter could henceforth be judged by a special agency, as though it were an object, the forsaken object. In this way an object-loss was transformed into an ego-loss and the conflict between the ego and the loved person into a cleavage between the critical activity of the ego and the ego as altered by identification" (14: 249). The conflict strongly resembles Victorian constructions of melancholy made inevitable by the recognition even in Wordsworth of the "two consciousnesses" in the mind: the "dialogue of the mind with itself" described by Arnold, the "return of the mind upon itself" described by Hallam as characteristic of melancholy, and Tennyson's idea of a "Second-rate Mind not in Unity with Itself."[6]

Freud's association of melancholy with conscience is almost certainly indebted to Hegel's dialectical analysis of unhappy consciousness in the *Phenomenology*, but for my purpose it is more significantly akin to Carlyle's diagnosis of his age's disease as the division of wholeness of mind into self-contemplation in which conscience first emerges as one part of the mind to chastise another (*Works*, 28: 7–8). Nothing could be more fundamentally Victorian than this formulation, in which "character," if not necessarily personality, is defined as the mastery of conscience over other elements of mind. This model of mind, fundamental to Victorian understanding of the self as identical with the will and self-control, is the same model that leads to Victorian earnestness.

Less systematically, Carlyle and other post-Kantian writers in England were engaged in a project much like Hegel's as they attempted to analyze the "unhappy consciousness" at the base of the modern subject. The division of mind described in Carlyle's analysis, the dialogue of the mind with itself, and the return of the mind upon itself are all versions of the modern formation of melancholy as recently described by Judith Butler, for whom Melancholia "returns us" to the figure of the "turn" as a founding trope in the discourse of the psyche:

> In Hegel, turning back upon oneself comes to signify the ascetic and skeptical modes of reflexivity that mark the unhappy consciousness; in Nietzsche, turning back on oneself suggests a retracing of what one has said or done, or a recoiling in shame in the face of what one has done. In Althusser, the turn that the pedestrian makes toward the voice of the law is at once reflexive (the moment of becoming a subject whose self-consciousness is mediated by the law) and self-subjugating. (168)

As my citations of Maudsley and Freud suggest, melancholy in the Victorian age involved not only the continuation of a literary discourse but also a social pathology in need of diagnosis. The diagnosis ultimately came in the form of Freud's *Civilization and Its Discontents,* but the discontents manifested in Victorian melancholy are historically specific to Victorian culture, since the introjection of the conscience, whether it is called the "superego," "the law of the father," "the symbolic order," or simply "character," is the introjection of the hegemonic cultural values of the age: as Samuel Smiles put it, "Character is human nature in its best form. It is moral order embodied in the individual" (quoted in Rylance, 132). Our postmodern anti-essentialism may lead us to question Smiles's invocation of "human nature," but we will all the more clearly see "moral order" as a socially constructed product of the historical moment. In fact, one reason why Victorians did not generally see melancholia as akin to genius is that they saw it not as an access to transcendent eternal truths but as historically conditioned: Maudsley argued that delusion is precipitated "in a mind saturated with the feeling of inexpressible woe; and it takes different forms according to the degree of the patient's culture, and the social, political, and religious ideas prevailing at the particular epoch" (Radden, *Nature,* 253). As Butler points out,

> the account of melancholy is an account of how psychic and social domains are produced in relation to one another. As such, melancholy offers potential insight into how the boundaries of the social are instituted and maintained, not only at the expense of psychic life, but through binding psychic life into forms of melancholic ambivalence. (167–68)

The specifically Victorian causes of melancholy are numerous, complex, and intertwined, but among the most pervasive are the emergence of an economic system alienating the products of consciousness from the working consciousness, the emergence of a rigid moral code enforcing the dictates of conscience as self-control, subordination of individual desires to the gospel of work, and, in general, the cultivation of such ideals as earnestness, character, and duty. Other major historical sources of the severity of conscience contributing to melancholy include the intellectual and scientific advances leading to the disappearance of God, the emptying of the heavens, and displacement of a providential teleology by a sense of immeasurable stretches of time in which human history is just a passing moment. For poets, the single greatest source of melancholy poetics may have been a version of Schiller's sense of the conflict between infinite inwardness and finite actuality: the incompatibility of a Romantic sense of the infinite, mysterious depths of the self with a Victorian sense of the finite socially constructed "character."

Perhaps more than any other age, the Victorians experienced the melancholy of time confronting eternity. Adding to the sensed emptiness of the cosmos was a sense of lost vitality in an emergent economic system that, as Marx showed, led to the reification and petrifaction of the human world. Further, the legacy of Romantic introspection combined with the loss of divinity and vitality in the world led to a perceived conflict between the demands of the individual and of society, especially the sense that the social order diminishes the claims of the individual. The "dialogue of the mind with itself" is, in effect, the dialogue of the ego with the cultural demands of the age, and Arnold represented it in *Empedocles on Etna* with the figure of a great poetic nature overwhelmed by the little natures that constitute the social order:

> The brave, impetuous heart yields everywhere
> To the subtle, contriving head;
> Great qualities are trodden down,
> And littleness united
> Is become invincible. (xi: 90–94)

Arnold blamed the melancholy, or anomie,[7] of his age on the "absence of great natures" (*Letters*, 1: 156), and Carlyle, similarly, saw the spiritlessness and lack of direction in the age as due to the absence of "heroes." Tennyson also lamented the loss of great natures amidst the multitudinousness of modern life: "the individual withers, and the world is more and more" ("Locksley Hall," 142). Further, his Ulysses feels diminished when called from the wide world of heroic adventure to the social demands of domesticity and duty, and much of Tennyson's other early poetry represents the difficulty of reconciling a creative individual mind with the demands of conscience or duty. The anomie of the age was paradoxically the product of a rage for moral order, just as, according to Freud, the melancholy of individuals is caused by the rage of the superego against the ego. Arnold's contrast of the "impetuous heart" with the "subtle, contriving head" is one of many Victorian references to the displacement of oceanic, infinite emotional depths by the finite moral order bounded by rationalist ideology. The suppression of "oceanic" depths of the self prevents the interpretation of such depths as either exaltation or infinite sorrow, but in itself it constitutes melancholia as a striving against inchoate and possibly mutinous depths of feeling.

As Foucault has extensively argued, the social structure of modern Western nations is based emphatically on the internalization of legal and moral policing within the self as conscience. The connection of melancholy with the development of conscience clarifies Hallam's enigmatic comment that for the belated melancholy poet "repentance is unlike innocence." The suggestion that belated poetry is somehow guilty, or transgressive, may be further glossed by reference to Nietzsche's analysis of the origins of bad conscience in *The Genealogy of Morals*.[8] Nietzsche's analysis is strikingly akin to Freud's discussion of conscience in melancholy, but it is more emphatic about the connection of guilt to the division of mind against itself. For Nietzsche, the internalization of social control within the self produced "bad conscience [as] nothing other than the instinct of freedom forced to become latent, driven underground, and forced to vent its energy upon itself" (220). Examining the same "modern" condition as Freud and Foucault, Nietzsche more immediately links his discussion with both transgression and the artistic production of beauty:

> This secret violation of the self, this artist's cruelty, this urge to impose on recalcitrant matter a form, a will, a distinction, a feeling of contradiction and contempt, this sinister task of a soul divided against itself, which makes itself suffer for the pleasure of suffering, this most energetic "bad conscience"—has it not given birth to a wealth of strange beauty and affirmation? Has it not given birth to beauty itself? (221)

The association of bad conscience with artistic production has been well discussed by Butler as a "moral laboring on oneself":

> This fundamentally artistic production of bad conscience, this production of a "form" from and of the will, is described by Nietzsche as "the womb of all ideal and imaginative phenomena." Bad conscience

is fabricated, but it in turn is credited with the fabrication of all ideal and imaginative phenomena. Is there, then, any way to answer the question of whether artistry precedes bad conscience or is its result? Is there any way to postulate something before this "turning back upon itself" which is the tropic foundation of the subject and all artistry, including all imagination and conceptual life? (76)

Butler's questions imply that the "dialogue of the mind with itself" is not, as Arnold thought, an obstacle to poetry but rather, as Hallam intimates in his essay on Tennyson, is the condition of the creative modern subject. Her comments, moreover, almost seem a description of the most important Victorian innovation in genre, the artistic production of subjects in dramatic monologues, which most characteristically involve speaking subjects imposing form on their own subjectivity as self-contemplation produces a self to be contemplated, and as the poet produces a poem for the reader's contemplation, but of course the association of unhappy consciousness with English poetry had already been definitively established by Byron's production of "Byronic heroes" as objects of aesthetic contemplation. Further, of course, for both Browning and Byron, the production of the poem involves the melancholy production of the self as a commodity. Late in the century R. L. Stevenson's *The Strange Case of Dr. Jekyll and Mr. Hyde* is a parable of the division of the conscience against the self to produce imaginative phenomena. Ronald Thomas convincingly argues that Hyde "is the text of Jekyll's own self-censorship" (251).

The disconcerting Victorian sense that the artist produces the self as a commodity, moreover, suggests that in this particular historical moment the division of mind into ego and conscience entails a further division of mind into producer and product, a division that suggests how melancholy must be further historicized within the capitalist marketplace and emergent commodity culture of the age. The cultural consequences of subject formation in modern capitalism have been well studied by the Frankfurt school critics, particularly Adorno, Benjamin, and Lukacs, whose views are deftly and concisely brought together by Beatrice Hanssen:

> [O]ffering a comparative reading of Lukacs' *Theory of the Novel* (1914–15) and [Benjamin's] *Trauerspiel* book, Adorno established that both works shared a common purpose, namely the transvaluation of nature and the natural. As he noted, Lukacs diagnosed the effects of modern capitalism in his theory of "second nature," a term that signaled the world of convention, reification, and petrifaction, as well as the ensuing alienation of the subject and his life-world, an alienation giving rise to a "charnel-house of long dead interiorities." (15)

The economic conditions contributing generally to the melancholy of the Victorian age (and our own) also contributed in very specific ways to the particular melancholy of authors in the newly developing capitalist marketplace of ideas described by Carlyle as an "angry, noisy forum" (*Works*, 1: 10), a "stunning hubbub, a true Babel-like confusion of tongues" (28: 33). Beginning in the mid-1820s changes in the economics of the publishing industry and in the political climate imposed new working conditions and expectations on authors. Even in the Romantic period Coleridge had already felt that the expanding but debased reading public was an obstacle to serious art, and later in the century Walter Bagehot and others regretted the effects of extended literacy in creating a debased reading public that included women and the undereducated lower classes. As Lee Erickson has shown, the industrialization of printing, papermaking, and even the textile industry altered the relations of authors to the means of production. For economic reasons that Erickson describes in detail, publishers almost entirely abandoned the publication of volumes of poetry by new poets, so the aspiring poet could hardly hope to come before an audience as the seemingly autonomous Romantic poets had done a generation before. As Benjamin observed, moreover,

> Around the middle of the century, the conditions of artistic production underwent a change. This change consisted in the fact that for the first time the form of the commodity imposed itself decisively on the work of art, and the form of the masses on its public. Particularly vulnerable to these developments . . . was the lyric. It is the unique distinction of *Les Fleurs du Mal* that Baudelaire responded to precisely these altered conditions with a book of poems. It is the best example of heroic conduct to be found in his life. (*Arcades*, 337)

Pace Benjamin, however, Baudelaire was scarcely unique in his response,[9] and his "heroism," as Benjamin himself notes, corresponded with a widely shared sense of "the unavoidable necessity of prostitution for the poet" (*Arcades*, 337).

As Elizabeth Barrett continually remarks in her letters, the only significant publisher of poets at this time was Moxon, who was himself wary of publishing any but the most proven of poets, specifically Barrett herself and Tennyson. The major venue of literary publication of all kinds had become the periodical press, so authors, as Carlyle complained, were forced to merge their identities with the corporate identities of the periodical to which they sold their work. In this way the social identity of the author, the "character," became explicitly reduced to and identifiable with the machinery of ideology. Worse, the very condition of selling their work in the literary marketplace involved an alienation of authors from the means of production and a commodification of their genius that Carlyle and others viewed as nothing less than the prostitution of genius: "I have said a thousand times," he said once again, "that the trade of Literature was worse as a trade than that of honest Street Sweeping: that I knew not how a man without some degree of prostitution could live by it" (*Letters*, 5: 237). This sense of prostitution within a commodity culture was widespread. Tennyson lamented "these dark ages of the Press" and hated submitting his genius to the "public thumb" (Ricks, 148–50). Browning spoke with chagrin of the need to retail his poetry where "verse-merchants most do congregate" and compared the sale of his own genius with the selling of cabbages. By marketing much of his early work in cheap pamphlets (the series called *Bells and Pomegranates*), he even attempted to create an audience beyond the reach of the "verse-merchants" by underselling the market, though with the result that he seemed to value his genius at something like the price of a cabbage. Similarly, R. H. Horne made a market for his epic *Orion* in the early 1840s by selling it for a farthing, and later in the century, John Ruskin attempted to circumvent the bourgeois marketing of literature by selling directly to working men in the letters of *Fors Clavigera*. Influenced by Ruskin, William Morris attempted to merge socialism with aestheticism, but his intervention in the cultural marketplace led to the contradictory position of his aesthetic "firm," selling beautiful objects for everyday life at prices that made them accessible not as art for the people but only as luxury items for the wealthy. Also, as Jerome McGann (1988) has argued, D. G. Rossetti's struggles to avoid the prostitution of selling his genius reveal the difficulties of achieving artistic autonomy in a capitalist economy. Perhaps the strongest example of the Victorian artist's sense of alienation in the modern marketplace is R. L. Stevenson's remark that even his subconscious mind, the source of his art, produced ideas that would sell because it was so thoroughly saturated with the values of the market. Even at their most apparently creative, he said, artists "are whores, some of us pretty whores, some of us not: whores of the mind, selling to the public the amusements of our fireside as the whore sells the pleasures of her bed" (quoted in Arata, 49). Stevenson's comment is only a more emphatic account of the division of authorial self experienced by other Victorian authors: the depths of the self are constrained by the controlling demands of public culture, and the production of the self, the author's unique "genius," as a commodity simultaneously produces the unhappy consciousness of "selling out," even though it is ultimately only selling out to itself, to the author's own conscience as the internalized moral order of the culture. Placing the author in his contemporary marketplace, then, underscores and historically contextualizes rather than answers Butler's question: "Is there . . . any way to answer the question of whether artistry precedes bad conscience or is its result?"

The economically induced shift from publications of books to a market flooded with journalism not only diminished the poet's sense of autonomous wholeness of being but also created a marketplace that inhibited the inward infiniteness of poetic feeling with public discourse. Early in the century Wordsworth had described the effects of newspapers as among the main causes of the reduction of modern consciousness to "a state of almost savage torpor,"[10] and at mid-century Arnold complained that newspapers were one of the leading causes of the fundamentally unpoetic nature of the Victorian age: "these are damned times—everything is against one—the height to which knowledge is come, the spread of luxury, our physical enervation, the absence of great *natures,* the unavoidable contact with millions of small ones, newspapers, cities . . . our own selves, and the sickening consciousness of our difficulties" (*Letters*, 1: 156).

It seems odd that the excitement of news should be associated with a "savage torpor" or even a "physical enervation," but Walter Benjamin has suggested how melancholy, newspapers, and modern commodity culture are interrelated. Describing the conditions that led to the melancholic art of Baudelaire and Proust, Benjamin discussed the effects of commodity culture:

> Man's inner concerns do not have their issueless private character by nature. They do so only when he is increasingly unable to assimilate the data of the world around him by experience. Newspapers constitute one of many evidences of such an inability. If it were the intention of the press to have the reader assimilate the information it supplies as part of his own experience, it would not achieve its purpose. But its intention is just the opposite, and it is achieved: to isolate what happens from the realm in which it could affect the experience of the reader. (*Illuminations*, 158)

Benjamin's claim that newspapers contribute to the "issueless private character" of "Man's inner concerns" suggests yet again that the effect of modern culture is to fence in the deep self with the social order, to bury melancholy consciousness within itself, a notion put still more forcefully by Theodor Adorno. Speaking of Kierkegaard, that second most melancholy Dane, Adorno argues that "in the reified world itself,"

> by its very history, mythical nature is driven back into the inwardness of the individual. Inwardness is the historical prison of primordial human nature. The emotion of the trapped is melancholy. In

> melancholy truth represents itself, and the movement of melancholy
> is one toward the deliverance of lost "meaning." A truly dialectical
> notion. (60–61)

Adorno's reference to the "emotion of the trapped" is suggestive of such Victorian representations of the claustrophobically imprisoned mind as Tennyson's "Mariana," "Lady of Shalott," and "The Palace of Art" as well as Walter Pater's famous description of solipsistically enclosed consciousness in the "Conclusion" to *Studies in the History of the Renaissance*. Further, though intimating a solution, Adorno's comments also suggest the difficulty of bringing the "truth" of melancholy to consciousness as cognitive thought or recovered "meaning." The difficulty of speaking the truth of melancholy was universally recognized: Maudsley spoke of "inexpressible woe" and "unutterable real suffering" (Radden, *Nature*, 253) and Freud's essay, notoriously vague about the cognitive content of melancholy, emphasizes that the sufferer himself "cannot consciously perceive what it is he has lost" (127), with the inevitable result that his inability to express himself, his "inhibition," "seems puzzling to us because we cannot see what it is that absorbs him so entirely" (127). The ineffable source of melancholy appears to be an infinite inwardness, a sublime of interiority or, in Maudsley's phrase, a "feeling of infinite within as of infinite without." This sense of infinite inwardness as sublime, ubiquitous in English poetry from the time of Wordsworth, is perhaps given its most emphatic form by Gerard Manley Hopkins in "No Worst There Is None": "O the mind, mind has mountains; cliffs of fall / Frightful, sheer, no-man-fathomed. Hold them cheap / May who ne'er hung there" (ll.9–11). As Hopkins's lines suggest, the "oceanic" that could be interpreted as a source of religious feeling could also be interpreted as a source of what Maudsley called vague, ineffable woe. Forceful as these lines are, however, they do not enunciate a cognitive content for melancholia but only an analogy for inward depth in the outward sublime. In effect, they domesticate the sublime in a Kantian sense, subordinating the potentially devastating power of the buried self to the critique of judgment, to the merely rational ego that projects the undiscovered country of the unconscious back into the natural world rather than delivering "lost 'meaning.'"[11]

The difficulty of representing melancholy is still more evident in Arnold's "The Buried Life," a work dedicated to the problem of depicting the depths of the inner self, specifically a "nameless sadness," a vague "something in this breast" (ll.3, 6), unavailable to consciousness and intuited as vast, infinite, but entrapped interiority:

> Still, from time to time, vague and forlorn,
> From the soul's subterranean depth upborne
> As from an infinitely distant land,
> Come airs, and floating echoes, and convey
> A melancholy into all our day. (ll.72–76)

Arnold's poem ends on a note of calm, as though he had succeeded in giving his "nameless sadness" a local habitation and a name, but like Hopkins, Arnold only substitutes an analogical outward landscape for inner depth:

> And what we mean, we say, and what we would, we know.
> A man becomes aware of his life's flow,
> And hears its winding murmur: and he sees
> The meadows where it glides, the sun, the breeze. (ll.87–90)[12]

The difficulty of representing the depths of melancholy was as great for Freud as for Arnold and Hopkins, and his essay would only have been able to characterize melancholy as the mute and inglorious depression known to the psychiatric discourse, if he had not turned suddenly to the older literary discourse about melancholia. Turning to the older tradition, and particularly to *Hamlet,* he gives the genius of melancholy a voice, or at least a spokesperson, in an eminently Victorian icon, and he locates melancholy in the peculiarly "modern problems" that Arnold located in "the dialogue of the mind with itself" inherited from Hamlet and Faust.

The special significance of *Hamlet* (and incidentally of *Faust*) for the Victorians was well stated by A. C. Bradley at the close of the century:

> wherever we are forced to feel the wonder and awe of man's godlike "apprehension" and his "thoughts that wander through eternity," and at the same time are forced to see him powerless (it would appear) from the very divinity of his thought, we remember Hamlet. And this is the reason why, in the great ideal movement which began towards the close of the eighteenth century, this tragedy acquired a position unique among Shakespeare's dramas, and shared only by Goethe's *Faust*. It was not that *Hamlet* is Shakespeare's greatest tragedy or most perfect work of art; it was that *Hamlet* most brings home to us at once the sense of the soul's infinity, and the sense of the doom which not only circumscribes that infinity but appears to be its offspring. (108)

Like other Victorians, Bradley saw Hamlet as overwhelmed by the unlimited possibilities of his own thought, paralyzed by the multitudinousness of possibilities brought on by "thinking too precisely on the event" (IV.iv.41). For Bradley, and for the Victorians more generally, Hamlet embodied the tendency of the melancholic described by Klibansky, Panofsky, and Saxl to "feed on the metaphysical contradiction between finite and infinite, time and eternity . . ." (234). Evidently for Bradley, as for Arnold, Hamlet and Faust were the prototypes of a modern subjectivity that came more widely into being with Romanticism. What Edward Alexander has described as a widespread Victorian "malady of Hamletism" (132) was caused by the sensed incompatibility of the infinite and inexpressible depths of a self "which passeth show" (I.ii.85) with the character represented by the "outward trappings" including not only clothing (Hamlet's "suits of woe") but other social signifiers including language itself. That is, the melancholy of Hamletism was caused by the incompatibility of the infinite Romantic self with the bounded Victorian "character."

Bradley's comments most vividly call to mind the work of Browning, who described his own poetry as an attempt to fit the infinite into the finite forms of his poems, but the Victorian poets most evidently suffering the "malady of Hamletism," as Alexander has argued, were Arnold and Arthur Hugh Clough, who, as Masao Miyoshi puts it, "has often been dismissed as a sort of agonized Hamlet mourning for a lost identity" (165). Both Arnold's and Clough's poetry consistently displayed the doubts, vacillations, and general incapacity for socially directed action of protagonists unable or unwilling to limit themselves within the bounds of conventional beliefs (unwilling, in a sense, to accept limited identities, to become characters). The most prominent melancholic among all Victorian poets was Tennyson, who described *Maud* as a "little *Hamlet.*"

The Victorian and Freudian preoccupation with *Hamlet* indicates a desire to preserve the traditional association of melancholy with genius and even hints that the "modern problems" once depicted so brilliantly by Shakespeare were not altogether beyond the scope of poetry, but it still does not indicate just how to free melancholy from its "inhibition," how it could find issue from its apparent entrapment, buried within the self. As I will argue in the next section, however, the example of *Hamlet* did provide a starting point for the Victorians to develop a poetics of melancholy, as they struggled to develop a poetic mode adequate to make sense of the "metaphysical contradiction between finite and infinite, time and eternity."

II. A Poetics of Melancholy

The tension in Victorian poetry between the poet's use of available public language for the expression of character as ideology and his or her effort to express the ineffable, idiosyncratic feeling of inwardness results in what Isobel Armstrong has called a "crisis of representation" (*Victorian Poetry,* 6). Armstrong's account posits the "double poem" (13) as the characteristic product of an ideology in which a historicized and "deeply politicized consciousness" is set against a more intimate and vital "aesthetic realm" (6). Armstrong's account of the divided consciousness of Victorian poets corresponds closely with my own account of melancholy as a split between a politicized Victorian "character " and an infinite Romantic self, but her account of the "double poem" leads to an assertion that "the task of a history of Victorian poetry is to restore the questions of politics" (7), whereas I am more concerned with exploring the ways that the "buried life" of the infinite self, perceived as anterior to language, could find expression.

The Victorians never seem to have doubted the "truth" of the innermost feelings, though they occasionally thought that modern life both made it difficult to feel intensely or on a grand scale and that modern subjectivity was to a degree anesthetized by the constant barrage of stimuli. After the death of Wordsworth, Arnold wondered "who, ah! Who, will make us feel?" in "this iron age / Of doubts, disputes, distractions, fears" (Memorial Verses,11.67, 43–44), and Arthur Hallam sensed a "decrease of *subjective* power, arising from a prevalence of social activity, and a continual absorption of the higher feelings into the palpable interests of ordinary life" (190, his emphasis). For just this reason, however, it seemed especially urgent to promote a poetic mode that would cultivate the feelings. In *The City of Dreadful Night,* in fact, Thomson asserted that only by stripping away the trappings of ideology, of "ordinary life" in an age of "doubts, disputes, distractions, fears," could one "break the seals of mute despair" (1.6), drawing on melancholy for poetic authority. The poet "wail[s] life's discords" (1.7)

> Because a cold rage seizes one at whiles
>   To show the bitter old and wrinkled truth
> Stripped naked of all vesture that beguiles
>   False dreams, false hopes, false masks and modes of youth;
> Because it gives some sense of power and passion
> In helpless impotence to try to fashion
>   Our woe in living words howe'er uncouth. (ll.8–14)

Here and throughout the opening sections of the poem, however, Thomson suggests that the uncouth, esoteric language of "power and passion" remains entrapped in melancholy consciousness, incommunicable beyond the "sad Fraternity" (1.36) of fellow melancholics:

> No secret can be told
> To any who divined it not before:
> None uninitiate by many a presage
> Will comprehend the language of the message,
>   Although proclaimed aloud for evermore. (ll.38–42)

The difficulty of finding apt language to express the deepest feelings was equally apparent to Hallam, even as he advocated a shift away from the Wordsworthian "poetry of reflection" to the "poetry of sensation" of Shelley, Keats, and Tennyson. He both recognized that such poetry was characteristically melancholy and implied that it was also difficult to disengage from the depths of the poet's psyche: "Hence the melancholy, which so evidently characterizes the spirit of modern poetry; hence that return of the mind upon itself, and the habit of seeking relief in idiosyncrasies rather than community of interest" (190). As Thomson suggests, even if the poet finds "community of interest," it is only within the limited community of the "sad Fraternity," and Hallam similarly recognized that the modern poet could hardly hope for a wide audience because his melancholy was dissonant with ideology. In a sense, Hallam and Thomson conceded a diminished cultural role for poetry even as they drew on the authority of melancholy as the key to something like "primordial human nature," drawing its imagery from a "charnel-house of long dead interiorities."

Audrey Jaffe has recently discussed both the Victorian belief in the truth of feeling and the difficult necessity of finding communal representation of idiosyncratic inwardness. Commenting on Richard Sennett's description of the "constant attempt [of the nineteenth-century 'personality'] to formulate what it is one feels," Jaffe notes that the authority and value of feeling are due precisely to its idiosyncrasy, its separateness from "community of interests": "In a modern dispensation . . . ideologies of feeling draw their power from feeling's presumed self-evidence: feeling, ostensibly emerging from the deepest interiority, seems by definition beyond the reach of social regulation, and its cultural value depends on that inaccessibility." Yet, Jaffe continues, for that feeling to have any social or cultural meaning, it must issue from interiority as representation: "though the ideological power of feeling relies on the idea of an essence or truth to which language and representation are said to remain inadequate, the specific nature of that power becomes visible in the terms of its representation" (14). In the terms of my argument, to reach a general audience the inchoate interiority of the inner self must be shaped for public discourse, and is limited and thus shaped *by* public discourse in the form of conscience and its rage for order. The dialogue of the mind with itself, as melancholy, is the site of artistic production, but what shape can this production take within that discourse?

Hallam's solution to these difficulties was to advocate poetic representation of feeling at the level of the senses—a "poetry of sensation" that speaks to and of the senses with an immediacy not to be found in the philosophical poetry of Wordsworth. Hallam's essay, insisting on the root meaning of the "aesthetic" in feeling and on the pursuit of beauty as the sole purpose of art, announces the tradition that would lead through Shelley, Keats, and the young Tennyson to D. G. Rossetti, William Morris, and Swinburne and on to Yeats, and he preemptively designated the "aesthetic" tradition of Victorian poetry as "so evidently" melancholy that the point did not need to be argued.

Hallam's view of sensation as the source and end of poetry was consistent with a general tendency of the post-Romantic period to value feeling above thought in poetry. John Stuart Mill, for example, was arguing at this time that the truest poets are those who have the deepest capacities for feeling, and his primary example of a "born poet" was the wailing Shelley. Moreover, in describing the particularly "poetic" element in other arts, he not only stressed the expression of deep feeling but also emphasized specifically melancholy feeling: "the very soul of melancholy exhaling itself in solitude" in "Winter's beautiful "Paga fui'" and the "grandeur and melancholy" of Beethoven's overture to *Egmont* (557). Once poetic authority is attributed especially to "persons who have most feeling of their own" (556), as by Mill, it is only a small step to attributing such authority to persons suffering the intense feeling of melancholy. For Shelley and Byron melancholia was the source and theme of poetry, and for Keats, "the wakeful anguish of the soul" described in the "Ode on Melancholy" was inseparable from "Beauty—Beauty that must die" (1.21).

Like Hallam and Keats, Edgar Allan Poe took it for granted that "Beauty is the sole legitimate province of the poem" (106), but more explicitly and emphatically than they, he also insisted that "Beauty of whatever kind invariably excites the sensitive soul to tears. Melancholy is thus the most legitimate of the poetical tones" (107). Unlike Arnold, moreover, Poe also knew how melancholy could find issue in representation: it could issue in the form of his poem, "The Raven." More usefully, however, for those who had not written "The Raven," he affirmed that "the death, then, of a beautiful woman is, emphatically, the most poetical topic in the world" (109).[13] The surprising prevalence of this opinion is evident in the many Victorian paintings of the dead or dying Ophelia and Lady of

Shalott as well as in poems like Tennyson's "The Lady of Shalott" and "Oriana." Perceiving a link between lyric poetry and melancholia, Hallam selected "Oriana" as representative of Tennyson's ability to capture the "effect by *sound*" (194, his emphasis) of "shades of fine emotion in the human heart . . . which are too subtle and too rapid to admit of corresponding phrases."[14] The ballad of Oriana's death, in Hallam's view, perfectly represents the kind of melancholy beauty prescribed by Poe: "The strong musical delight prevails over every painful feeling and mingles them all in its deep swell until they attain a composure of exalted sorrow, a mood in which the latest repose of agitation becomes visible, and the influence of beauty spreads like light over the surface of the mind" (195).

Obviously not every poem can be "The Raven" or "Oriana" or yet another variation on the theme of the dead or dying woman. A more comprehensive mode of apprehending and expressing the depths of melancholy is suggested by the ways in which the late Romantics and early Victorians brooded on death to allegorize the depths inaccessible to the outward senses. Wordsworth's "deep power of joy" enabled him to see into "the life of things," but for later generations "the life of things" had been displaced by a "world of convention, reification, and petrifaction," and it became the burden of melancholy imagination to see into the death of things. Arnold's sense of the innermost life as "buried" is to be taken literally and grouped with the speaker of *Maud* imagining himself as literally buried, with Heathcliff's notion that his soul was in the grave, with Lucy Snowe's identification with the figure of a nun buried alive in *Villette*, with Dickens's Dr. Manette, buried alive in the Bastille, with George Eliot's description of Dinah Morris's spiritual beauty in terms of a "lovely corpse" (158).

Eliot's reference to the "lovely corpse" calls to mind the late-twentieth-century revisions to Freud's theory of mourning and melancholy by Nicholas Abraham and Maria Torok, who argue that for the melancholic the lost ego-ideal is not only cast over the ego as a shadow but is cast into the ego as an "exquisite corpse," entombed in what they describe as a psychic "crypt" that simultaneously protects it and renders it an issueless interiority, a buried self hidden from consciousness. As in Arnold's "The Buried Life," the interior ego-ideal is hidden from consciousness so that the ego cannot betray it, and like Arnold and Freud, Abraham and Torok insist that however much the conscious self might long to represent this encrypted "Reality," however much the ego might want to "spill the beans and come clean," the buried ideal remains "unnameable."[15] Still, for Abraham and Torok the unspeakable encrypted truth is not mute and issueless, but finds representation in literally cryptic language. As Derrida points out in his foreword to *The Wolf Man's Magic Word*, "the appearance of an exquisite corpse," though "apparently illegible and devoid of meaning," is ultimately readable: the corpse can be "exhumed" by analysis (xxxv). For postmodern psychoanalysis, as for Arnold and Hopkins and Victorian studies generally, the unnameable buried self is spoken in other words. For Abraham and Torok the language of the hidden interiority is "cryptonomy," but for the Victorians the crucial point is that the buried life speaks itself as the other, speaks itself as allegory. The corpse, of course, is itself an allegorical representation and even, as we shall see, the ultimate allegorical referent in the eyes of Walter Benjamin.

For the Victorians, as for Benjamin, the awareness of the inner life as corpse and the fragmentation of the reified world into emptied out, meaningless ruins is the precondition for the brooding of the melancholy gaze that can assign (or seem to find) subjective meanings and attempt to articulate a redeeming coherence in the structure of allegory. William James, describing the alienated perception of "melancholy subjects" in a world that has become "remote, strange, sinister, unnerving" (151), accounts for the brooding tendency of melancholia:

> Now there are some subjects whom all this leaves a prey to the profoundest astonishment. The strangeness is wrong. The unreality cannot be. A mystery is concealed, and a metaphysical solution must exist. If the natural world is so double-faced and unhomelike, what world, what thing is real? An urgent wondering and questioning is set up, a poring theoretic activity. (152)

The allegorical structure of *The City of Dreadful Night* reveals a possible poetic form to represent the uncanny world of melancholia by representing the "charnel house of long dead interiorities." Thomson's poem represents a journey through the "Great ruins of an unremembered past" (1.79), a "drear pilgrimage to ruined shrines" (1.153), culminating in a monumental shrine to Melancholia herself, as imagined in Albrecht Dürer's famous allegorical engraving (ll.1040–1053).

Whether associated specifically with ruins and melancholy or more generally with the Utilitarian, scientific, rationalist spirit of the age, allegory seemed the almost inevitable mode of the Victorian age. From the 1820s, the nineteenth century was notoriously a "Mechanical Age . . . the Age of Machinery" in which man had become reified: "Men are grown mechanical in head and in heart, as well as in hand" (Carlyle, "Signs of the Times," *Works*, 27: 63). Lamenting this condition, Coleridge notoriously identified allegory as the literary mode of a "mechanical understanding, which in the blindness of self-complacency confounds SYMBOLS with ALLEGORIES. Now an Allegory is but a translation of abstract notions into a picture language which is itself nothing but an abstraction from objects of the senses; the principle being more worthless even than its phantom proxy, both alike unsubstantial, and the former shapeless to boot" (*The Statesman's Manual*, 30).

For Coleridge the "symbol" participated in the "life of things," while allegory, like the "dead letters" of "literal language," could only systematize or articulate dead things. Perhaps the clearest example of the tendency to articulate dead things in Victorian poetry is to be found in William Morris's "Concerning Geffray Teste-Noire," in which the narrator describes finding the bones of a slain woman, reassembling the skeleton, falling in love with it (her), adorning it with hair of spun gold, and building a shrine for this aesthetically "resurrected" exquisite corpse. But the post-Romantic allegorist is best represented by another "articulator of human bones," Mr. Venus of Dickens's *Our Mutual Friend*, who embodies the tendency of the age to build systems in which dead matter can be instilled with the semblance of life, as in Saussure's work showing how words and dead letters find meaning only within articulated linguistic systems, and in Marx's account of the "life" of commodities. As the nineteenth century came to understand itself in structuralist terms, as an order of *things*, or as a "Social System" (Carlyle, "Signs of the Times," 27: 600) "that knows its own structure" (28: 13), the system building of allegory was perhaps its inevitable literary expression. The skeletal articulation of Mr. Venus epitomizes Walter Benjamin's account of modern allegory as summed up by Teresa Kelley: "allegory offers emblematic images that are, as it were, skeletal reminders of a system of meaning" (254). Franco Moretti has pointed out that, for Goethe, as for Coleridge, allegory, "being conventional," "acquires a whole series of pejorative connotations. It is an artificial figure, mechanical, dead" (78). Yet, Matthew Arnold notwithstanding, Goethe's use of allegory in *Faust* "is a sign of his historical intelligence: of his having understood that allegory is *the poetic figure of modernity*" (78, Moretti's emphasis). As Moretti notes, since Benjamin allegory has been seen as structurally parallel with Marx's analysis of the commodity: "like the commodity, allegory humanizes things, making them move (and speak), and it reifies human beings" (78).[16]

It should not be wholly surprising that attempts to represent the buried life of the self should concern themselves with articulating dead matter or making dead matter articulate, like Yorick's skull. Both Thomas Carlyle and John Ruskin devised theories of the imagination akin to Hamlet's melancholy insight, and Ruskin, in particular, offered a distinctively Victorian sense of melancholy imagination as opposed to the Wordsworthian and Coleridgean model of joy wedding self, language, and nature in the divine logos. In the second volume of *Modern Painters*

(1846) Ruskin defined what he called the "imagination penetrative," with an eye toward Coleridge's influential distinction between the fancy and the imagination. Although imagination remained the important authoritative faculty, Ruskin did not see it as an echo of divine creation and evidence of a holy plan, but rather as an access to "the melancholy deeps of things" (4: 257). Ruskin argues that the truth of things is to be found in the mysterious depths below "outward images of any kind."[17] Like Ruskin, James argues that "No prophet can claim to bring a final message" (162) unless he accounts for the "taint of nausea," a "whiff of melancholy, things that sound a knell, for fugitive as they may be, they bring a feeling of coming from a deeper region, and often have an appalling convincingness" (136). Similarly, Thomson characterizes melancholics as those who

> fill their living mouths with dust of death
> And make their habitation in the tombs,
> And breathe eternal sighs with mortal breath,
> And pierce life's pleasant veil of various error
> To reach that void of darkness and old terror
> Wherein expire the lamps of hope and faith. ("The City of Dreadful Night," ll.559–64)

Again, as Ruskin puts it, imagination

> ploughs [surface images] aside, and plunges into the very central fiery heart; nothing else will content its spirituality; whatever semblances and various outward shows and phases its subject may possess go for nothing; it gets within all fence, cuts down the root, and drinks the very vital sap of that it deals with . . . ; its function and gift are getting at the root, its nature and divinity depend on its holding things always at the heart. (4: 250–51)

Not surprisingly, Ruskin's ultimate example of the "imagination penetrative" is Hamlet's meditation upon Yorick's skull.

Walter Benjamin's twentieth-century thoughts on melancholy and allegory bring the terms of the nineteenth-century discourse into sharp focus. Replacing the Romantic imagination with melancholy, the allegorical mode in Benjamin takes as its starting point the ruin, or corpse, or skull and, like Mr. Venus, articulates the dead bones of the past into a system of meaning:

> If the object becomes allegorical under the gaze of melancholy, if melancholy causes life to flow out of it and it remains dead, but

eternally secure, then it is exposed to the allegorist, it is unconditionally in his power. That is to say it is now quite incapable of emanating any meaning or significance of its own; such significance as it has, it acquires from the allegorist. He places it within it, and stands behind it; not in a psychological but in an ontological sense. In his hands the object becomes something different; through it he speaks of something different and for him it becomes a key to the realm of hidden knowledge; and he reveres it as the emblem of this. This is what determines the character of allegory as a form of writing. It is a schema; and as a schema it is an object of knowledge, but it is not securely possessed until it becomes a fixed schema: at one and the same time a fixed image and a fixating sign. (*Origin*, 183–84)

Ruskin's discussion especially clearly distinguished the melancholy Victorian imagination from the Coleridgean Romantic: for Coleridge, the imagination, as opposed to the "fancy," is the cheerful expression of the entirely healthy mind, sharing in "the one Life within us and abroad" ("The Eolian Harp," 1.26) to echo the eternally creative faculty of logos itself, but Ruskin, maintaining the Coleridgean distinction, continues to see "fancy" as a juggling of externals but sees imagination as essentially melancholy:

> She sees too far, too darkly, too solemnly, too earnestly ever to smile. There is something in the heart of everything, if we can reach it, that we shall not be inclined to laugh at. And thus there is reciprocal action between the intensity of moral feeling and the power of imagination; for, on the one hand, those who have keenest sympathy are those who look closest and pierce deepest, and hold securest; and on the other, those who have so pierced and seen the melancholy deeps of things are filled with the most intense passion and gentleness of sympathy. (4: 257)

Such reverie, the "emotion of the trapped," to take Adorno's phrase, is apparent early in the post-Romantic period in the intensity of longing in "Mariana" and throughout the works of Elizabeth Barrett, and it eventually became the "malady of reverie" that Pater saw characterizing "aesthetic poetry."

The shift from a poetics of pleasure to a poetics of melancholy was not as clear-cut or abrupt as the juxtaposition of Ruskin's "imagination penetrative" with Coleridge's theocentric imagination implies, but it was paradoxically an inevitable result of the very success of the Wordsworthian,

Coleridgean model. Once Wordsworth made "the Mind of Man" his "haunt" and the "main region of his song" ("Prospectus" to *The Recluse*, ll.40–41), the poetic tradition was turned inward and the mind was divided against itself into at least two states of consciousness: the mind observing and the mind observed. Though Wordsworth did not put the matter in these terms, it is clear that the mind observing corresponds with conscience and that it has authorial control over the mind observed, the subject. By the time of Byron, Shelley, and Keats, and more explicitly by the 1830s, such self-consciousness came to seem morbid, even diseased: Wordsworth's ideal wholeness of mind came to seem impossible as the irreconcilable conflict of the mind observing and the mind observed became increasingly painfully felt. Carlyle's great essays analyzing the spirit of the age, "Signs of the Times" (1829) and "Characteristics" (1831), emphatically registered the association of modern (late Romantic) literature with morbidity and disease, and promoted the authority of a "piercing" imagination to penetrate the surfaces of things and locate the "deep truth" that Shelley had declared "imageless."[18]

The emergence of melancholy poetics was obviously problematic for Carlyle, who famously instructed his age to move beyond the morbidity of late Romanticism, to "close thy Byron" and to eschew the "wailing" Shelley, so it is not surprising that he carefully distinguished himself from the "melancholic speculators" (*Works*, 27: 80) that he evidently resembled. He nevertheless saw his age through the lens of the period's icon of melancholy, Hamlet, whose "'large discourse of reason' *will* look before and after" (27: 36, and see *Hamlet*, IV.iv.36–37)[19] and he felt that "the time is sick and out of joint" (27: 80; *Hamlet*, I.v.188), sunk in languidly restless discontent. More pertinently still, he argued that because of the loss of other sources of spiritual authority, "At no former era has Literature . . . been of such importance as it is now" (27: 77), but he specifically denied modern literature the Coleridgean authority to disclose "to our senses the deep, infinite harmonies of Nature and Man's soul" (27: 78). Carlyle apparently believed that in other times literature might have divine authority, but like many of his contemporaries, he feared that his unpoetic age could not claim any such authority, and he lamented "the diseased self-conscious state of literature" (28: 24) as a symptom of the age's degradation. Yet he also saw that to have any authority in a melancholy age, literature must itself be melancholy: the age is diseased, but "The self-consciousness is the symptom merely; nay, it is also the attempt towards cure" (28: 20). Carlyle himself, moreover, wrote as a melancholic, appropriating the cultural authority of Hamlet's penetrating imagination to pierce the infinite depths of the soul and look beneath the "film" that supports life over the "boundless Deep, whereon all human things fearfully and wonderfully swim" in the "neighbourhood of an inevitable Death" (27: 3). Even though, like Ruskin, he wanted to penetrate beyond the mere surfaces of things, he wrote in a mode of melancholy allegory, diagnosing the "signs" and "characteristics" of the age as emblems or symptoms of "horror and disease and dead men's bones" (28: 20) beneath the fragile film. He even demonstrated the close connections among melancholy, piercing imagination, and allegory, the inward sublime and its outward manifestation:

> So cunningly does Nature, the mother of all highest Art, which only apes her from afar, "body forth the Finite from the Infinite"; and guide man safe on his wondrous path, not more by endowing him with vision, than, at the right place, with blindness! Under all her work, chiefly under her noblest work, Life, lies a basis of darkness, which she benignly conceals; in Life too, the roots and inward circulations which stretch down fearfully to the regions of death and Night, shall not hint of their existence, and only the fair stem with its leaves and flowers, shone on by the fair sun, shall disclose itself, and joyfully grow. (*Works*, 28: 4)

For Carlyle, as for Ruskin and Thomson, the outward show of things is semblance, "a vesture that beguiles," but as Benjamin would argue, the veil that hides the deep truth may also emblematically body it forth.[20]

Carlyle seems to welcome an ignorance that is bliss, but he recognizes that the deep truth is ascertainable only as melancholy allegory in which the flowers are emblems writ on a delicate film that "any scratch of a bare bodkin will render asunder" (*Works*, 28: 3). Such signs on the painted veil of Life signify allegorically "in a deeper than metaphorical sense" (27: 78).[21] Carlyle's allegorical mode, most obviously represented in the clothes philosophy of *Sartor Resartus*, thus originates, like Hamlet's, in the classical tendency to "feed on the metaphysical contradiction between finite and infinite, time and eternity" (*Works*, 28: 28–29). Time itself is the clothing of infinity, so that the semiology of clothes represents the embodiment of eternity in time: "Time itself reposes on Eternity: the truly Great and Transcendental has its basis and substance in Eternity; stands revealed to us as Eternity in a Vesture of Time" (*Works*, 28: 38–39). Carlyle's allegory, which anticipates and may have influenced a recurring motif of clothing as allegory in Browning's poetry, is best understood in modern terms in relation to Benjamin's arguments in *The Origin of German Tragic Drama* that allegory retains the traces of lost divinity—Benjamin even allegorizes these traces *à la* Carlyle as clothing: "The attire of the Olympians is left behind, and in the course of time the emblems collect around it" (225). Further, like Carlyle, Benjamin sees the confrontation of time and eternity as the underlying basis of allegory: "Allegory established itself most permanently where transitoriness and eternity confronted each other most directly" (224), and he also argues that the deep truth, if imageless, is accessible as allegory: "The Sense of the abyssal is to be defined as 'meaning.' Such a sense is always allegorical" (*Arcades,* 271).

Carlyle's allegory resembles Adorno's comments on the emotion of the trapped, since he reads the cast-off clothing of time to restore meaning to the world, to free the human soul from its historical prison, "that 'Time element,' wherein man's soul here below lies imprisoned,—the Poet's task is, as it were, done to his hand: Time itself, which is the outer veil of Eternity, invests, of its own accord, with authentic, felt 'infinitude' whatsoever it has once embraced in its mysterious folds" (*Works,* 28: 79). Carlyle's example helps make sense of Adorno's enigmatic argument that the "deliverance of lost meaning is necessarily allegorical":

> For if truth presents itself in melancholy, it indeed presents itself to pure inwardness exclusively as semblance. . . .
>
> Thus truth subordinates itself to melancholic semblance through semblance's own dialectic. In its semblance melancholy is, dialectically, the image of an other. Precisely this is the origin of the allegorical of Kierkegaard's melancholy. In the face of melancholy, nature becomes allegorical. . . . Melancholy itself, however, is the historical spirit in its natural depth and therefore, in the images of its corporeity, it is the central allegory. (60–61)

As is often the case, Adorno's comments are rather oracular than lucid, but at the very least he is suggesting that man's "private character" is the realm of an authoritative melancholy and that such melancholy, though imprisoned as "inner concerns," is not necessarily "issueless" but might find expression in allegory, "the image of the other." Adorno's "semblance" ("*schein*") refers to the "images of [the historical spirit's] corporeity," and both terms refer to the outward dress, the "clothing" of Time. For Adorno the fragile film or painted veil of allegory as *schein* is subjectively constituted, and as semblance is ultimately delusive, but for Carlyle and other post-Christian theists the clothing of time represents the lineaments of Truth, hidden from human perception but still existent behind the appearances of things.

An influential poststructuralist account of melancholy and allegory may elucidate the issues more clearly. Like the Frankfurt critics, Paul de Man displaced the aesthetic primacy of the Romantic symbol with his insistence on allegory as a poetic mode more adequately suited to represent the temporal reality of human experience. In his account of how Rilke's depth of feeling *seems* to be represented seamlessly in his symbols (*Allegories*, 48), de Man almost seems to be answering Arnold's question in "Memorial Verses" about who, after Wordsworth, will "make us feel" and more specifically, "Where will Europe's latter hour / Again find Wordsworth's healing power?" (ll.63–64). De Man asserts that "Rilke seems to be endowed with the healing power of those who open up access to the hidden layers of our consciousness" (20).

But this is semblance. De Man analyzes the illusion that melancholy speaks itself by demonstrating the poet's virtuoso displacement of his own unhappy consciousness with an "allegory of figuration" (*Allegories*, 45). He quotes Hermann Mörchen to demonstrate the extent to which Rilke's melancholy poetry, like Tennyson's (according to Hallam), seems to eliminate the gap or barrier between ineffable, private feeling and public representation: "The fundamental poetic practice, namely the elaboration of a metaphorical language, also derives from the experience of suffering. The metaphor is an act of identification: the actual suffering of the poet is made 'equal' with that of his symbolic figures" (25–26).

Mörchen's utopian argument is akin to Hallam's assertion that the very sounds of the poet's language may convey shades of inwardness too deep and too subtle for the denotative meanings of words to communicate, though Mörchen goes further to argue that poetic "truth" is communicated in language "that is not confined to acoustic affinities but . . . includes linguistic structures in general" (*Allegories*, 26).[22] De Man's reading of Rilke's poems demonstrates that Rilke both creates and deconstructs the illusion of the equivalency of feeling and language in a way that sheds some light on Adorno's remark that in melancholy truth presents itself as "semblance." Apparently thinking of Baudelaire's theory of *correspondances*, de Man argues that Rilke's metaphors characteristically *seem* to confirm a "'correspondence' between the inwardness of the subject and the outside world," but that they do so by displacing rather than embodying inwardness, substituting the *seeming* inwardness of things for the actual inwardness of the self by means of "analogical representation" (35). The means of at least *seeming* to communicate pure inwardness are allegorical, then, in something like the way Adorno cryptically describes as "semblance." Or, as de Man puts it, the poem that *appears* to be a confrontation of man and nature is in fact the "simulacrum of a description in which the structure of the described object is that of the figural potential in language" (38).

In de Man's view feeling does not achieve its own "deliverance" from the "historical prison of inwardness," and the semblance of feeling achieved by allegorical figuration is in fact *only* semblance: the "general pattern of substitution that all tropes have in common" allows one meaning to "substitute for the other without revealing the difference necessarily introduced by the substitution" (*Allegories*, 62).

The nature of melancholy allegory is clearer in Walter Benjamin's analysis, which both Adorno and de Man have in mind.[23] In his *The Origin of German Tragic Drama* Benjamin had rehabilitated allegory at the expense of the Romantic idealization of the symbol, primarily by debunking the Romantic belief that the symbol could seamlessly unite experience and language and arguing that allegory has the salutary but melancholy function of signifying the inability of language to capture and communicate moments of pure being. The symbol claimed to arrest and immortalize moments, but allegory, a sequential and temporal mode like language itself, acknowledges in its ongoing course that each moment is temporary and incomplete, so that the images of allegory are only transiently meaningful and soon give way to "disappointed abandonment of the exhausted emblem" (185). Benjamin asserts that nature appears to the allegorist "not in bud and bloom but in the overripeness and decay of her creations . . . as eternal transience" (179). Allegory describes the truth of mortal existence, but it is a disillusioned, thoroughly melancholy truth. "Within the decisive category of time," Benjamin argues,

> Everything about history that, from the very beginning, has been untimely, sorrowful, unsuccessful, is expressed in a face—or rather in a death's head. And although such a thing lacks all "symbolic" freedom of expression, all classical proportion, all humanity—nevertheless, this is the form in which man's subjection to nature is most obvious and it significantly gives rise not only to the enigmatic question of the nature of human existence as such, but also of the biographical historicity of the individual. This is the heart of the allegorical way of seeing, of the baroque, secular explanation of history as the Passion of the world; its importance resides solely in the stations of its decline. The greater the significance, the greater the subjection to death, because death digs most deeply the jagged line of demarcation between physical nature and significance. But if nature has always been subject to the power of death, it is also true that it has always been allegorical. (166)

Benjamin's comments are historically specific to seventeenth-century Lutheran Germany, but as he came to see, his comments apply also, with only slight modification, to nineteenth-century Europe since in important respects the culture of the baroque coincides with Victorian culture. In the first place, almost as if describing the conflict between the overstrained Victorian conscience and the "joy" of the Romantic life of things,

Benjamin described "[t]he allegorical outlook" as having its "origin in the conflict between the guilt-laden physis, held up as an example by Christianity and a purer [pagan, but also Romantic] natura deorum" (226).[24] Second, Benjamin's argument that the sense of time confronting eternity underlies the melancholy that produces allegory is entirely consonant with the new Victorian awareness that time spans millions of years of astronomical and geological change rather than the mere thousands of years of biblical history, and that this perspective of time confronting eternity discredited any notion of a teleologically purposeful divine plan with human life at the center. The changed perspective rendered human life and human history insignificant within a vast span now perceived as "an endless succession of discrete moments—in other words as inauthentic, empty infinitude" (Hanssen, 58). The new Victorian sense of emptiness in infinite time was cogently expressed by Edward Fitzgerald, who noted that the new sense of geological time "must wither the poet's sense of immortality" (*Letters*, 1: 566) and commented that "we all live in a ridiculous parenthesis of Time on a shelf made by insects and planted by stray seamews."[25] Benjamin argued that within a cosmic scheme that reduced life to insignificant transience, the only meaning to be redeemed from time is found in the monuments of transience, the ruins of history. As Carlyle said, whatever time "once embraced in its mysterious folds" is redeemed in melancholy brooding as an emblem, a key to the "felt infinitude" (*Works*, 28: 79) of the imprisoned inner self. When the ultimate truth of human existence is death and the true self of the individual is "buried," the ultimate representation of human life is the corpse or the death's head. Benjamin had just enough religious hope to fancy that the *caput mortuum* retained the residue of former life and even former divinity ("the residue of the creative word of God" [quoted in Duttman, 59]), and similarly, many Victorians, still Christian under empty skies, could hope, as Carlyle did, that the ruins of time, the cast-off clothes of history, might still represent something "truly Great and Transcendental."[26]

As we have seen, for Benjamin the emotion of the trapped could find issue in the articulation of "dead objects" ("in its tenacious self-absorption [melancholy] embraces dead objects in order to redeem them" [*Origin*, 157]). Looking at the seventeenth-century world of the *trauerspiel*, when Lutheranism had rendered "good works" irrelevant to salvation, Benjamin saw a world in some respects strikingly like Victorian England, where the conduct of earthly life ("creaturely existence") had no cosmic consequences, no ultimate meaning. In both eras the "rigorous morality" of official discourse "did, it is true, instill into the people a strict sense of obedience to duty, but in its great men it produced melancholy" (138). For both eras the futility of human endeavor produced the dilemma of the dispirited

Hamlet: "What is a man / If his chief good and market of his time / Be but to sleep and feed? A beast, no more" (138, and see *Hamlet* IV.iv.33–35). Again seeming to describe Victorian England as much as Lutheran Germany, Benjamin suggests that "There was no answer to this except perhaps in the morality of ordinary people—'honesty in small things,' 'upright living'—which developed at this time, forming a contrast to the taedium vitae of richer natures. For those who looked deeper saw the scene of their existence as a rubbish heap of partial, inauthentic actions" (139). And the looking deeper of the melancholy gaze (the brooding described by James) resulted in seeing the vesture of allegory, reviving "the empty world in the form of a mask," because "[e]very feeling is bound to an a priori object, and in the representation of this object is its phenomenology." Nameless "feelings, however vague they may seem when perceived by the self, respond with a motorial action to a concretely structured world" (139). To the melancholic gaze, "the most simple object appears to be a symbol of some enigmatic wisdom" precisely because "it lacks any natural creative relationship to us" (140). Consequently, the representation of feeling, of interiority, shifts from the abstract language of subjectivity to phenomenology of subjective experience in the articulation of a structure of objects, rather like Mr. Venus articulating bones into a human form. Crucially, the introduction of a severe conscience, of rigorous public morality, produces the melancholic gaze that then finds expression as allegory.

Though Benjamin developed his thoughts on allegory in relation to the baroque German drama, his analysis depended on a post-Romantic discrediting of the Romantic symbol and a return to the baroque conception of the symbol as emblem—the kind of emblem well described by Giorgio Agamben:

> Metaphor, as the paradigm of signifying by improper terms (and according to baroque theorists, both the emblem and the impresa fall under this framework), becomes thus the principle of universal dissociation of each thing from its own form, of every signifier from its own signified. . . . Each thing is true only to the extent to which it signifies another, and each thing is itself only as it stands for another. For the allegorical project of the baroque, this mortification of the proper form is a token of redemption that will be rescued on the last day, but whose cipher is already implicit in the act of creation. (142–43)

Since Benjamin's understanding of the baroque depended on his post-Romantic discrediting of the symbol, it is not surprising that his later writings focus on the melancholy of nineteenth-century European post-Romanticism for which the industrialized and reified world presented itself as a congeries of things, emptied of intrinsic meaning but able to signify other things. From this perspective, melancholy and its expression in allegory simultaneously see the object world as an anomic phantasmagoria and suggest the possibility of its redemption. Describing what he calls the "antinomies of the allegorical," Benjamin writes that

> any person, any object, any relationship can mean absolutely anything else. . . . [A]ll of the things which are used to signify derive, from the very fact of their pointing to something else, a power which makes them appear no longer commensurable with profane things, which raises them to a higher plane, and which can, indeed, sanctify them. Considered in allegorical terms, then, the profane world is both elevated and devalued. (175)

Despite his collapsing of the baroque age of reformation with the nineteenth-century age of commodity culture, for Benjamin melancholy allegory is profoundly historical, though unlike what he calls "universal history," it presents not the triumph of the victors but sites of loss where the "historical materialist" "recognizes the signs of a Messianic cessation of happening, or, put differently, a revolutionary chance in the fight for the oppressed past" (*Illuminations,* 263). Elsewhere, arguing for the dialectical character of allegory, he remarks that

> The word "history" stands written on the countenance of nature in the character of transience. The allegorical physiognomy of nature-history . . . is present in reality in the form of the ruin. . . . And in this guise history does not assume the form of the process of eternal life so much as that of irresistible decay. Allegory therefore declares itself to be beyond beauty. Allegories are, in the realm of thoughts, what ruins are in the realm of things. (177–78)

Not surprisingly, Benjamin's argument for the dialectical nature of allegory has been superseded by the implications of his preemptively poststructuralist sundering of the signifier from the signified. Benjamin's account of the function of signs obviously anticipates the postmodern version of allegory that, in de Man's version, functions as a system of *différance:*

> it remains necessary, if there is to be allegory, that the allegorical sign refer to another sign that precedes it. The meaning constituted by the allegorical sign can then consist only in the *repetition* (in the Kierkegaardian sense of the term) of a previous sign with which it

can never coincide, since it is the essence of this previous sign to be pure anteriority. (*Blindness* 1983, 207)

The work of art is a sign of the pure anteriority of the artist's consciousness, an emblem of forever lost origins.

Melancholy allegory was an effective poetic mode in the works of Tennyson (especially *Maud*), Browning, and other Victorian poets, but, as Arnold and many others saw it, not only was melancholy ineffectual earlier in the century, but by his hopelessly belated age, even his own melancholy was an "outworn theme." On the other hand, Arnold's own best poetry, *malgré lui,* was relentlessly melancholic; however "outworn" he thought it, melancholy is the persistent tone and even theme of "Stanzas," "The Scholar Gypsy," "Thyrsis," "The Buried Life," "Dover Beach," and of course the rejected *Empedocles*. Further, though Arnold manifestly described melancholy as unpoetic in the preface to *Poems,* he praised the melancholy poetry of Keats, and he even described a penetrating imagination akin to that of Ruskin as he traced the element of natural magic in British poetry to its Celtic strain. In "On the Study of Celtic Literature," he argued that the Celts are responsible for English culture's streak of "Titanism," a "penetrating passion and melancholy" (*Works,* 3: 361). For that matter he only found it necessary to write the preface in order to combat the view that "a true allegory of the state of one's own mind . . . is perhaps the highest thing that one can attempt in poetry." Arnold's rejection of "allegories of one's own mind" is much better remembered than the advocacy of such allegories by a critic he declined to name (J. M. Ludlow), but Arnold was well aware that he was actually questioning the authority of Goethe, whose criticism was being elucidated by Ludlow.

Goethe's version of allegory was a mode designed to represent subjective truth, not the "real" world, and as Stanley Corngold has shown, the authority of Goethe also stood behind both de Man's and Benjamin's formulations of allegory, allegories of the poet's own mind. As we have seen, Benjamin's account of the allegorist notes that "for him" the appropriated emblem "becomes a key to the realm of hidden knowledge." As the crucial phrase "for him" suggests, the melancholic's allegory creates a symbolic order unique to the allegorist, hence an "allegory of his own mind," not of universal knowledge or truth. Allegory then generates both semblance, the *appearance* of truth, and a genuinely true index of the poet's subjectivity. In Hamlet's terminology, the semblance, or seeming, is communally apparent in his "suits of woe," but the deep truth of his inner self is also spoken by the outward show of emblems.

Twentieth-century theorists from Freud to Benjamin and Adorno to de

Man seem to be describing Victorianism as well as later modes of thought not so much because they all share in an "epistemic" celebration of the self, but because they all share in a post-Romantic sense of loss described by de Man:

> Romanticism can appear as a high point, a period of splendor, and the subsequent century as a slow receding of the tide, a decay that can take on apocalyptic proportions. A reversed image of the same model sees Romanticism as a moment of extreme delusion from which the nineteenth century slowly recovers itself until it can free itself in the assertion of a new modernity. (*Allegories*, 81)

Even within the high Romantic era what appears as splendor at one moment appears as delusion the next, as is made emphatically clear in Wordsworth's "Elegiac Stanzas," which explicitly characterized the delusional splendor as semblance: "the gleam, / the light that never was, on sea or land, / The consecration and the poet's dream" (ll.14–16). For all post-Romantics who are no longer able to believe in the logocentrism of Coleridgean metaphysics, Romanticism is bound to look like a splendid delusion, as it did for Tennyson, the Brownings, Carlyle, and Arnold as well as Benjamin, Adorno, and many postmoderns. The sense of lost splendor, moreover, is characteristic of chastened melancholy: the Romantic symbol unifying god, man, and nature is displaced by a more limited sense of the possibilities of poetic language, and particularly by an allegorical mode that acknowledges the gap between language as the dress of thought and the imageless deep truth, the melancholy deeps of things. Like Hamlet, it is aware of a distinction between the inward truth that passes show and the outward "trappings and the suits of woe," the allegorical semblances that cover the truth, but simultaneously "body it forth."

The characteristic content of melancholy allegory, moreover, represents a melancholy consonant with Freudian and post-Freudian theory, and it was already available to the early Victorians in works of disillusioned Romanticism beginning at least as early as Coleridge's "Kubla Khan" and conspicuously including such works as Byron's *Manfred*, Shelley's *Alastor*, and Keats's *Endymion*. In the face of excessively sanguine beliefs about the Romantic symbol, even the poets of the Romantic era began to replace logocentric symbolism with allegoric representations of failed quests for transcendental vision or expression. Byron, Shelley, and Keats all rewrite vision as brooding, objectifying the deep self as an other under the scrutiny of the observing self, displacing miraculous epiphanies of the spirit with allegorical narratives of brooding on the self, and they all displaced imagination as achieved transcendence with imagination as melancholy love, a desire to possess and incorporate the unattainable imaginary. The extent to which these works anticipated a postmodern definition of melancholy is evident in Schiesari's account of the Lacanian scheme in which the melancholic is recognized as

> a self split against itself, fleeing the social into a perpetual dialogue with its own Imaginary.... Such a morbid turning-in on itself, however, frustrates the implicit desire for a fusion of selfhood because a distinction is thereby established between the self and its *objectification* of itself. The "sufferer" thus bemoans this inability to suture the self or to overcome the necessity of lack. As elaborated since the Renaissance, the discourse of melancholia glorifies this frustration as heroic suffering and consecrates the situation of lack as blessed. (8)

Lacan's analysis of melancholy, like Freud's, draws on a reading of *Hamlet:* for Lacan, the melancholy of Hamlet is for the loss of the phallus as ego ideal (imaginary fullness of being, complete identity), and the play represents his hopeless desire for the imaginary and his actual pursuit of death. Further, for Lacan as for Benjamin, mourning is an ideal condition for the deployment of substitute objects for the lost ideal—evidently, therefore, for the production of allegory. Postmodern psychoanalysis, Marxist theory, and even poststructuralist literary theory provide a framework from which to view Victorian melancholy, but I would not wish to argue that the Victorian poets thought through the possible meanings of melancholy in a precociously postmodern way. Rather, they inherited a fully elaborated poetics of melancholy directly from the Romanticism of Coleridge, Byron, Shelley, and Keats, who had all developed their poetry in response to a Wordsworthian model that they could neither escape nor imitate. In allegorical narratives by all of these poets the creative imagination is presented as originating, at least at times, in melancholy narcissism and a dialogue with its own "imaginary" conceived as a female love-object. Byron's and Shelley's narratives, in particular, can be glossed more convincingly than *Hamlet* itself with Lacan's account of the pursuit of the imaginary ego-ideal and of actual death.

Perhaps the best model of such a construction of poetic imagination is Coleridge's "Kubla Khan." Coleridge, of course, presented the poem as a "psychological curiosity" rather than as a parable of the visionary imagination, but the poem nevertheless presents a vision of absolute authority in the representation of an Oriental despot whose simple "decree" brings into being not merely a vision but the realization of that vision in material terms, as well as a despotic control over the created world. The "psychological curiosity" Coleridge had in mind was concerned with the effects of an "anodyne" (opium) on the imagination, but Coleridge also saw opium as a "will-destroying" drug and the poetic imagination and the poet's very self as the faculty of will (the most important element in Victorian "character"). The psychological curiosity is at least in part an experiment to see whether the poetic will could control the most voracious appetites that attack willpower, including not only the opium but also the "Abyssinian maid" who is, perhaps, an allegorical figure for the pleasures of opium itself. The poem's melancholy nature may also be seen in the dialogic structure of the preface and the two distinctly different sections of the poem as representative of the dialogue of the mind with itself, of a multitudinous and possibly melancholy consciousness. The possibility of the poet's realizing in himself the Khan's extreme version of poetic authority as power is entirely dependent on satisfaction of melancholy desire, on the appropriation of female sensibility in the person of the Oriental "damsel with a dulcimer":

> Could I revive within me
> Her symphony and song,
> To such a deep delight 'twould win me,
> That with music loud and long,
> I would build that dome in air,
> That sunny dome! those caves of ice!

The poem explicitly displays the loss of a transcendental power to create the thing itself in the Romantic symbol, the desire to revive it, and the sense that the revived objectification (the damsel) would suture the wholeness of self. The melancholic is doomed to ultimate failure: the fantasized woman cannot lead the poet out of his own interiority into authoritative communication with the world because she is herself finally a narcissistic ego-ideal, only existing as the shadow of the loved object that has fallen on the ego. She exists only in the interior dialogue of the mind with itself.

In addition the poem follows a prefatory account of a "vision" in which signifier and signified are magically fused as "images rose up before [the poet] as *things,* with a parellel production of the correspondent expressions." The poem itself records not the attainment of this vision, but the loss of it, and the parallel sundering of signifier from signified: that is, the poem presents itself not as the material and allegoric over the spiritual and symbolic, since fantasy and allegory are characteristically perceived in Romantic aesthetics as Oriental despots, like the khan himself. Kelley points out that in Hegel's *Aesthetics* "*Phantasie* is an oriental despot whose proliferation of sensuous shapes to represent divinities works against the spiritual in art" (137). And finally, the publication of "Kubla Khan" as a fragment suggests that the loss of wholeness described in the poem finds its fullest representation as a ruin, representing only the loss of divinity and the decay of vision.

A similar melancholy quest is more fully represented in the construction of the poetic character in Shelley's *Alastor* and Keats's *Endymion*. In both of these poems the protagonist is explicitly represented as a solitary, melancholy character troubled by a dream of transcendence to be achieved through an Orientalist erotic quest. In *Alastor* the skeptical Shelley presents a parable that, like Coleridge's, finally reveals the impossibility of transcendence through narcissistic brooding. The narrative structure of *Alastor* evidently enacts a complex "dialogue of the mind with itself" akin to the Freudian dialogue of the ego divided against itself. The Poet protagonist is represented within the frame narrative of a poet-narrator, and both poet figures are represented within the critical discursive frame provided by the preface. In addition, the Poet is clearly characterized by his narcissism as he is metaphorically compared to the narcissus flowers that, like him, "For ever gaze on their own drooping eyes, / Reflected in the crystal calm." As in "Kubla Khan" the Poet is enamored of an ideal that is patently a projection of his own ego, or soul, a "fair fiend" (1.297) whose "voice was like the voice of his own soul / Heard in the calm of thought" (ll.153–54) and is driven on a narcissistic quest to locate in the material world a being who can only exist as a part of his own mind. Like "Kubla Khan," *Alastor* presents the visionary quest within an Orientalist discourse that suggests at least a latent cultural imperialism even as it examines a manifestly Romantic imperialism in the attempt to appropriate a feminine sensibility that is "other" at least to the extent that it is gendered as feminine, and yet at the same time is already appropriated as the ego's idealization of itself. An interesting variant on the theme is also present in *Alastor* since Shelley represents the Poet "fleeing the social into a perpetual dialogue with its own Imaginary," his rejection of an actual woman, the "Arab maiden," as a cause of the Poet's punishment, his alienated solitude—it is as if the melancholy quest could be fulfilled by turning from poetic idealism to actual cultural imperialism, the actual appropriation of a living "Arab maiden."

Significantly also, the Poet of *Alastor*, like the protagonist of Byron's *Childe Harold*, seeks for truth among "The awful ruins of days of Old" (1. 107), "poring on memorials/ Of the World's youth" (ll. 121–22) and attempting to articulate the truths of the dead world. Describing the ruins of ancient shrines, the Poet almost seems to anticipate Benjamin's theory of the redemptive power of allegory by attempting, as Shelley would put it in "A Defence of Poetry," to redeem "from decay the visitations of the divinity in man" (505).

Keats's *Endymion* was evidently modeled in part on *Alastor*, though its archaic Elizabethanism and its mythic sources introduce a supernatural element that enables Endymion's eventual transcendence to godhood. Keats's uses of the Narcissus myth (1.890–989) make it clear that he was as aware as Shelley of the ultimately narcissistic character of pursuing the transcendent vision of a dream, but his deliberately anachronistic Elizabethanism nevertheless provides a happy ending as it is used in the service of a neo-Platonic version of melancholy desire. Endymion is characterized from the start as a melancholy character for whom the world is impoverished:

>   all the pleasant hues
> Of heaven and earth had faded: deepest shades
> Were deepest dungeons; heaths and sunny glades
> Were full of pestilent light; our taintless rills
> Seemed sooty. . . . (ll.691–95)

His transcendence from earthly melancholy to heavenly fulfillment precisely follows the neo-Platonic trajectory described by Ficino and others. Endymion is made to speculate on this possibility as early as book i, and he concludes that, originating in "ardent listlessness" (i. 825), "this earthly love has power to make / Men's being mortal, immortal" (i. 843–44). Keats enables his protagonist to climb the neo-Platonic ladder of love to eventual immortality partly because he does not follow the example of *Alastor* and have Endymion scorn human love in the form of an Oriental woman. Instead, Endymion is made to fall in love with an Indian maiden who is the virtual embodiment of "sorrow," and only through this love, this wedding to sorrow, or embrace of melancholy, is he finally "spiritualized" from "this mortal state" (iv. 991–93). Endymion is made a god only by allegorically embracing the melancholy that Keats later invoked in his great odes: transcendence is reached when the mind miraculously achieves unity with itself by satisfying its own melancholy desire. The Orientalism of "Kubla Khan," *Endymion, Alastor,* and, for that matter, *Childe Harold's Pilgrimage* and *Manfred* anticipates the cultural imperialism of the Victorian age in a startling way, but these poems only represent a particularly exaggerated version of the Romantic imagination as an imperial faculty. In the examination of inwardness, the melancholic, like the lover and like the Romantic imagination, creates the ego-ideal in his own image, falls in love with his own "Imaginary," and seeks to appropriate this infinite inwardness (the soul within the soul, as Shelley puts it).

My focus in the following chapters will be on the allegorical figurations of melancholy in the poetry of Tennyson, Elizabeth Barrett Browning, and Robert Browning, the poets most immediately inheriting the legacy of what Masao Miyoshi has called "the romantic failure in self-discovery"

(107) and struggling with the problems of the divided self. Before proceeding, however, it will perhaps help to draw together some of the diverse strands in my argument with a brief glance at the most programmatically allegorical of the melancholy Victorians, Dante Gabriel Rossetti.

Not coincidentally, in such ostentatiously allegorical works as *The House of Life* Rossetti was the Victorian most emphatically credited with finding means to express the buried life of the inmost self with precision. As Walter Pater put it, Rossetti's poetry was able to find "exact equivalence of those data within," to produce "the just transcript of that peculiar phase of soul which he alone knew, precisely as he knew it" (200). In part, as Pater recognized, Rossetti's allegorical mode was a legacy from Dante:

> This delight in concrete definition is allied with . . . Dante, the really imaginative vividness, namely, of his personifications—his hold upon them, or rather their hold upon him, with the force of a Frankenstein, when once they have taken life from him. Not Death only and Sleep, for instance, and the winged spirit of Love, but certain particular aspects of them, a whole "populace" of special hours and places, the "hour" even "which might have been, yet might not be," are living creatures, with hands and eyes and articulate voices. (201)

The extent to which Rossetti believed in the Christian symbolism that he inherited from Dante and deployed in "The Blessed Damozel" and the early poems and paintings of the virgin Mary has been debated, but I have argued that the use of such images was entirely agnostic, and I would add now that the efficacy of these images as allegorical representations of the poet's own mind was due, precisely, to their status in post-Christian thought as ruins, emptied-out emblems of dead faith (*Rossetti and Limits*, 53–76). Even the natural world, for Rossetti, provided emblems emptied of divine truth but allegorical of the speaker's own mind. "The Woodspurge" is an account of melancholic brooding:

> My eyes, wide open, had the run
> Of some ten weeds to fix upon;
> Among those few, out of the sun,
> The woodspurge flowered, three cups in one.
>
> From perfect grief there need not be
> Wisdom or even memory:
> One thing then learnt remains to me,—
> The woodspurge has a cup of three. (*Poems*, ll.9–16)

The woodspurge can no longer represent the divine Trinity but rather, in Benjamin's terms, presents itself to the melancholy gaze in which the most simple object "lacks any natural creative relationship to us" but "appears to be a symbol of some enigmatic wisdom."

Rossetti's most elaborate allegory, however, is *The House of Life*, which, as I have argued at length elsewhere, is emphatically a poem of divided consciousness, perhaps the most powerful "account of personality dismemberment in the language" (*Rossetti Revisited*, 133). As I have also argued elsewhere, *The House of Life*, especially in the "Willowwood" sonnets (49–52), is squarely in the tradition of the poems that I have here described as allegories of melancholy:

> The lover of "Willowwood" is first cousin to the questing poet of *Alastor*, and is almost as closely related to Keats's Endymion and Byron's Manfred. Except for Endymion, however, these narcissistic questers seeking their vision beyond the confines of mortal life are all ultimately seeking not fuller life, but death. Not just Rossetti, but the romantic tradition generally . . . reduces the female to the unattainable vision that keeps [the poet] questing. (*Rossetti Revisited*, 132)

As this account indicates, *The House of Life*, like its Romantic predecessors, lends itself readily to the analysis of melancholy drawn from *Hamlet* by Lacan: it is an allegory of desire for the lost ego-ideal in which the melancholy divided self broods on death to explore its own innermost depths and seek its lost unity of being.

Rossetti is the clearest practitioner of melancholy allegory in the late Romantic tradition, but allegories of melancholy take many forms in the Victorian period. As we shall see, the Romantic allegorization of imagination as desire for the veiled otherness of the inner self is at the heart of Tennyson's poetic project, and is the model for Browning's *Pauline* and *Paracelsus*, Fitzgerald's "Salámán and Absál," and, in a transgendered form, Elizabeth Barrett's *Sonnets from the Portuguese*. More generally, the Victorian dialogue of the mind with itself characteristically leads poets into allegories of their own minds that shadow forth the dialectical struggle of conscience and a "buried life," a subterranean deep self, or, in more characteristically Victorian terms, "character" and the "abysmal deeps of personality" (Tennyson, "The Palace of Art").

Chapter Two

Tennyson's Hollow Oes and Aes

I. The Abyss of Sorrow

As has always been recognized, Alfred Tennyson's characteristic mood and poetic mode was melancholy. He himself often spoke of the "black blood of the Tennysons," and in the brilliant essay that ushered him onto the literary stage in 1831, Arthur Hallam described him as a "poet of sensation" in the line of Shelley and Keats, and a poet of the "melancholy, which so evidently characterizes the spirit of modern poetry" (190). Early-twentieth-century criticism tended to see him as a poet with little to say but with a remarkable virtuosity for expressing the mood of melancholy. In fact, once Harold Nicolson generated the "two Tennysons" concept in 1923, the "Tennyson problem" for criticism was to separate the "real Tennyson," the melancholy mystic of the wolds, from the factitious Tennyson, the dull-witted spokesman of Victorian values. In effect, the two-Tennyson theory has long distinguished between Tennyson's intimate self and his public "character," his depth of feeling and his conscience.

Among the critics of this period, T. S. Eliot offered the most eloquent account of the two Tennysons and also came closest to fusing them back into one: the Victorian period, he wrote,

> had, for the most part, no hold on permanent things, or permanent truths about man and God and life and death. The surface of Tennyson stirred about with his time; and he had nothing to which to hold fast except his unique and unerring feeling for the sound of words. But in this he had something that no one else had. Tennyson's surface, his technical accomplishment, is intimate with his depths: what we most quickly see about Tennyson is that which moves between the surface and the depths, that which is of slight importance. By looking innocently at the surface we are most likely to come to the depths, to the abyss of sorrow. ("*In Memoriam*," 620)

Eliot's "one body of water theory" almost seems to unite Tennyson's surface "character" with his deep self, but his metaphor preserves the lurking dualism, since surface and depth signify language and feeling. Like all major post-Enlightenment poets, Tennyson attempted to fuse the two, the inner self, or subject, and the public world of language, the subjective and the objective, but Eliot can only explain how this is done by recapitulating Hallam's notion that the sheer sounds of the verse communicate "shades of fine emotion in the human heart . . . which are too subtle and too rapid to admit of corresponding phrases" (Hallam, 194). On the other hand, Tennyson's use of surfaces to conjure depths, especially within an "abyss of sorrow," suggests that he was writing in the melancholy allegorical mode, that the surface is semblance, a painted veil. The surface that "stirs about with his time" is the Carlylean time-vesture, the ideological character of the age, the conscience and public character of the poet. Like Thomson's, Tennyson's poetry is allegorical as it seeks to reveal "that void of darkness and old terror" beneath "life's pleasant veil of various error."

Later twentieth-century criticism of Tennyson tended to preserve the old notion of two Tennysons in one way or another. For Christopher Ricks, as well as other critics of the last generation, Tennyson is "the poet of the nursery," whose essential self (his depths) are purely "natural" and pre-ideological, something like Adorno's "primordial human nature," and the factitious Tennyson is the superficial overlay of Victorian cant. The problem remains, however, of explaining how Tennyson manages to express "primordial human nature" through the public discourse of language. One solution seems to be offered by turning to Julia Kristeva's theory that the divided self, the subject split between conscious and unconscious, expresses itself in a poetic language in which the conscious mind speaks in the "language of the Father," and the unconscious speaks in a "semiotic" mode, a natural language of rhythm and sound patterning that refers not to conscious rationality but to the Platonic *chora*, the "unnamable, improbable, hybrid, anterior to naming, to the One, to the father, and consequently, maternally connoted" (*Desire*, 133). Kristeva's theory is especially suggestive for Tennyson since it seems to explain the often noted discrepancy between Tennyson's apparent ideological meanings and his subversive emotions, conveyed from the abyss of sorrow in prosodic measure. Moreover, since "semiotic" language is associated by Kristeva with the babbling of infants, her theory would enable us to hold on to the notion of Tennyson as the poet of the nursery, uttering a language that must be authoritative because it is utterly "natural," uncorrupted by ideology. Unfortunately, however, even if Kristeva's theory is accepted, the prelinguistic utterances of the semiotic would not be comprehensible in the public domain of symbolic language, and, in any case, though Tennyson's unconscious mind and even his poetic rhythms may often work against his apparent meaning, his unconscious is not purely "natural" but is also subject to ideology. Despite Kristeva, it remains unclear, in Eliot's terms, how the surface expresses the depths, the "abyss of sorrow," in comprehensible terms. For my purposes the issue is clearer if we resolve Tennyson's "two selves" into the single but conflicted melancholy self, the conscience turned against the oceanic depths. From this point of view, the "surface" expresses the conscience, or character, always available to the symbolic order of language, and the "depths" are intimated allegorically. In short, the two-Tennyson problem is the problem of Victorian melancholy.

As Carlyle might put it, the "surface" of Tennyson consists wholly of the outward trappings of socially available discourses, but beneath them lies a "basis of darkness . . . [that] stretches down fearfully to the regions of death and Night" (*Works*, 28: 4). Carlyle's account of the darkness of infinite depths and the "blindness" needed to perceive them suggests the inadequacy of Eliot's visual approach to Tennyson's depths. Eliot's analysis founders, I think, on his use of visual metaphors to describe responses to Tennyson's poetry—we *look* through the surfaces to the depths, but trying to do this only brings us to an undergraduate notion of peeling off the superficial and apparently superfluous "level" of language to get at the hidden meaning beneath, as though poetry were a palimpsest on which the words are a mere encumbrance to be cleared away before getting to a hidden meaning that must somehow exist prior to language. The common though misleading metaphor that speaks of levels of meaning has a kind of Tennysonian sanction, since Tennyson himself speaks of words that half-conceal and half-reveal the thought within, but if we read his surface as allegorical we do not look past words to another level but look at them as signifiers of an anterior, lost meaning—the abyss of sorrow available to the penetrative imagination, perhaps even a feminine chora, which would help to explain Tennyson's characteristic use of women as allegorical signifiers of the melancholy depths of things.

Eliot's aural response is probably more helpful than his visual imagery, since one cannot simply look through the veil of Tennyson's surfaces, let alone "plough it aside," as Ruskin would seem to suggest. Though I will argue that Tennyson's poetry is ultimately allegorical, the allegorical mode is supplemented by another element of melancholy poetics suggested by Hallam's and Eliot's perception of the communicative possibilities of sound and rhythm. As Herbert Tucker argues, Tennyson's "unnamable" depths are accessible in his rhythms. Drawing on Tennyson's many references to a "measure of doom," to "Aeonian music measuring out / The steps of Time, the shocks of Chance—/ The blows of Death," Tucker argues that Tennyson's "rhythms imitate the experience of unconditional being, which he feels as a pulse at the core of consciousness and intuits at its outer limits as a patterned, governing force; they also express the deep if restricted range of moods that arise in owning the fatal necessity which that experience discloses" (*Tennyson*, 30).

Of course Tennyson is here allegorizing the abstractions of doom and death with the sensual imagery of music, but it is true that readers must *sound* the depths of Tennyson's verse to identify the sensual veil of the allegory. A similar contention has been strongly argued by Matthew Campbell, though Campbell approaches Tennyson less by sounding the depth of his melancholy than by stressing the "rhythm of his will" when Tennyson speaks as the advocate of his age's and his own strong will to self-control. For Campbell, the occurrences of rhythmic lassitude or hesitation in Tennyson's verse are measures of the poet's sense of the resistance that must be overcome by the strong will. Campbell and Tucker may not agree on which of Tennyson's rhythmic tendencies to use as a baseline, but both suggest that, as Campbell puts it, the sonic qualities of Tennyson's verse communicate "a concern with sounding a sense of self or character" (4–5). In my terms, of course, "self" and "character" are not synonymous, but character is the "strong will to self control," so I would recast Campbell's argument slightly by suggesting that the "rhythm of will" is the imposition of the constraints of character on the self. The poet's inwardness is expressed or contained in the pulses of his measures, which are, at times, described as the pulses of his own heart beating. Armstrong and Tucker both note that at his most "visionary" Tennyson is also at his most solipsistic. In his youthful "Armageddon," vision offers no visual image at all (Tucker, *Tennyson*, 44) but the speaker, attuned to his own heartbeat, affirms that

> There was a beating in the atmosphere,
> An indefinable pulsation
> Inaudible to outward sense, but felt
> Through the deep heart of every living thing,
> As if the great heart of the Universe
> Heaved with tumultuous throbbings on the vast
> Suspense of some grand issue. (iv. 28–34)

For Tucker, "this ontological throb is *the* Tennysonian signature . . . it communicates the poet's need to find in the rhythmic evidence of his own heartbeat a means of sympathetic contact with a power beyond anything he could see or touch" (*Tennyson*, 48). This does sound very much like Tennyson was, or felt himself to be, reverberating or echoing some anterior truth, possibly something like what Adorno calls "primordial human nature," and it certainly seems to be the case that he was representing his own inmost emotions, perhaps even his unconscious, in the throbbings of his verse. Ideally a reader would sound the depths of Tennyson's poetry and of his inmost self precisely because the depths sound themselves, as Tennyson says in "The Epic," by the poet's "mouthing out his hollow oes and aes, / Deep chested music" (50–51). These echoic, resounding vowels are, like his "Aeonian" measures, a hallmark of his verse and seem a direct expression from his "abyss of sorrow," from the "abysmal deeps of Personality" ("Palace of Art," *Poems,* 1: 223).

Tennyson would seem, in Kristeva's terms, to have pioneered a "specific economy of imaginary discourses . . . [that] are constituently very close to depression and at the same time show a shift from depression to possible meaning" (*Black Sun,* 100). These discourses include the transmutation of the *imaginary* into artifice specifically through "the means of prosody, the language beyond language that inserts into the sign the rhythm and alliteration of semiotic processes . . . which unsettles naming and, by building up a plurality of connotations around the sign, affords the subject a chance to imagine the nonmeaning, or the true meaning, of the Thing" (*Black Sun,* 97). Kristeva's attempt to identify a language beyond language is inevitably obscure, but her emphasis on the ability of poetic artifice, and particularly rhythm, to express the truth of melancholy is consistent with Hallam's and Tucker's analyses of the acoustics of Tennyson's melancholy verse and with the perception most notoriously expressed by Eliot that although Tennyson had little of note to say, as the "saddest of English poets" he was able to communicate from the abyss of sorrow because of his remarkable "technical accomplishment."

Matthew Rowlinson's intricate psychoanalytic reading of "Armageddon" as allegorical is more helpful than Kristeva's generalizations. Rowlinson's account is much too involved to recapitulate here, but he sees Tennyson's visionary mode as an attempt to recover a vision, a memory, of an ideal that is always already lost and that only ever existed as an ego-ideal. Though Rowlinson does not associate the poem with "Kubla Khan," he does note that the ideal is imagined as a fabulously splendid city presided over by an "oriental despot," in a version of the "imperial sublime" (45), and we may be reminded of Coleridge's "Abyssinian maid" by Tennyson's attempts to recover the visionary city "represented . . . as a woman." Moreover, just as the "shadow of the dome of pleasure / Floated midway on the waves" in Coleridge's poem, the vision of Armageddon "is visible as [a woman] only as a reflection in a river" (47). Rowlinson's reading of the poem as allegory is far more psychoanalytically technical than anything I propose, but it is consistent with seeing the reflected vision as *schein* or semblance, and the poem generally as melancholy allegory in the tradition I have traced.

The poetics of melancholy, adumbrated in "Armageddon," anticipate a thematic interest in exotic Orientalism that I discuss more fully in the next section, but first the remarkable "technical accomplishment" that enabled Tennyson to speak from the "abyss of sorrow" may be described through close examination of his poetry, and for the remainder of this section I will look at a few of his best poems to discuss both the characteristics of his prosody and the subjective "truth" of the melancholia it expresses. Tennyson's most explicit poem to express these concerns is the beautiful lyric from *The Princess*, "Tears, Idle Tears."

"Tears, Idle Tears" appears, somewhat incongruously, at a point in *The Princess* when Princess Ida calls for a cheerful song to "lightlier move / The minutes" (iv. 17–18) over the preprandial wine. For Tennyson, if not for Princess Ida, the music of the lyrical mode does not abridge the time but rather sounds the abyss, as the singer of the lyric is immediately engulfed in her own melancholy music:

> Tears, idle tears, I know not what they mean,
> Tears from the depths of some divine despair
> Rise in the heart, and gather to the eyes,
> In looking on the happy Autumn-fields,
> And thinking of the days that are no more. (iv. 21–25)

Speaking through the medium of a nameless woman, Tennyson sounds the depths of an impersonal, apparently universal sorrow that lies too deep for words but wells from the depths to drown the self in tears. The nameless singer has no identity, no character, beyond the "divine despair" that speaks itself through her in the form of tears. Rather like the Indian maid of *Endymion*, she is simply a personification of sadness, and far from providing amusement for an idle moment, she brings a corpse to the feast, the corpse of dead love, days that are no more, the "Death in Life" (iv. 40) of the past buried in memory. Though the singer presents herself as the medium of "divine despair," the consolation of melancholy presents itself, in language suggestive of Benjamin's emphasis on ruins and corpses, as a spirit that "haunt[s] / About the moulder'd lodges of the past" (iv. 44–45), as a "death's-head at the wine" (iv. 69).

The "divine despair" is allegorized as universal, but correspondences with *In Memoriam* indicate that the poem allegorizes Tennyson's own grief for the death of Arthur Hallam, that it gains its force as an allegory of the poet's own mind. The "fair ship" bearing "lost Arthur's loved remains" in

In Memoriam (ix. 1–3) is strongly paralleled in the second stanza of "Tears, Idle Tears":

> Fresh as the first beam glittering on a sail,
> That brings our friends up from the underworld
> Sad as the last which reddens over one
> That sinks with all we love below the verge,
> So sad, so fresh, the days that are no more. (iv. 26–30)

More subtly, yet even more significantly, the imagery of the third stanza allegorizes and generalizes the personal grief expressed in *In Memoriam* by the melancholy brooding on Hallam's tomb and coating it over with the semblance of divine glory, what Wordsworth called the "gleam, / The light that never was, on sea or land, / The consecration and the Poet's dream" ("Elegiac Stanzas," ll.14–16):

> When on my bed the moonlight falls,
>   I know that in thy place of rest
>   By that broad water of the west,
> There comes a glory on the walls:
>
> Thy marble bright in dark appears,
>   As slowly steals a silver flame
>   Along the letters of thy name,
> And o'er the number of thy years.
>
> The mystic glory swims away;
>   From off my bed the moonlight dies;
>   And closing eaves of wearied eyes,
> I sleep till dusk is dipt in gray:
>
> And then I know the mist is drawn
>   A lucid veil from coast to coast,
>   And in the dark church like a ghost
> Thy tablet glimmers to the dawn. (lxvii. 1–16)

In the song from *The Princess* this fantasy of the risen spirit is evoked by the matter-of-fact and seemingly less meaningful image of the dawn slowly illuminating the bedroom window: the "divine despair" is

> sad and strange as in dark summer dawns
> The earliest pipe of half-awakened birds

> To dying ears, when unto dying eyes
> The casement slowly grows a glimmering square;
> So sad, so strange, the days that are no more. (iv. 31–35)

The passage from *The Princess* replaces the wholly imagined glimmer of Hallam's tomb with the perfectly familiar, matter-of-fact "glimmering square" of the casement, providing an allegorical signifier of subjective grief with an enigmatic image from the object world and demonstrating, in Benjamin's terms, the power of the melancholic gaze to transform an image "incapable of emanating any meaning or significance of its own" into "something different: a key to a realm of hidden knowledge" (see chapter 1, section II). Though spoken through an already allegorized figure of "divine despair," the lyric is manifestly an allegory of the poet's own mind, and its images, incapable of speaking any universal truth, speak with the absolute ontological authority of subjective truth.

Tennyson provided several explanations of the poem, as well as of the phrase "divine despair," including the comment that "This song came to me on the yellowing autumn-tide at Tintern Abbey, full for me of its bygone memories. It is the sense of the abiding in the transient" (*Poems*, 2: 232n). The remark obviously invites comparison with "Tintern Abbey," but Tennyson's poem darkens Wordsworth's nostalgia, replacing its renovating virtue with a deeper melancholy that does not renovate but does provide the transient individual a sense of communion with an abiding, eternal power, and of separation from it in the transience of mortality. As the last stanza makes clear, the poem is not a tribute to renovating power but a lament for irredeemable loss:

> Dear as remembered kisses after death
> And sweet as those by hopeless fancy feigned
> On lips that are for others; deep as love,
> Deep as first love, and wild with all regret;
> O Death in Life, the days that are no more. (iv. 36–40)

Nostalgia can only bring the dead past into the life of the present as the corpse of dead love. In another comment on the poem, however, Tennyson hinted at a more positive, though no more expressible reading of melancholy inwardness: "It is in a way like St. Paul's 'groanings which cannot be uttered.' . . . It is what I always have felt even from a boy, and what as a boy I called the 'passion of the past'" (*Poems*, 3: 32n). "Groanings" hardly seems a reassuring word, but this explanation at least carries a theological hope, like St. Paul's, that once freed from the transient, from "the body of this death" (Romans 7:24), the self may fully reach its union with the "abiding." The poem's mourning for the self expressed as a passion for the past thematizes melancholy as a source of transpersonal authority on the basis of idiosyncratic personal associations but also, on the surface, in the apparently wholly natural form of felt sensation, tears. In this way melancholy is its own seal of authenticity, not produced by the mere individual but coming to him from an unimpeachable if unidentifiable source.

In "Tears, Idle Tears," but even more obviously in "Mariana," "The Lady of Shalott," and "The Palace of Art," Tennyson represents melancholy as theorized by Adorno: "Inwardness is the historical prison of primordial human nature. The emotion of the trapped is melancholy. In melancholy truth represents itself, and the movement of melancholy is one toward the delivery of lost 'meaning.' A truly dialectical notion. For if truth presents itself in melancholy, it indeed presents itself to pure inwardness exclusively as semblance" (60–61). Quite possibly something like "primordial human nature" is what Tennyson had in mind by "the abiding," though more likely he was thinking of a transcendent cosmic power made immanent in the emotion of melancholy. Tennyson's decision to mimic the sensibilities of women, particularly of abandoned women, to represent the emotion of the trapped, however, is not "natural" but a response to the Victorian gender ideology that saw women as more subject to emotional lability than men and also more or less literally entrapped them in the domestic parlor and, more abstractly, in confined roles within the social structure. It is perhaps worth noting that Kierkegaard, who largely inspired Adorno's thought on melancholy, in the long section of *Either/Or* entitled "Silhouettes" centered one of his most extensive meditations on the dialectic of inwardness in the analysis of the sensibilities of three imagined women abandoned by their lovers.[1] Tennyson's imagining of the melancholy Mariana is no more purely natural than Kierkegaard's imaginative creation of three complex female melancholics—both assume that women are more a prey to sensations than men because they are less reflective and intellectual and more at the mercy of circumstances. Instead of a dialectical movement of inwardness, however, Tennyson represents the emotion of the trapped as a helpless emotional emptiness and stasis.

Mariana is not physically trapped in the moated grange, but from the first stanza it is clear that she is stuck there:

> With blackest moss the flower-plots
>   Were thickly crusted, one and all:
> The rusted nails fell from the knots
>   That held the pear to the gable-wall.
> The broken sheds looked sad and strange:

> Unlifted was the clinking latch;
> Weeded and worn the ancient thatch
> Upon the lonely moated grange.
> She only said, "My life is dreary,
> He cometh not," she said;
> She said, "I am aweary, aweary,
> I would that I were dead!" (11.1–12)

The moat is presumably not filled with crocodiles, and the latch is "unlifted," not "unliftable": evidently the most oppressive physical restraints on Mariana are the "shadow of the poplar" that "fell / Upon her head, across her brow" (11.55–56) and the "thick-moted sunbeam" that "lay / Athwart the chambers" (11.78–79). Even Mariana should be able to fight her way through a shadow and a sunbeam, so students reading the poem make a kind of sense when they ask, "why doesn't she just leave and find the guy?" But the question misses the point. As an objectified image of the poet's "imaginary," she is segregated from the faculty of will and is not trapped in the grange but in her own brooding passivity, by her own melancholy. John Stuart Mill famously selected "Mariana" as the poem that best represented Tennyson's "power of *creating* scenery, in keeping with some state of human feeling; so fitted to it as to be the embodied symbol of it, and to summon up the feeling itself, with a power not to be surpassed by anything but reality" ("Tennyson's Poems," 561–62). Mill's remark suggests that Tennyson's scenery, his visible surface, is to be read as a bodying forth of the inward invisible as in melancholy. It is a form of allegory in which the subjectivity fixates on the "*a priori* object[s]" that represent its phenomenology. In "Mariana" the strong emotion is melancholia, and James Richardson's superb reading of the poem reveals some of the ways Tennyson created it through the setting:

> [R]eading "With blackest moss the flower-plots were thickly crusted," one thinks of Keats's "To bend with apples the *moss'd* cottage-trees"—in both lines, moss is not just an object, but something that *happens*. Similarly, the nails are "rusted," not "rusty," and the thatch is in an ambiguous disarray because "weeded," a word that usually means "cleared of weeds," is forced to mean "weedy" as well. Things have *happened* to helpless objects, and there is a sense of causeless effect. Not "no one lifted the latch," but "unlifted was the clinking latch," which refuses even to imagine a being capable of working a latch. Its silent clinking therefore becomes a ghostly attack. Similarly, nails work loose often enough but having them fall emphasizes the unpredictability of a Tennysonian world in which the stabilizing forces of friction and process often fail. (45)

As Richardson's description makes clear, the poems creates its feeling of melancholy through images of decay as Mariana's mind fixates on transience and her grange visibly decomposes into a ruin. The entire setting is an allegorical emblem of decomposition and the mortality of all things human.

Mariana projects her own sense of helplessness on the poem's objects, or, rather, Tennyson projects a sense of melancholy onto Mariana, who projects it onto the objects. Numerous critics have described how Tennyson's prosodic virtuosity further engenders the state of helpless entrapment: rhythmically, the iambic tetrameter lines are slowed by strong caesuras: "With blackest moss // the flower-plots / Were thickly crusted // one and all." Even the three syllables of "one and all" must be further stretched to match the length of the longer feet. Similarly, the verse is further slowed, even to a stop, as the stanza reaches the refrain with its trimeter lines that must be stretched to match the rhythm of the dominant tetrameter. The verse is further slowed by the heavy punctuation of the refrain and by the long vowel sounds—not only the "hollow oes and aes" but especially the interminable "ees" of "dreary . . . aweary, aweary." The rhyme scheme adds further to the sense of stasis with its constant resoundings of the long vowels and with the echoing double rhymes of the refrain. In addition, and most obviously, the repetition of the almost unvarying and always wearying refrain at the end of every stanza generates a frustrated sense of always returning to where we started. Combined with Tennyson's masterful orchestration of vowels, diphthongs, and impeding consonant clusters, the sound of the verse effectively sounds Mariana's depths. The cumulative effect of the dense patterning of sound is, as Tucker well describes it (reversing the negative polarity of Pound's complaint about the "gumminess" of Victorian verse), a kind of "'gum' or mucilage of a rare vocalic and consonantal music" in which "discretely observed details are held together by the power of sound" (*Tennyson*, 73), and, for that matter, Mariana is herself stuck in place, trapped in the poem's viscous language and in her own obsessive refrain. The echoic sounds, moreover, suggest a kind of hollowness at the core of Mariana's consciousness, a desolation that bespeaks the loss at the origin of desire. What Mariana most obviously has lost is the absent lover, but as the discreteness of the observed detail implies, she more fundamentally lacks the organizing power of a shaping will or fully coherent self. Tennyson's imitation of a female passivity and sensibility, of Mariana's melancholy, is embodied in the poem's stasis, its lack of a "rhythm of will" (see Campbell, 71–85). In this claustrophobic sense of entrapment each object seems to lie crushingly athwart Mariana's consciousness and, as Carol Christ says, the "mesmerizing" "acuteness" of the objects "conveys the blankness of a mind that under prolonged emotional strain seizes upon any object to find some release. Only through the sensation of objects can Mariana escape her despair within. Yet the sharpness of the images shows this impression is painful as well. The isolation of images from each other suggests her own isolation" (19–20).

As Christ discusses at length, in Victorian literature grief and melancholy frequently produce a heightening of sensation at the expense of reflection.[2] This form of brooding is most conspicuously present in "Mariana," in the speaker of *Maud* brooding on a seashell, and in Rossetti's speaker in "My Sister's Sleep" and, especially, "The Woodspurge," but it is also evident in Ruskin's turning the precisely observed details of Pre-Raphaelite painting into narratives, in the paintings themselves, and even in Lockwood's analogy comparing a prisoner's scrutiny of a spider with country dwellers' observations of their neighbors in the prison of rural isolation. Intense melancholic brooding generally lacks the organizing will to produce narrative on the order of *Wuthering Heights,* but it does engender a hyperesthesia like that in Hallam's poetics of sensation as described by Armstrong: "Since self is composed of 'fragments of being,' and is 'the common character' of a series of 'momentary beings,' the way to transform 'self' or consciousness is to attack through sensation the 'ligatures' of habitual thought which bind the self in a coherent chain of association" (*Victorian Poetry,* 63). The experienced self is, of course, the coherent self bound by the ligatures of habitual thought, except when sensation overwhelms reflection in the blankness of melancholy; for Hallam the "ultimate fact of consciousness [is] that the soul exists as one subject in various successive states" (137). Consequently, loosing the ligatures of thought may have the possibly salutary effect of subverting ideology, as Armstrong suggests, but it obliterates the unified self, and brings about the loss of the ego-ideal theorized by Freud as the fundamental characteristic of melancholy. On the other hand, this melancholic hyperesthesia is obviously a heightening of the aesthetic sense, and it indicates one strong reason for the close link in Victorian poetry between melancholy and poetic sensibility in a tendency to articulate dead but enigmatic objects into an allegorical structure representative of feeling. This link is still more clearly apparent in "The Palace of Art," in which the soul is separated from the organizing self ("I") of the speaker:

> I built my soul a lordly pleasure-house,
>   Wherein at ease for aye to dwell.
> I said, "O Soul, make merry and carouse,
>   Dear soul, for all is well!" (ll.1–4)

The soul is an aesthete who does not possess the will to make distinctions among her many artistic treasures. Without a will, she is also without a self since, as J. F. Ferrier argued, a person without a "will . . . is not a conscious or percipient being, not an *ego*" (Campbell, 69). The opening stanza of "The Palace of Art" obviously draws on the aesthetic pipe dream of "Kubla Khan," but more significantly it anticipates the aesthetic hedonism of "The Rubaiyat of Omar Khayyam" and the "new hedonism" of late Victorian aestheticism. But this hyperesthesia inevitably turns out to be its own punishment, the stagnant entrapment of solipsistic melancholy, a hell found in the "abysmal deeps of Personality" ("The Palace of Art,"1.223).

As is implicit in "Mariana" and explicit in "The Palace of Art," Tennyson's representation of the aesthetic reveries of entrapped women is a form of melancholy brooding on death, or at least "Death in Life." Mariana is, in effect, buried alive in the moated grange, and the soul in her pleasure house is ultimately seen as a corpse "mouldering with the dull earth's mouldering sod" (1.261) and "Shut up as in a crumbling tomb, girt round / With blackness as a solid wall" (11.273–74). Consequently, poring on emblems in the object world, especially on works of art, ultimately amounts to brooding on death, on corpses: where once she had seen works of art, the soul comes to see "corpses three months old" (1.243). That brooding women and works of art both allegorize death and decay is startling, but this point has been extensively and convincingly argued in Elizabeth Bronfen's *Over Her Dead Body*. Examining Poe's infamous identification of the dead or dying woman as the most poetic thing in existence, Bronfen argues that

> Part of the equation between femininity and death resides precisely in the fact that Woman as man's object of desire (*objet a*) is on the side of death not only because she repeats the always already lost primordial mother but because she so often serves as a non-reciprocal "dead" figure of imaginary projection, given that, in Lacan's terms, "the whole of [man's] realization in the sexual relation comes down to fantasy." (63)

In terms more accessible to Tennyson, the pursuit of beauty in Romantic allegory is always a pursuit simultaneously of beauty as the fantasized ego-ideal and of death. Bronfen draws on the work of Sarah Kofman to offer the provocative suggestion that

> all effective art is the work of melancholy precisely because . . . the creation of beauty allows us to escape from the elusiveness of the material world into an illusion of eternity (a denial of loss), even as it

> imposes on us the realization that beauty is itself elusive, intangible, receding. Because it is created on the basis of the same elusiveness it tries to obliterate, what art in fact does is mourn beauty, and in so doing it mourns itself. (64)

Tennyson's simultaneously emphatic and enigmatic representation of these issues is another poem about an entrapped woman, "The Lady of Shalott." "The Lady of Shalott" is a far more self-evidently allegorical work than "Mariana" or even "The Palace of Art," and most commentators have seen the Lady as a figure for the artistic vocation, weaving representations of the world as it passes by at an appropriately aesthetic distance from her tower, already framed both in her window and in her mirror. From the start the artist figure is presented as removed from life in a haunted realm where only "Shadows of the world appear" (1.48). Tennyson himself said that the key to the poem is the end of part ii, when the lady sees "two young lovers lately wed" and declares herself "half sick of shadows": "The newborn love for something, for some one in the wide world from which she has been so long secluded, takes her out of the shadows into that of realities" (Hallam Tennyson, *Memoir,* 1: 117). What tempts the Lady, however, is not a reality but an image, the shadow of an ideal from the fantasy world of romance, "bold Sir Lancelot" in a flashing of the light that never was on sea or land. The climax of the poem literalizes the allegorical linking of feminine beauty, desire, aesthetic image, and death in the figure of the Lady's corpse, a signifier floating into Camelot as a signed and titled work of art. The "lovely" corpse (1.169) is Poe's most poetical thing in existence *par excellence,* and the poem is the perfect emblem of Tennyson's representation of beauty as a result of the melancholy allegorical gaze brooding on death. It is no wonder that it became a Victorian icon.

Tennyson's usual gendering of the melancholy/aesthetic temperament as female is not a compliment to women but an aspersion on the aesthetic sensibility as lacking the masculine powers of reflection and productive will, so it is not surprising that he also represents melancholia in the male mind only if it is sufficiently "second rate" and "sensitive" as in "Supposed Confessions," drugged into passive stupor as in "The Lotos-Eaters," or decayed by senescence as in "Tithonus." The poems featuring women may, if only incidentally, provide a critique of the stupefying effect of Victorian gender ideology, but "The Lotos-Eaters" and "Ulysses" offer an apparently more calculated representation of the demoralizing, melancholy effects of emergent capitalism even on vigorous men.

Entrapped in effeminate passivity by the drug, the mariners of "The Lotos-Eaters" epitomize the buried life, speaking as "voices from the grave" (1.34) to brood on "death, dark death" (1.98) and on the death in life of memory sepulchred in the depths of the mind as "Two handfuls of white dust, shut in an urn of brass" (1.113). An even greater prosodic tour de force than "Mariana," "The Lotos-Eaters" similarly fuses the strong emotion of the perceiving mind with the perceived world in a "rich vocalic music." The strong emotion once again is melancholy and constitutes a morbid withdrawal from the world of action, but in this case it is "mild-minded melancholy," an addictively pleasant respite from labor. The shifting rhythms of the sleepily seductive choric song are perhaps even more masterfully lulling than the introductory Spenserian stanzas, but the opening stanza will serve to illustrate the comparison to "Mariana":

"Courage!" he said, and pointed toward the land,
"This mounting wave will roll us shoreward soon."
In the afternoon they came unto a land
In which it seemed always afternoon.
All round the coast the languid air did swoon,
Breathing like one that hath a weary dream.
Full-faced above the valley stood the moon;
And like a downward smoke, the slender stream
Along the cliff to fall and pause and fall did seem. (ll.1–9)

Ulysses' brief dramatic monologue of nine words is the only counterpoint in the poem to the mariners' longing for peace, and even this brief speech invites submission to the elements: "Courage! . . . This mounting wave will roll us shoreward soon." Aside from the single word, "Courage," the whole stanza, and the whole poem, submit to a lassitude that, in the context of the Victorian work ethic, can only be regarded as unmanly idleness, degrading sloth. The mariners never mount more than a weak sophistic argument in favor of abandoning their work, their king, their country, and their families. The argument amounts to an affirmation that the life of a vegetable is preferable to the life of a laboring man, and their whole lengthy song can be described as unmanly whining: "why / Should life all labour be? / Let us alone . . . / Let us alone . . . / Let us alone . . . (ll.86–93). The argument of the poetry, however, is stronger than that of the logic; even the speaker of the opening stanza provides a prosodic narcotic stronger than any rational argument. The Spenserian stanza, with its intricate recursive rhymes and its full stop in the closing alexandrine and couplet, is particularly well suited to create a "Mariana"-like sense of hollowness and stasis, and Tennyson adds to and exaggerates these effects with hypnotic power. In the first four lines the sense that mariners and verse alike are going nowhere is achieved not only by the echoic recursive rhymes but also by the outrageous repetition of the word "land" as its own rhyme, by eliminating the forward momentum "shoreward," stalling it in the internal near double-rhyme of "toward," and by impeding the momentum of "soon" with the premature internal rhyme of "afternoon," which returns the verse to where it started by rhyming with itself in line 4. The "land" of line 3 is still the "land" of line 1, and repeating the word "afternoon" twice in two lines does make it seem "always afternoon," as if time were standing still, like the uncanny downward smoke of the waterfall. It would be tedious and superfluous to review all of the tricks of assonance and alliteration that further contribute both to the sense of stasis and to an echoing that seems to reverberate from hollowness. I will, however, jump to the end of the stanza to note the eeriness of the waterfall that pauses, not coincidentally, at the pause of the caesura in the final line, and to the brilliant use of the alexandrine's gratuitous sixth foot to glance back at the whole of the preceding stanza, and call everything into doubt with the implication that it may all be, indeed, a "weary dream" that only "did seem." These seductive effects are a reminder that melancholy is not all bad—even Mariana's house was "dreamy" (1.61)—but they also increase the sense of being mastered by sensation, giving in to solipsistic isolation, to a distorted and distorting subjectivity that may be only hallucinatory semblance. Tennyson's representation of melancholy inwardness in "Mariana" has been likened to Walter Pater's powerful recommendation of hyperestheticism as the best use of the solipsism he posits as the unavoidable human condition, but Pater's account is in some ways even more strongly suggestive of "The Lotos-Eaters":

> [T]he whole scope of observation is dwarfed to the narrow chamber of the individual mind. Experience, already reduced to a swarm of impressions, is ringed round for us by that thick wall of personality through which no real voice has ever pierced on its way to us, or from us to that which we can only conjecture to be without. Every one of these impressions is the impression of the individual in his isolation, each mind keeping as a solitary prisoner its own dream of a world. (60)

Like Mariana, the lotos-eating mariners are prisoners of their own consciousness, and despite their solidarity as a chorus, each evidently lives within his own dream of a world. As was the case for the visionary poet of "Armageddon," the apparently cosmic cadence that each man hears as a confirmation of his own rhythm of existence turns out to be only his own heartbeat, and voices from without seem to be spoken by fellow mariners sealed off in the narrowest of all prisons:

>   to him the gushing of the wave
> Far far away did seem to mourn and rave
> On alien shores; and if his fellow spake,
> His voice was thin, as voices from the grave;
> And deep-asleep he seemed, yet all awake,
> And music in his ears his beating heart did make. (11.31–36)

This music would seem to be the "Aeonian music" that Tucker persuasively argues is the authoritative source of Tennyson's inspiration and prosodic practice, and combined here with the phrase "far far away," which Tennyson said had always had a powerful influence on him, the stanza suggests both that the lotos inspires poetic apprehension akin to Tennyson's own and that such apprehension involves a melancholy withdrawal of the isolated self. The choric song further develops the attraction of dreamy, self-enclosed, poetic reverie as the mariners praise the "Music that gentlier on the spirit lies, / Than tired eyelids upon tired eyes" (11.50–51). In his revisions for the 1842 version of the poem, Tennyson added lines in which the mariners clearly put themselves morally in the wrong by hubristically identifying themselves with the Epicurean gods in their indifference to human suffering, but in the 1832 version it was quite possible to read the poem as a paean to the inspiring power of the lotos and a justification both for the mariners' withdrawal from labor and for the poet's withdrawal from the strenuous business of the world. In fact, in his often perceptive, if also hostile and supercilious, review of the 1832 volume, John Wilson Croker easily associated Tennyson's singing with that of the mariners: "How they got home you must read in Homer;—Mr. Tennyson—himself, we presume, a dreamy lotos-eater, a delicious lotos-eater—leaves them in full song" (594). Such a reading leaves the poet open to charges of an unmanly shirking of responsibility, so it is not surprising that Croker's review, like John Wilson's in *Blackwood's*, is rife with ridicule of Tennyson's supposed effeminacy. Probably because of the poem's susceptibility to such a reading, Tennyson's revision for 1842 made clear his condemnation of the mariners' attitudes.

Still, the poem's close association of melancholy and song suggests that, for good or ill, melancholy does have an undeniable poetic allure and power, and even the 1842 insertion about the Epicurean gods may be seen as an anticipation of the so-called "new hedonism" of Pater and the aesthetic movement later in the century. To the extent that "The Lotos-Eaters" is seen to endorse withdrawal from labor for the sake of the beauty of sweet music, the poem may be seen as subversive of the Victorian ideology of work, if only because labor is implicitly characterized as weakening the individual self. Isobel Armstrong, however, convincingly argues that the poem is not simply subversive in its withdrawal from the labor force but is an active and powerful "critique of oppression" (*Victorian Poetry*, 86):

> It is no accident that the mariners' need for Lotos is to allay the horrors of labour, for opium was often taken by industrial workers for the same reason. . . ."The Lotos-Eaters" is both the *expression* of the addictive desire in which the drug requires further drugging, and an *analysis* of the conditions under which the unhappy consciousness of the unhappy body comes into being. (87; emphasis in original)

Armstrong further shows how Tennyson produces a Carlylean, proto-Marxist critique of the alienation of labor: "Tennyson brilliantly renders . . . the psychological state" of laborers reduced to cogs in the industrial process:

> For the Lotos-Eaters all experience is always emptying out, because identity itself is transformed, "taken from us" (91), into an estranged past when consciousness has no direct access to what it makes: *production*, materially and psychologically, is a *subtraction* from identity; "ah, why / Should life all labour be? . . . Let us alone. What is it that will last? / All things are taken from us, and become / Portions and parcels of the dreadful Past." (87–88, 90–92; emphasis in original)

Armstrong is right, I think, about what the poem accomplishes, though it is impossible to say whether Tennyson fully intended his alienated mariners to represent the alienated conditions of modern industrial labor or whether the implication presents itself as an inevitable analogy with the poet's alienated self as the laboring consciousness allegorizes it in externalized imagery. The same is true of "Ulysses," a poem that only *seems* to reverse the situation of "The Lotos-Eaters" as Ulysses, addressing his mariners, who have somehow returned to Ithaca, develops his call for "Courage!" in an exhortation "To strive, to seek, to find, and not to yield" (1.70). Although "Ulysses" is clearly "a poem of will," as Campbell says (131), in recent years most readers have agreed with Robert Langbaum that Tennyson's "emotional bias," "a certain life-weariness, a longing for rest through oblivion," is "all the more powerful because it appears to be subconscious . . . it even conflicts in a poem like *Ulysses* with what seems to be his intent" (89). The emotional drag on Ulysses' call for active will is evident in the rhythm, in what Langbaum calls the "enervated cadence" (90) of Tennyson's emotional bias. The usual and surely correct way to account for this emotional drag is to recall Tennyson's comment that

"Ulysses" was a poem of mourning for Arthur Hallam: "The poem was written soon after Arthur Hallam's death, and gave my feeling about the need for going forward, and braving the struggle of life perhaps more simply than anything in 'In Memoriam'" (Hallam Tennyson, *Memoir*, 1: 196). But though Tennyson was mourning for a friend, the tone of the poem is not one of mourning but of melancholy, because Ulysses is mourning the loss of an ego-ideal. Rhetorically, he encourages his mariners and himself with the affirmation that "Though much is taken, much abides; and though / We are not now that strength which in old days / Moved earth and heaven; that which we are, we are" (ll.65–67), but emotionally and prosodically the poem grieves for the much that is taken, "that strength," and laments that "that which we are" is old and comparatively decrepit. As in "Tears, Idle Tears," the poem expresses "wild regret" for the "Death in Life, the days that are no more!" (1.40). Consequently, Ulysses' remark that "I am a part of all that I have met" (1.18) is less a boast about his fame than a lament akin to the Lotos-Eaters' regret that "All things are taken from us, and become / Portions and parcels of the Dreadful Past" (ll.91–92). Even for kings, experience seems not to create a self by the cumulative accretion of the past, but rather seems to use up the self: the events he has met have not become a part of him, but he has left parts of himself behind, with all that he has met:

> I am a part of all that I have met;
> Yet all experience is an arch wherethrough
> Gleams that untravelled world, whose margin fades
> For ever and for ever when I move.
> How dull it is to pause, to make an end,
> To rust unburnished, not to shine in use!
> As though to breathe were life. Life piled on life
> Were all too little, and of one to me
> Little remains. (ll.18–26)

The "untravelled world" for which Ulysses yearns is one of the poem's several echoes of *Hamlet,* recalling Hamlet's description of death as the "undiscovered country from whose bourn / No traveler returns" (III.i.80–81): as Tennyson's traveler moves forward in time, toward death, the horizon recedes before him. But Ulysses is not thinking only of the future and death but also of the "Death in Life," the remembered past, which also presents a fading horizon as he moves away from it. Ulysses, spent in the past, fades into a ghostly "gray spirit yearning in desire" (1.30) for his irrecoverable past self as well as for the dubious "new things" (1.28) of the future. The melancholy drag of the rhythm, moreover, is almost thematized in the metrical puns of line 22, which assert that it is "dull" to pause and make an end, but pause on "pause" at the caesura and make an end on "end." The enervated cadence of the poem becomes more dramatically apparent as Ulysses' exhortation reaches what ought to be its rhetorical climax:

>   My mariners,
> Souls that have toiled, and wrought, and thought with me—
> That ever with a frolic welcome took
> The thunder and the sunshine, and opposed
> Free hearts, free foreheads—you and I are old;
> Old age hath yet his honour and his toil;
> Death closes all: but something ere the end,
> Some work of noble note, may yet be done,
> Not unbecoming men that strove with Gods.
> The lights begin to twinkle from the rocks:
> The long day wanes: the slow moon climbs: the deep
> Moans round with many voices. (ll.45–56)

Just as the speech gathers speed and approaches a "rhythm of will," Ulysses' free forehead crashes into the frolic welcome of a full stop with the heavy caesura of line 49, and only sputters for a few words more before shuddering to another halt with the heavily stressed closing syllable that only returns him to the grim truth he has been trying to overcome: "You and I are old." From here the cadence proceeds by fits and starts, punctuated with the undeniable melancholy of mortality: "Death closes all"; "the long day wanes." The slow spondaic feet and the trademark "hollow oes and aes" assimilate Ulysses' speech to the many other voices moaning round the deep. The split between Ulysses' exhortation and his moaning tone seems perfectly to epitomize melancholy dialectic: the symbolic language of rational understanding says one thing, and the semiotic language of prosody says another. But of course this only returns us to Langbaum's formulation that the subconscious emotional bias in Ulysses conflicts with what seems to be his intent. The overall effect, however formulated, is to present Ulysses as etiolated to a gray spirit, a ghost of his former self, now become a name in a sign system in which words no longer correspond to things.

In both "The Lotos-Eaters" and "Ulysses" the melancholy cadences suggest an alienation of the self from its striving and labor and reflect the economic conditions of Victorian England, but the overdetermined melancholy of the poems is also a function of literary history. The moaning of the deep and the echoing of the twilight are in part a result of

Tennyson's belated position in literary history. At least since Burton's excessively allusive introduction to *The Anatomy of Melancholy* in the name of Democritus Jr., a heavily allusive style has been characteristic of the literature of melancholy in the English tradition, and in "Ulysses" the deep moans round conspicuously with the voices of Homer, Dante, Milton, Shakespeare, and lesser poets. Ulysses' voice, like those of the Lotos-Eaters, is one among others that seem to speak from the hollow of the grave, or at least from the ghostly afterlife of poetic language.³ Except for the echoes of Tennyson's sources in Homer and Dante, the most conspicuous echoes are of *Hamlet* and particularly of Hamlet's melancholic tendency to "feed on the metaphysical contradictions between finite and infinite, time and eternity." For Ulysses as for Hamlet, the time is out of joint, or at least he is out of step with time, and for all his speechmaking he is unable to whip himself into action and fulfill the duty he sets himself. On the other hand, as has been often observed, it would hardly seem that Ulysses' desire to abandon his "aged wife," his country, and his people is in accord with Victorian values, so even his conscious intent, like that of the Lotos-Eaters, may be seen as an ideological critique of the conditions that wear down not only laborers but even the Captains of Industry. If so, the melancholy of the poem is not, perhaps, at odds with the apparent intent but rather reinforces the debilitating effects of an ideology of strenuous adherence to duty.

The poem, however, is probably best seen as an affirmation of "character" and an expression of conscience meant to reinforce rather than subvert Victorian ideology. Ulysses' desire to set off from his island home to seek undiscovered lands is certainly consistent with Tennyson's love for the literature of discovery and with the Victorian admiration of naval heroes, and by Tennyson's own account the poem was meant to enforce the Victorian call to strive with the conditions of life: it was a call for "going forward, and braving the struggle of life" (Hallam Tennyson, *Memoir*, 1. 96). Consequently, the poem may be seen as an exhortation to the Victorian work ethic, and possibly even to imperial adventure, only attenuated by the emotional bias of Tennyson's melancholy.

Certainly Ulysses' desire to seek, to find, and not to yield seems to epitomize the Victorian imperial ideal, and it has been widely thought in part to serve that ideological purpose, but aside from the technical point that the poem is too early to be properly called "Victorian" at all, Matthew Rowlinson points out that it is much too early to speak the imperial idiom that only emerged in the last third of the century. Further, as Rowlinson demonstrates, the use of the poem to promote an ideology that created "the high visibility of 'Ulysses' in the canon of Tennyson's poetry was the result of historical developments that considerably postdate its writing and publication" (267). Moreover, the tone of Ulysses' instructions to Telemachus, Rowlinson notes, is preposterously akin not to the rhetoric of the dawn of empire but to its twilight. A poem expressing apparent enthusiasm for the noble work yet to be done in old age, the final lines of "Ulysses" are frequently read at retirement parties, and Rowlinson's comments capture some of the incongruity of this: "[H]e seems to be imagining between himself and his subjects not just differences of class, but bizarrely, cultural and even racial differences. He sounds, in fact, like a colonial administrator turning over the reins to a successor just before stepping on the boat to go home. But, of course, Ulysses in Ithaca already is at home" (267).

Rowlinson's argument against reading "Ulysses" as an endorsement and encouragement of imperial ideology is entirely convincing, but as his readings also suggest, the melancholy tone that empowers and characterizes "Ulysses" and all of Tennyson's best poetry is not ideologically neutral. Though the authority of melancholy is surely its seemingly "natural" source in intense feeling, and though in Tennyson's verse it seems to inform the rhythms with the bodily pulse of unmediated sensation, I will argue in the next section that Tennyson's melancholia, though not yet a direct expression of imperial ambition, is heavily mediated by an internalized social discourse combining Romantic, sexist, and Orientalist presuppositions that anticipated and paved the way for the imperialist ideology of the later nineteenth century. The poetry that made Tennyson's verse so useful for promoting the late Victorian imperial purpose was forged to a great extent from the abyss of his melancholy.

II. The Poetics of Melancholy and the Imperial Imagination

Tennyson's emblematic use of female or feminized subjectivity to brood on death and art and to allegorize melancholy is a clear reflection of the post-Romantic literary history of his age, and his representation of emasculating melancholy is an apparent representation of the effects of his age's economic structure, but his melancholy is also a product of political discourse internalized as conscience to structure anomic inwardness within a framework of current sexist and colonialist discourses. Since melancholy is a physical sensation that seems unarguably natural, not ideological, it is not surprising that generations of critics have seen Tennyson's best and most characteristic poetry as unpolitical, but this perception is itself political and is marked as such in Hallam's early essay. Even while denying that Tennyson had a political agenda, Hallam noted that the "melancholy which so evidently characterizes the spirit of modern poetry" would ultimately exercise a politically conservative function as "a check acting for conservation against a propulsion toward change." Though Hallam worried that such poetry "in proportion to its depth and truth is likely to have little immediate authority over public opinion" (190), his reference to "depth and truth" suggests that the authority of melancholy proceeds from the depths of the poetic self and carries with it the truth of feeling that Carlyle called the "felt indubitable certainty of experience" (*Works*, 1.156).

The most influential Tennysonians of the last generation, Christopher Ricks, Jerome Hamilton Buckley, and A. Dwight Culler, all attempted to disengage the "essential genius" of Tennyson's melancholy from the encumbrance of its historical moment. Culler's view of Tennyson's poetry as the expression of "natural" feeling, however, hints at a reading of Tennyson as an imperialist of the imagination: "Unlike the youthful Keats, Tennyson did not remain silent upon a peak in Darien—rather he plunged volubly into its thickets and claimed province after province for his own" (9).

Tennyson was deeply interested in the possibilities of the Romantic imagination as an imperial selfhood capable of entering into and even appropriating provinces and forms of consciousness initially outside the self, and his "sympathy" enabled him to enter into the feelings of the many female figures who are generally thought to represent his own poetic sensibility. The imaginative imperialism here is spelled out at length in Arthur Hallam's essay "On Sympathy." Hallam's "sympathy" is an emotional process that enables the individual self to avoid solipsism and to achieve some awareness of another's subjectivity. The poet whose "soul transfers at once her own feelings and adopts those of the new-comer" (*Works*, 1: 137) is necessarily expanding the individual self to engage with a historically specific "other," so that when Tennyson is at his most apparently Tennysonian, as in "Mariana," it is usually through identification with, or sympathy with, a specifically female other, as femaleness was constructed in the nineteenth century. In those poems in which Tennyson seems to gender his own poetic sensibility as feminine, it is within a degrading gender ideology that sees women as more emotional than men but less rational. Also, since women were by definition excluded from political thought, the adoption of female perspectives made it "natural" to disengage the poetic sensibility from the masculine political concerns of the day. When Hallam sought to praise Tennyson as an emotional poet in his review of *Poems* of 1830, he did so by distinguishing between "poets of reflection, such as Wordsworth," and what he characterized as the superior, Tennysonian "Poets of sensation," who possess the "powerful tendency of imagination to a life of immediate sympathy with the external universe" (186). Poets of sensation are implicitly feminized: "Susceptible of the slightest impulse from external nature, their fine organs trembled into emotion at colors, and sounds, and movements, unperceived or unregarded by duller temperaments" (186). Hallam, moreover, was well aware that the poets of sensation, Shelley and Keats, were not ideologically neutral, but Shelley especially, and Keats by association, was seen as politically radical, even as Jacobinical, so in a futile attempt to defang conservative reviewers he made a point of extricating Tennyson from the politics associated with sensation: "he has also this advantage over [Keats] and his friend Shelley, that he comes before the public unconnected with any political party or peculiar system of opinions" (191). Even though Hallam recognizes that the poetry of sensation has a possibly democratic tendency because poets of sensation "keep no aristocratic state, apart from the sentiments of society at large; they speak to the hearts of all," he affirms that they are at the top of the human hierarchy so that they "elevate inferior intellects into a higher and purer atmosphere." Hallam even goes so far as to imply that Milton and Shakespeare were poets of sensation in England's golden literary age, and that the effect of their writings was nothing less than the construction of national identity, of Englishness: the "knowledge and power" drawn from reading their works was "ours as Englishmen; and amid the flux of generations and customs we retain unimpaired this privilege of intercourse with greatness" (189).

Hallam further observes that the golden age of poetry is long gone in the present unpoetic age, and in so doing he takes the opportunity to position the melancholy Tennyson as a conservative, paradoxically preserving the essential elements of England's greatness by the melancholy of modern poetry: "In the old times the poetic impulse went along with the general impulse of the nation; in these it is a reaction against it, a check acting for conservation against a propulsion towards change" (190).

For Hallam even the melancholy generally thought a primary characteristic of Tennyson's essential genius is to be regarded as a product of the historical moment, and despite its effeminate form, it is ideologically aligned with Burkean conservatism and the preservation of Englishness.[4] Hallam and Tennyson paradoxically arrive at the conservative counterforce to the masculine, muscular spirit of the progressive age by colonizing and appropriating the realm of the "weaker" sex, by constructing a feminized version of the powerful imagination of "poets of sensation." Both Englishness and melancholy are cultural constructions brought into being by a remarkable indulgence in a feminized sensibility. Ultimately, though, such indulgence is structured and controlled by a masculine discourse of personal restraint and social order.

Tennyson's melancholy exploits the poetic power of dangerous feminine emotional lability and passion that threatens his ideal of masculine self-control and public order, and makes use of such elements even as it displaces and controls them. His use of feminine personae to represent his poetic sensibility enabled him both to represent erotic longing and to distance himself from what was self-evidently "other." Since female eroticism was threatening to social order, and was suppressed in middle-class English life and thus unavailable to direct observation, let alone sympathetic colonization, it is not surprising that Tennyson drew on the current discourse of Oriental sensuality both to find sources of erotic, sensual beauty and to push the threat from the center of British bourgeois life. The appropriation of the feminine, of course, suggests not only admiration but also desire and control of it.

As Edward Said has argued, to understand the culture of an imperial nation, we must take into account the relation of that culture to the empire, even, and especially, when the cultural products seem unconcerned with empire. If Said is right, it should not be surprising that Tennyson's centrality as the generally acclaimed greatest poet of his age was made possible in part by his use of the current discourse of Oriental sensuality. Such a use was almost overdetermined for Tennyson, since the imperial center's ethical control of rebellious tendencies allegorizes the ethical restraints of the poet's conscience over the anomic tendencies of the inner self. Though Tennyson's Orientalist sources often displace his poetic anxieties, they also provide him with a means to explore otherwise forbidden interests in a feminized eroticism, at least as refracted from "Fatima" to "Mariana" or from "A Dream of Fair Women" to "The Palace of Art." What he hesitated to say as a socially concerned masculine poet, he could say within the more detached, even scholarly voice of Orientalism. And what he was unable to say directly because of the vast, vague, and ineffable quality of inwardness, he could give a local (or colonial) habitation and name by allegory, speaking the other.

A closer look at specific poems in which Tennyson is evidently concerned with his own place in the ethical discourse of his age indicates that he constructed a poetic self not only in terms of the imperial, though feminized, Romantic imagination but also in terms of explicitly political and cultural imperialism. Frequently, Tennyson's English power is expressed in poems about exploration and discovery, figuring the poet more as a "stout Cortez" than as a Keatsian "chameleon poet" of negative capability. Tennyson could have found the analogy of the poet and the explorer in Keats's sonnet, or in the many Byronic figures like Childe Harold who cultivate melancholy poetic sensibility in extensive travels to remote regions, but as Alan Sinfield has pointed out, he would also have seen the idea of the poet converge with that of the explorer in Washington Irving's *Life and Voyages of Christopher Columbus*. The continuity of the explorer with the poet was set up for Tennyson by Irving, who represents Columbus's "poetic temperament" as spreading "a golden and glorious world around him." As Sinfield notes, "The poetic spirit is the advance guard of capitalism and imperialism, and cannot escape this involvement" (53).

In "On Sublimity" (1827) Tennyson collapses the poetic imagination with the wonder evoked by the literature of voyage and exploration; he allegorizes the inward sublime not in Romantic landscapes of the transforming imagination but in actual exotic, faraway wonders of the natural world. Tennyson sought the sublime in tales of adventurers and explorers reporting on the wonders of the world, from the more or less familiar Fingal's Cave in the Island of Staffa, and the by then well-known "Niagara's flood of matchless might," to the more exotic "stupendous Gungotree," "Cotopaxi's cloud-capt majesty," and "Enormous Chimborazo's naked pride." Another poet might have used Mount Snowden or Mont Blanc, but Tennyson's construction of sublimity called for the remote and exotic or, in the phrase that so influenced his childhood, the "far, far away." Like Keats, but unlike Cortez, Tennyson's "realms of gold" were literary, but whereas Keats was discovering the wonders of the literary tradition as he read Chapman's Homer, Tennyson was exploring the discoveries of Cortez's followers in the colonial tradition, reading Ulloa's *A Voyage to South America*. In general, as Paden's still important *Tennyson in Egypt* reveals, the reading that most influenced the poetry of early Tennyson was overwhelmingly constituted of books of exploration and discovery, and such Orientalist writings as Savary's *Letters on Egypt* and the works of Sir William Jones.

For Tennyson the danger of the visionary mode was a too complete withdrawal into his own interiority, unmediated by public discourse. Problems of articulating the inner self appear in the early "Armageddon" as a sense of transgression, of sin, at the presumptuousness of the prophetic mode. The speaker sees "such ill-omened things / That it were sin almost to look on them" (i. 53–54). But beyond the sinfulness of gazing upon "Obscene, inutterable phantasies" (i.107) is the more obvious transgression of assuming the visionary perspective of "God's omniscience" (ii. 27). In language that anticipates the soul's hubris in "The Palace of Art," the speaker worships his own sublimity: "in that hour I could have fallen down / Before my own strong soul and worshipped it" (ii. 49–50). To avoid total incoherence, the poet must move beyond the speaker's foundering in the abyss of the inexpressible and introduce comprehensible content into the sublime, which he accomplishes by mediating his inwardness with publicly available discourses, his sources in the literature of exploration and discovery, calling upon "Cotopaxi's cloud-capt altitude" (i. 100) and other wonders to give content to his vision. When

Tennyson's father insisted that he submit a poem for the Cambridge prize competition on the theme of Timbuctoo, he transformed the seemingly incongruous "Armageddon" for the purpose. "Armageddon," as a visionary poem almost without content, could easily be filled with the content of Tennyson's favorite literature of exploration and discovery. What he did to transform "Armageddon" into "Timbuctoo" was to muse on "legends quaint and old" (16) of other lost cities that had stirred the European imagination: "divinest Atalantis" and "Imperial Eldorado" (11.22, 24). And now, when the angel appears, he remains too dazzling to be looked upon, but nevertheless he offers a very clear vision of the celestial city as beheld by St. John on Patmos. Finally, near the end of the poem the poet achieves a vision of Timbuctoo, or rather of a rich Oriental city that he imagines as Timbuctoo. He sees

> The argent streets o' the city, imaging
> The soft inversion of her tremulous Domes,
> Her gardens frequent with the stately Palm,
> Her Pagods hung with music of sweet bells,
> Her obelisks of ranged Chrysolite,
> Minarets and Towers. . . . (ll.227–32)

In "Timbuctoo," however, Tennyson exhibits his distrust of the visionary mode—the speaker recognizes that Atalantis and Eldorado are fables, and that even Timbuctoo, when it is discovered rather than imagined, will lose its luster. Before the eyes of "keen *Discovery*" the "brilliant towers" (1.240) of the city will dissolve like the visions of Prospero's masque, will "Darken, and shrink and shiver into huts, / Black specks amid a waste of dreary sand, / Low-built, mud-walled, Barbarian settlements" (ll.242–45).

Despite his recognition that discovery is a way of discrediting the imagination, and that actuality always falls short of imagination, Tennyson continued to stimulate his imagination with tales of modern adventure that still provided possibilities of magnificence, possibilities to which "Men clung with yearning Hope which would not die" ("Timbuctoo,"1.27). He believed, however, that the poetic sensibility must ultimately submit to the discipline of rational Victorian discourse: Timbuctoo is only imagined as an earthly paradise, and then demoted to sordid actuality as the "Barbarian" huts of an inferior race that evidently need to be "improved" by European discovery and appropriation. In "Timbuctoo" Tennyson pushed the dangerously anarchic sublime from the religious centrality of "Armageddon" to the edges of the world and then controlled it completely by substituting "keen Discovery" for imaginative wonder.

Tennyson's discipline of imaginative longing for wonders at the far edge of the known world with the scourge of conscience remained important in his more mature works. Notoriously, in "Locksley Hall" (1842) when the speaker seeks escape from his emotional entanglement and suffocation in England, he avoids guilty discontent with England by allegorizing the turn inward as a retreat to the vast expanses of the Empire, "some retreat / Deep in yonder shining Orient" (ll.153–54). Better yet he imagines some faraway island, free of all restraints, "all links of habit—there to wander far away" in "Breadths of tropic shade and palms in cluster, knots of Paradise" (ll.157–60). Not only does the speaker of "Locksley Hall" imagine an earthly paradise waiting to be discovered, but so of course do Tennyson's Ulysses, the poet of "The Hesperides," and the mariners of "The Lotos-Eaters." These retreats, however, form only one part in the dialectic of inwardness, for they exist in part to be castigated by the conscience, the inward voice of Victorian ideology.

Sinfield has pointed out that Tennyson's imaginative flight to the remote edges of the world is a defining quality of the poet who sought imaginative escape from an England less characterized by imagination, beauty, or passion than by the rush for progress characterized in "Locksley Hall," "in this march of mind / In the steamship, in the railway, in the thoughts that shake mankind" (ll.165–66). Sinfield describes the process cogently: "Finding imaginative impetus marginalized theoretically and politically in Britain, he invested it in remote places. Finding himself expected to explore states of mind, he did so by using the people and scenery of remote places, and their impact on Europeans" (39). This is, I think, an accurate account of Tennyson's imaginative activity, but also his flights from the center tend to be associated with transgression, with kinds of experience forbidden to an English gentleman. Seemingly the flight from the center is, in itself, a form of transgression in its refusal to participate in the communal life, but of course the kinds of transgressive experience Tennyson imagines *are* at the center of British imperial culture—Tennyson only makes them seem marginal, in the same way that Victorian culture generally relegated forbidden experiences to the margins. The notoriety of the speaker's desires in "Locksley Hall" is not associated with his desire for a tropical paradise but with his desire for an unlimited range of sexual passion: "There the passions cramped no longer shall have scope and breathing space; / I will take some savage woman, she shall rear my dusky race" (ll.167–68). The transgressive, imperialist fantasy is almost immediately rejected, simply because the center *is* more valued than the periphery—or more crudely, because the English and their modern age are immeasurably superior to the lower races at the far end of empire:

> I *know* my words are wild,
> . . . I count the grey barbarian lower than the Christian child.
>
> I, to herd with narrow foreheads, vacant of our glorious gains,
> Like a beast with lower pleasures, like a beast with lower pains!
>
> Mated with a squalid savage—what to me were sun or clime?
> I the heir of all the ages . . . (ll.173–78)

The speaker of "Locksley Hall" is not to be simply identified as Tennyson, but elsewhere Tennyson shares this speaker's fantasy of escape from restraint by detours through some exotic and erotic paradise preceding a return to the center with reinforced belief in its values, especially the value of conscience and self-control. Ultimately, rebellious feelings are subjugated to the ethical character but the conflict ending in this subjugation constitutes the melancholy dialogue of the mind with itself as both an allegory of the poet's own mind and an allegory of imperial control.

"Anacaona" (1830), a poem based on material from Irving's biography of Columbus, describes just such an escape in the context of imperial exploration. According to Irving, Anacaona was the beautiful and intelligent queen of an island paradise. Tennyson's poem makes the most of her exotic beauty and setting and heightens her erotic appeal: she is "A dark Indian Maiden . . . Wantoning in orange groves / Naked and dark-limbed and gay" (ll.1–6). Though "wantoning" is a rather more loaded term than any authorized by Irving, Tennyson did have ample precedent in Irving for stressing the naked beauty of Anacaona. Irving described the welcome offered the European explorers: "[T]he young women were entirely naked, with merely a fillet round the forehead, their hair falling upon their shoulders. They were beautifully proportioned; their skin smooth and delicate, and their complexion of clear and agreeable brown" (351). According to Irving, however, Anacaona was later killed by the Spaniards, and, further, the discovery of this island paradise, so far from the authority and restraints of home, helped tempt the sailors into mutiny against Columbus. Tennyson's poem does not mention any of this, though it introduces a somber, foreboding tone in the last stanza: "never more upon the shore . . . wandered happy Anacaona" (ll.77–82). Still, despite the somber ending, "Anacaona" remains a poem of untroubled erotic fantasy—in this case with no apparent sense of guilty transgression. But Tennyson never published it, giving various unconvincing reasons, but perhaps providing the real reason in an unguarded comment describing "that black b_____ Anacaona and her cocoa shadowed *coves* of niggers—I cannot have her strolling about the land in this way—it is neither good for her reputation nor mine" (*Poems*, 1: 308). According to Culler, "'Anacaona' is perhaps the least ambiguous" of the many poems akin to "The Lady of Shalott" in presenting an image of the Poet's sensibility; Tennyson "could use [Anacaona] as a symbol of the poet not only because she danced and sang the traditional areytos, or ballads, of her people but also because her name and that of her country were so melodious that Tennyson, weaving them into his rhymes, could make it seem as if she and her island were of music all compact" (56). As Culler's allusions to Prospero's island might suggest, and given the mutinous behavior of the Spaniards in Tennyson's source, this poem and others like it (conspicuously "The Lotos-Eaters") may be attempting a kind of cultural work comparable to that which Stephen Greenblatt attributes to *The Tempest*. Greenblatt argues that the discovery of an apparent island paradise by the survivors of the shipwrecked "Sea-Venture" of the Virginia Company led to a crisis of authority, since the temptations to remain in paradise rather than proceed to colonial work were almost overpowering at such an extreme distance from governmental authority. *The Tempest*, he argues, represents Prospero's staging of "salutary anxiety" to bring the mutineers of a similar shipwreck back to a proper respect for authoritative order. For Tennyson in particular, I would suggest that what Greenblatt calls "salutary anxiety" is melancholy as I have described it, an inner conflict in which conscience or duty always castigates mutinous feeling. The analogy to Greenblatt's reading of *The Tempest* is strengthened by the echoes of *The Tempest*, particularly of Ariel's song, that, as Isobel Armstrong has said, "haunt" Tennyson's early poems (*Victorian Poetry*, 58). Further, like Shakespeare, Tennyson was using narratives of colonial exploration as his source. Certainly his relocation of excesses of eroticism to the edges of the imperial world provides an outlet for overflow that might otherwise threaten the orderly authority at the imperial center—in "Locksley Hall" the deranged speaker can dissipate his dangerously excessive passions in erotic fantasies of tropical paradises. Similarly mutinous fantasies lead Ulysses to abandon his "aged wife" and the Lotos-Eaters to abandon their families.

In "Anacaona," "The Lotos-Eaters," "The Hesperides," and "Ulysses" Tennyson explores the remote margins of the West, but even the discourse about the West was "Orientalist," as indicated by the word "Indians" to represent Native Americans. Much more often, however, Tennyson drew on the burgeoning discourse of explicit Orientalism for his representations of transgressive exotic otherness. In "Persia" (1827), for example, he makes poetic capital of Oriental names before warming to his theme of the destruction of Persia:

> Land of bright eye and lofty brow!
>> Whose every gale is balmy breath
>>> Of incense from some sunny flower,
> Which . . .
>> Sheds perfume. (ll.1–6)

Persia is personified as an exotically perfumed courtesan, suggesting the effeminacy that made her easy prey to Alexander's armies. Still more significantly, within colonialist ideology the conquest of the Orient is an Englishman's duty, so the erotic conquest of the female is appropriated within the sphere of manly duty. Here, as in "The Expedition of Nadir Shah into Hindostan" (1827), which draws on Sir William Jones's account of the Persian destruction of the Mogul empire in 1738, Tennyson chronicles the loss of Oriental glory and implicitly the concomitant transfer of prestige to the West. The armies of Nadir Shah reduce a paradisial realm to a wasteland: "The land like an Eden before them is fair, / But behind them a wilderness dreary and bare" (ll.19–20). The displacement of the Mogul empire by an anarchic wasteland opened the door to British expansion in India in the eighteenth century, and Tennyson's poetry seems to open the same door by justifying British control of the undisciplined East.

I do not want to attribute sinister motives to Tennyson but only to note that his numerous early poems on Oriental subjects inevitably took the tone of the dominant Orientalist discourse of his age, that the discipline of unruly states of the empire allegorized the discipline of unruly states of the inward self. For Tennyson's own poetic development, the most important characteristic of Orientalism is its eroticism. The eroticism that was unsuitable in speaking of the chaste English seemed perfectly "natural" in descriptions of the Orient or Oriental women. In "Thou camest to thy bower my love" (1827), for example, Tennyson was able to write with uncharacteristic erotic directness because he was drawing heavily on Sir William Jones's translation of the erotic poem the *Gitagovinda*.[5]

"The Lotos-Eaters" was primarily based on a passage describing the idyllic lassitude of a colonialist dream in Irving's *Columbus,* but the lotos itself comes not only from Homer but from Tennyson's characteristic accounts of Oriental lushness and luxuriance. The full importance of Orientalist eroticism in forming Tennyson's poetic sensibility is especially clear in "Fatima" (1832), by far the most impassioned of Tennyson's female impersonations:

> Last night, when some one spoke his name,
> From my swift blood that went and came
> A thousand little shafts of flame

> Were shivered in my narrow frame.
>   O Love, O fire! once he drew
>   With one long kiss my whole soul through
>   My lips, as sunlight drinketh dew. (ll.15–21)

"Fatima" expresses an unashamed sexual desire, akin to but more outward than the suppressed yearnings of "Mariana," and this sexual frankness is made possible for Tennyson by displacing it onto an Oriental subjectivity. Like "Mariana," it is a poem about waiting and facing the alternatives of sexual fulfillment or death, but in the case of "Fatima" much more clearly than of "Mariana," it is explicitly a longing for erotic fulfillment *as* death:

> My whole soul waiting silently,
> All naked in a sultry sky,
> Droops blinded with his shining eye:
> I *will* possess him or will die.
>   I will grow round him in his place
>   Grow, live, die looking on his face,
>   Die, dying clasped in his embrace. (ll.36–42)

"Fatima" is important to our understanding of Tennyson if only because it represents an Oriental other that helps to externalize and express the buried Western subjectivity and especially to suggest the energy of suppressed passion in Tennyson's more canonical poems as well as the strength of moral consciousness in conflict with the libidinal desires of the deep self. Similarly, in "A Dream of Fair Women" (1832) the eroticism owes nothing to the apparent inspiration, Chaucer's *Legend of Good Women,* but rather is picked up on another detour into Oriental sensuality via Savary's *Letters on Egypt.* Savary, not Chaucer, stimulated reverie about "hushed seraglios" (1.36), and Cleopatra, the dominant figure of the poem, owes little to Chaucer's Cleopatra or even to Shakespeare's, despite her "swarthy cheeks" (27) from *Antony and Cleopatra.*

Tennyson's representation of Cleopatra is especially striking because it parallels his much better known representation of the soul in "The Palace of Art" (1832). The soul, generally assumed to represent the evil consequences of living in art, falls from grace by becoming a kind of hubristic inspiration to spiritual anarchy:

> "I take possession of man's mind and deed.
>   I care not what the sects may brawl.
>   I sit as God holding no form of creed,
>   But contemplating all." (ll.209–12)

Cleopatra, in "A Dream of Fair Women," makes an analogous claim: "I governed men by change, and so I swayed / All moods" (11.130–31). The implication is that Tennyson's fear of art detached from social good is at least in part a fear of the eroticism that both attracts and repels him in representations of the Orient.

In its original form "A Dream of Fair Women" was, like "The Palace of Art," a representation of the poetic spirit divorcing itself from the social order. The opening stanzas compared the poet with a balloonist raised high above humankind and, like the soul in "The Palace of Art" or like the Lady of Shalott, viewing humankind from a detached, "aesthetic distance":

> So, lifted high, the Poet at his will
>   Lets the great world flit from him, seeing all,
>   Higher through secret splendours mounting still,
>   Selfpoised, nor fears to fall. (*Poems*, 1: 480n)

An earlier version even more strongly suggests the similarities among the soul's, the poet's, and Cleopatra's ability to be an unmoved mover: "The poet's steadfast soul, poured out in songs, / Unmoved moves all things with exceeding might" (*Poems*, 1: 480n). "A Dream of Fair Women," structured like "The Palace of Art" as a series of tableaux, seems to have been an analogous effort to analyze the dangers of unrestricted art or imagination, of the excessive profusion of images that characterize allegory or an eastern despotism of sensual excess, and it seems, moreover, to have seen these dangers as analogous to the dangers represented by Eastern female sensuality and its supposed tyranny over the rational mind. Some of the influences of Orientalist discourse remain evident in "The Palace of Art" itself. Ricks points out that the poem "was probably influenced by Sir William Jones" and that there "are also affinities with George Sandys's account of Egyptian 'Palaces' in his *Travels*" (Tennyson, *Poems*, 1: 437n), but the most obvious Orientalist influence is Coleridge's Kubla Khan, whose "stately pleasure dome" is ostentatiously echoed in the "lordly pleasure-house" of Tennyson's opening line. In the 1832 version the soul's downfall in the midst of embroideries of "every legend fair / Which the supreme Caucasian mind / Carved out of Nature for itself" was given a somewhat Oriental cast by reference to a mysterious "Asiatic dame": "in her pride," the soul beholds in herself

> Madonna, Ganymede,
>   Or the Asiatic dame—
> Still changing, as a lighthouse in the night
>   Changeth athwart the gleaming main. (*Poems*, 1: 446n)

Whoever the "Asiatic dame" may be, anxiety about the possibly anarchic power of art is here associated with the threat of a disordered, feminized mutability.

The clearest example of Tennyson's early uses of Oriental lore to construct and express a poetic sensibility is the poem Hallam cited as characteristic of Tennyson's genius at its best, "Recollections of the Arabian Nights." Hallam's praise of the poem, not incidentally, coyly indicates how the source could be simultaneously innocent and expressive of forbidden desires: "our author," he says, "has, with great judgment, selected our old acquaintance, 'the good Haroun Alraschid,' as the most prominent object of our childish interest, and with him has called up one of those luxurious garden scenes, the account of which, in plain prose, used to make our mouth water for sherbet, since luckily we were too young to think much about Zobeide!" (192).

The poem itself is a colonialist's dream. The fantasy is distanced by setting it in childhood, and the "realms of gold" represented in the poem are of course literary realms. Still, the poem indicates that for Tennyson the "golden realms" of literature were often very like the "golden realms" dreamed of by imperial conquerors. Besides, as Said has made clear, the Orient only existed for the West as a literary realm, as the discourse of Orientalism. The childhood memories are recalled as a voyage into the Middle East "many a sheeny summer-morn, / Adown the Tigris I was borne, / By Bagdat's shrines of fretted gold" (ll.5–7). Arabia is transformed by the poet into a literal golden realm—everything he sees is a treasure: the "costly doors" (1.17), the "gold glittering" of lamplight" (1.18), the "broidered sofas" (1.19), even the natural landscape is "damask-work, and deep inlay / Of braided blooms" (ll.28–29). The stream is seen as wealth: "diamond rillets" and "crystal arches" all "silver-chiming" (ll.48–51); the lake is covered with "diamond-plots" (1.85); the leaves are "rich gold-green" (1.82); the flowers are "studded wide / With disks and tiars" (ll.63–64), and even the anchor is silver. The shallop eventually enters into the palace and harem of Haroun Alraschid, where still greater riches are exhibited, climaxing not in sherbet but in erotic voyeurism:

> Then stole I up, and trancedly
> Gazed on the Persian girl alone,
> Serene with argent-lidded eyes
> Amorous, and lashes like to rays
> Of darkness, and a brow of pearl
> Tressed with redolent ebony,
> In many a dark delicious curl,
> Flowing beneath her rose-hued zone. (ll.133–40)

The scene is reminiscent of Porphyro's voyeurism in Keats's "Eve of St. Agnes," but Tennyson arrives at this expression of erotic desire by a route that takes him like a conqueror through an Eastern version of Eldorado. Once again Tennyson's "poetry of sensation" is not an emanation of his autonomous essential genius but a social construct dependent on England's contemporary Orientalist discourse. As Culler notes, the poem's final vision brings the poet face to face with Haroun Alraschid: "[I]n the 185th tale of *The Arabian Nights,* on which the poem is based, there is nothing the young Prince, who has secretly stolen to an assignation with the Caliph's favorite, would less rather see than the Caliph himself. Yet this is what Tennyson has him do, and so the heady amorous vision dissolves in boyish laughter" (32). The voyeurism, for Culler, is whitewashed by the innocent boyishness of the poet, but one might argue that the apparent complicity of the Caliph, whose eyes laugh "With merriment of kingly pride," suggests a willingness to share his harem, and thus suggests precisely the triangulation of desire that Eve Sedgwick has argued is the paradigm of male homosocial desire in the nineteenth century. Peace is made with the colonial other, and the treaty is ratified by the exchange or sharing of the woman. It is under the approving glance of the Caliph that Tennyson's poetic, erotic, and cultural imperialism are all made acceptable, even "natural" within the hegemonic homosocial and colonialist culture of his day.

Tennyson's later works generally depend less on Orientalist discourse for their inspiration, despite such exceptions as "Akbar's Dream," but they continue to depend upon a representation and simultaneous distancing of emotions and modes of thought perceived as feminine. Killham has argued, for example, that the "erotic near Eastern setting invented for the Persian girl is carried over" to *The Princess* (*Poems,* 1: 125n), and Sedgwick's analysis of *The Princess* has convincingly shown that it represents not female liberation through education but rather an extreme form of male homosocial bonding through the exchange of women. Even in *In Memoriam* the authoritative masculine voice is achieved by personifying the poet's emotion, "Sorrow," as female, a weakness that is long indulged but must eventually be disciplined. As I discuss in the next section, Orientalist fantasies are also at the heart of *Maud,* Tennyson's most extensive experiment in the poetics of melancholy.

III. Tennyson's "Little *Hamlet*"

Tennyson's two great poems of mourning and melancholia, *In Memoriam* and *Maud,* can to some extent be seen as distinguishing between "'normal' mourning" that eventually finds hard-earned resolution in *In Memoriam* and the "'pathological' mourning" of *Maud* that is clearly a form of madness (Armstrong, *Victorian Poetry,* 255). To be sure, the mourning of *In Memoriam* is so extended and its resolution so dubious that its differentiation from melancholia is not entirely convincing, but the imposed resolution certainly makes it a more "hopeful" poem than *Maud,* which seems to have been written as a sequel to return Tennyson to his accustomed melancholy: "It's too hopeful [*In Memoriam*], more than I am myself. I think of adding another to it . . . showing that all the arguments are about as good on one side as the other, and thus throw men back more on the primitive impulses and feelings" (*Poems,* 1: 8). However sad and perplexed it may be, *In Memoriam* eventually disciplines the "primitive impulses and feelings" with the Christian ideology of the age, exalting "character" above the "abysmal deeps of personality." *Maud,* on the other hand, was a generic experiment designed to represent a pathological condition, evidently melancholia: "The whole was intended to be a new form of dramatic composition. I took a man constitutionally diseased and dipt him into the circumstances of the time and took him out on fire" (*Letters,* 2: 138). As critics have recognized, Tennyson's "new form" was recognizably akin to the spasmodic poems that Ludlow and Arnold characterized as allegories of the poet's own mind, though the word "dramatic" evidently distinguishes the diseased mind from the "poet's own." The autobiographical resonances of *Maud,* however, have long been recognized, and even though the speaker cannot be simply equated with Tennyson or the eponymous heroine with Rosa Baring, the poem is evidently a symbolic representation of the poet's own emotional experience, an allegory of his own mind.

Rather than being the representation of a specific woman known to Tennyson, Maud is a complex allegorical signifier of the Romantic beloved. Like the Poet's vision in "Alastor," she is the spectral figuration of the speaker's ego-ideal or "epipsyche," and the speaker's desire for her is allegorized within the courtly tradition as a quest for a queen of Romance ("Rose of the rosebud garden of girls" [i. 902]) and for the perfect beauty that is also death ("Dead perfection" [i. 83]). Like all allegorical emblems, according to Benjamin, Maud is a multivalent signifier, an emblem of beauty, of death, of "Honour that cannot die" (i. 177), of Englishness ("Bright English lily" [i. 738]), of wealth and class status and even, "Cleopatra-like" (i. 216), of the Oriental erotic temptation explored in many of Tennyson's earlier poems. *Maud* is, in short, a melancholy allegory very much in the tradition of *Alastor* and *Endymion,* and as the erotic pursuit of an insistently Orientalized sexual other, it reiterates Tennyson's fusion of the imperial Romantic imagination with the imperial spirit of the age. *Maud* is especially important because it is an allegory of both the poet's own mind and Victorian pathology generally. The "constitutionally diseased" speaker is explicitly enflamed by the "circumstances of the time" and particularly the economic condition of the age, as the poem represents the "history of a morbid poetic soul, under the blighting influence of a recklessly speculative age" (Hallam Tennyson, *Memoir,* 1: 96).

The allegorical character of *Maud* is, moreover, strikingly illustrative of Benjamin's thesis that melancholy is generative of allegory: the speaker "brood[s] / On a horror of shatter'd limbs" (i. 55–56), on a "corpse in the pit" (ii. 326), and generally on graves, corpses, and death throughout, beginning with the opening account of the "Mangled and flatten'd and crushed" corpse of his father in the "dreadful hollow," pausing also on Maud's mother "mute in her grave as the image in marble above" (i. 159), an anonymous funeral urn (i. 303), the "blacker pit" of yet another grave (i. 335), and culminating in a grim hallucination of his own buried life in a "shallow grave" (ii. 244). The poem is, in effect, the allegory of a consciousness diseased by its own failure to "bury [it]self in [it]self" (i. 75) deeply enough and particularly to "bury / All this dead body of hate" (i. 779–80).

The resultant allegory replays in sharper focus the process I have traced in the earlier poems. The multiplicity of meaning associated with Maud and the protagonist's quest imbricates the love story with social issues from the outset. Expressing his disgust with the sordid commodity culture of the age,[6] the speaker's initial desire is not for a woman but for a national cause to heal and unify the diseased spirit of the age, specifically a chivalric, martial spirit to end the economic civil war of each against all:

> When a Mammonite mother kills her babe for a burial fee,
> And Timour Mammon grins on a pile of children's bones,
> Is it peace or war? Better, war! loud war by land and by sea,
> War with a thousand battles, and shaking a hundred thrones! (i. 45–48)

When Maud attracts the speaker's attention away from brooding on shattered limbs, it is as a "chivalrous battle-song" (i. 383), a bugle call to action:

> She is singing a song that is known to me,
> A passionate ballad gallant and gay,
> A martial song like a trumpet's call!
> . . . .
> Singing of men that in battle array,
> Ready in heart and ready in hand,
> March with banner and bugle and fife
> To the death for their native land. (i. 164–66, 169–72)

The cure for the speaker's "diseased condition" is to replace the diseased condition of culture with a return to the chivalric spirit of the feudal past, specifically to replace "a time so sordid and mean" (i. 178) with a pursuit "of Death and of Honour that cannot die" (i. 177). The call is eventually realized not as an achieved erotic union with Maud but as a call to an Eastern war in the Crimean, and, as in "Locksley Hall" and other earlier poems, the melancholic anomie of the hero is subordinated to the demands of a militant ideology. As if recapitulating Tennyson's earlier career, *Maud* originates in a seemingly contentless melancholia and proceeds through the speaker's literal recollection of the Arabian Nights to a love synonymous with imperial appropriation of an Orientalized other and finally to outright imperial aggression as the hero enlists to fight in an Eastern war.

The "germ" of *Maud*, as Tennyson said, was the lyric "O that 'twere possible" (ii. 141–238), a poem written in 1833–34 during his early grieving for Hallam. But despite its emotional origins in Tennyson's mourning, the poem does not move toward a resolution of grief but rather displaces sadness to a mysterious, undeveloped heterosexual yearning that can have no resolution. As a result, it is not so much a poem of grief as a poem of such purely Tennysonian melancholy that Swinburne called it "the poem of deepest charm and fullest delight of pathos and melody ever written, even by Mr. Tennyson" (3: 125). Harvie Ferguson has pointed out that in modern thought "melancholy has no substance of its own, that it is 'only' the sombre mirror in which being reflects itself" (xvi), and Tennyson's lyric, describing a subject haunted by a vaguely perceived phantom, seems to epitomize a vision of melancholia as the representation of a "deathlike type of pain" that is explicitly a reflection of the subject: "'Tis the blot upon the brain / That *will* show itself without" (ii. 200–201). Quite possibly the reference to the brain rather than the mind indicates that Tennyson saw the hero's disease in terms of the age's "medical materialism," but the disease manifests itself in and as diseased signs of the times. As in Carlyle's account of the signs of the times, the deeper meaning is allegorically readable in the signs of the surface, where the infinite bodies forth the finite, and so shows itself without. The speaker can assert his own anguish, but the source of that anguish, its content, remains shadowy and undefined:

> Through the hubbub of the market
> I steal, a wasted frame,
> It crosses here, it crosses there,
> Through all that crowd confused and loud,
> The shadow still the same;

And on my heavy eyelids
My anguish hangs like shame. (ii. 208–14)

Maud was written, apparently, to provide a context that would make this lyric "intelligible," in effect to provide a referent, a substance for this nebulous "it," in response to "a suggestion made by Sir John Simeon, that, to render the poem fully intelligible, a preceding one was necessary. He wrote it; the second poem too required a predecessor, and thus the whole poem was written, as it were, *backwards*" (Hallam Tennyson, *Memoir*, 1: 379).

Tennyson's development of a love plot to represent the hopelessness of melancholy yearning is of a piece with the pattern traced in the early lyrics, and with the Romantic love represented by the "Alastor" poet's yearning for his insubstantial ideal likeness, with Endymion's longing for Cynthia, and with the "Kubla Khan" poet's longing for the Abyssinian maid. More specifically, however, it all but explicitly recalls the emotional entrapment of "Mariana":

> For am I not, am I not, here alone . . .
> Living alone in an empty house,
> Here half-hid in the gleaming wood,
> Where I hear the dead at midday moan,
> And the shrieking rush of the wainscot mouse,
> And my own sad name in corners cried,
> When the shiver of dancing leaves is thrown
> About its echoing chambers wide,
> Till a morbid hate and horror have grown
> Of a world in which I have hardly mixt,
> And a morbid eating lichen fixt
> On a heart half-turned to stone. (i. 254–67)

As in "Locksley Hall," the appropriate response would apparently be to turn from "feminine" "perversity" to mix with the world ("I myself must mix with action, lest I wither by despair" ["Locksley Hall," 1.98]).

In this case, the speaker does not explicitly embrace the imperialist fantasy of finding some dusky woman to rear his savage race, but he does envision a romance with Maud in strikingly imperialist terms. His fantasy of wedded bliss with Maud is grounded in an actual recollection of the Arabian Nights:

i

> Did I hear it in a doze
>   Long since, I know not where?

> Did I dream it an hour ago,
>   When asleep in this arm-chair?
>
>   ii
>
> Men were drinking together,
>   Drinking and talking of me;
> "Well, if it prove a girl, the boy
>   Will have plenty: so let it be."
>
>   iii
>
> Is it an echo of something
>   Read with a boy's delight,
> Viziers nodding together
>   In some Arabian night? (i. 285–96)

As Ricks points out, it *is* an echo of some Arabian night, specifically *The Story of Nourredin Ali and Bedreddin Hassan* (*Poems*, 2: 537n). In addition, Maud is imagined as an Oriental seductress:

> What if with her sunny hair
> And smile as sunny as cold,
> She meant to weave me a snare
> Of some coquettish deceit,
> Cleopatra-like as of old
> To entangle me when we met,
> To have her lion roll in a silken net
> And fawn at a victor's feet. (i. 212–19)

Further, Maud herself is represented in terms of wealth that resembles the bejeweled version of Oriental splendor set forth in "Recollections of the Arabian Nights": she is imagined both as the phantom of "O that 'twere possible" and as a gem: "Luminous, gemlike, ghostlike, deathlike" (i. 95). She is a "pearl," a jewel (i. 352), a "precious stone" (i. 498) with a "sweet purse-mouth" (i. 71). Further, as Tucker observes, the "exotic images the hero imports for Maud's beauty (the 'Arab arch,' the curiously male peacock's crest) suggest that his fantasies of erotic dominion are imperial fantasies as well" (*Tennyson*, 419). As in the earlier poems, however, the dreams of erotic or imperial conquest are dashed. In fact, Maud's interfering brother, referred to throughout as the Sultan, interrupts the fantasy exactly as the good Haroun Alraschid did in "Recollections of the Arabian Nights." When the Sultan claims possession of his own, he makes inevitable the climactic and disastrous duel that kills the brother and dooms the speaker's love. It is at precisely this defeat of the dream that the "ghastly Wraith" (ii. 32) appears to provide the antecedent for the shadowy "it" of "O that 'twere possible." Yet this antecedent hardly gives substance to the melancholy shadowed forth as "it"—the problem is not simply that it is not substance but spirit, but that it apparently negates the most likely reading of "it" as Maud's ghost, since Maud is still alive when it appears. The mystery only deepens around the meaning of the externalization of the "blot upon the brain."

Finally, as in the earlier poems, the seductive, unmanning imperial fantasy provides, perhaps, languorous reverie:

> There is none like her, none.
> Nor will be when our summers have deceased.
> O, art thou sighing for Lebanon
> In the long breeze that streams to thy delicious East,
> Sighing for Lebanon,
> Dark Cedar, though thy limbs have here increased,
> Upon a pastoral slope as fair,
> And looking to the South, and fed
> With honeyed rain and delicate air,
> And haunted by the starry head
> Of her whose gentle will has changed my fate,
> And made my life a perfumed altar-flame. (i. 611–22)

But this feminized, perfumed reverie must eventually give way to the masculine actualities of empire. In the case of *Maud,* masculine activity is vigorous indeed: the speaker not only kills the Sultan but joins his nation's imperial cause to fight against Eastern iniquities, to fight for the good, "to embrace the purpose of God and the doom assigned." Whether the dreadful warmongering at the end of *Maud* is attributed to Tennyson or to his speaker, it is certainly consistent with both Tennyson's earlier tendencies and with the psychological movement of *Maud* from reverie, through erotic and imperial fantasy, to actual imperial warfare and a reassuring solidarity with Englishness: "I have felt with my native land, I am one with my kind" (iii. 58).

The longing for a revival of chivalric honor in *Maud* is consistent with Tennyson's medievalism elsewhere and suggests that his "poems made on . . . chivalric bones" (Barrett Browning, *Aurora Leigh,* v. 198), like Morris's "Concerning Geffray Teste-Noire," are a product of melancholy brooding on the loss of a social ideal in the strife of modern commodity culture. John Lucas has persuasively argued that Tennyson as laureate had no problem as a spokesman for the chivalry idealized in the medieval rhetoric that depicted Victoria as Gloriana and Albert, in Tennyson's words, as "Scarce other than my king's ideal knight" (Dedication to *Idylls of the King*,1.6), but in the 1850s, at the time of *Maud*, Englishness was clearly aligned with the commercial, commodity culture celebrated at the First Great Exhibition of 1851, but excoriated in *Maud* as a particularly vile form of civil war (i. 21–52). The deepest source of melancholia in *Maud* is the speaker's inability to align himself with the commercial spirit that he associates with a "lust of gold" that is "Horrible, hateful, monstrous, not to be told" (iii. 39–41), akin to the degrading sexual lust described by Shakespeare as "Savage, extreme, rude, cruel, not to trust" (Sonnet 129,1.4). From this perspective, the courtly love tradition evoked by representing *Maud* as "Queen Rose of the rosebud garden of girls" (i. 902) is actively antithetical to the conditions of English culture.

A fuller account of the relation of melancholia in *Maud* to the spirit of the age is, perhaps, best achieved by considering Tennyson's reference to the work as a "little *Hamlet*" (Hallam Tennyson, *Memoir*, 1: 296). Like Hamlet, the speaker of *Maud* is melancholy because the time is out of joint, or at least because he is alienated from it. As I have discussed, the Victorian age was particularly attuned to Hamlet's melancholia as "at once the sense of the soul's infinity, and the sense of the doom which not only circumscribes that infinity but appears to be its offspring" (Bradley, 108), and a similar comment by Coleridge provides a useful suggestion regarding how Tennyson's "little *Hamlet*" might be read as an experiment in genre; speaking of Hamlet's "morbid excess" of meditation on his own mind, Coleridge remarks that

> The effect of this overbalance of the imaginative power is beautifully illustrated in the everlasting broodings and superfluous activities of Hamlet's mind, which, unseated from its healthy relation, is constantly occupied with the world within and abstracted from the world without,—giving substance to shadows and throwing a mist over all common-place activities. It is the nature of thought to be indefinite;—definition belongs to external imagery alone. Here it is that the sense of sublimity arises, not from the sight of an outward object, but from the beholder's reflection upon it;—not from the sensuous impression, but from the imaginative reflex. . . . Hamlet feels this; his senses are in a state of trance, and he looks upon external things as hieroglyphics. (*Lectures*, 344–45)

In terms of genre, *Hamlet* seems to have served both Romantic and Victorian poets as a model of what Coleridge represents as the melancholy sublime. Writing of a time when verse drama was effectively defunct, Romantic and Victorian poets characteristically chose closet drama or even, to use the term Tennyson chose for *Maud*, monodrama, to represent a melancholic monomania akin to Hamlet's. The most obvious English example is Byron's *Manfred* with its many echoes of *Hamlet*, but as Bradley and Arnold recognized, Goethe's *Faust* is an even more significant modern version of the melancholy sublime. The conspicuous Victorian examples are *Maud* itself and Arnold's *Empedocles on Etna*, so it is particularly appropriate that Arnold suppressed the Hamlet-like broodings, the melancholy of the modern world, in a phrase that applies equally well to all works that rely on hieroglyphics to shadow forth the "infinite within," to the Romantic and Victorian works I have mentioned, and to the poetic aspirations of the nineteenth century generally:

> [T]he modern critic not only permits a false practice; he absolutely prescribes false aims.—"A true allegory of the state of one's own mind in a representative history," the Poet is told, "is perhaps the highest thing that one can attempt in the way of poetry."—And accordingly he attempts it. An allegory of the state of one's own mind, the highest problem of an art which imitates actions! No assuredly, it is not, it never can be so; no great poetical work has ever been produced with such an aim. . . . *Faust*, itself, judged as a whole, and judged strictly as a poetical work, is defective. (*Prose Works*, 1: 8)

Coleridge's reference to "hieroglyphics" and Arnold's to "allegory" suggest a generic inheritance from *Hamlet* of greater significance than the use of dramatic form to depict melancholia. The most significant generic feature in all of these works is allegory or, more specifically, the melancholy allegory described by Benjamin.

Benjamin's discussion of allegory is all the more obviously pertinent to Tennyson's "little *Hamlet*" because it was developed to explain the seventeenth-century German tragic drama that ostentatiously used the same allegorical principles that *Hamlet* used far more indirectly (*Origin*, 191). Benjamin comments that "for *Hamlet*, as indeed for all Shakespearian 'tragedies,' the theory of the Trauerspiel is predestined to contain the prolegomena of interpretation" (228). *Hamlet*, like *Maud*, can be seen as a complex meditation and allegorical contextualization to cope with the figure of a ghost, and both revolve around the central character's contemplation of death and burial. "In the *Trauerspiel* of the seventeenth century," says Benjamin, "the corpse becomes quite simply the pre-eminent emblematic property" (218), as in *Hamlet* the pre-eminent emblematic properties are the dead king, the skull of Yorick, and the open grave of Ophelia, and as in *Maud* they are the corpses in the "dreadful hollow" and, eventually, the speaker's own corpse as he hallucinates his burial.

Perhaps the best way to describe allegory in this sense is to return once again to Coleridge's "Kubla Khan." In Coleridge's headnote the vision of his reverie is described as already formulated in language: "all the images rose up . . . as things, with a parallel production of the correspondent expression, without any sensation or consciousness of effort" (*Works,* 102). This is exactly what Benjamin describes as the spurious claim of the Romantic symbol, "which miraculously unites the beauty of form with the highest fullness of being" (164), but as Coleridge's work suggests, it is possible only in an opium-induced reverie. It is a pipe dream, and the only way to fix it in language in the waking world is by an allegory that "immerses itself into the depths which separate visual being from meaning" (165). Unlike the symbol, which is momentary and, in Blake's terms, finds "eternity in a moment," allegory is a sequential, temporal progression of signs that seek recovery, or "redemption" of the lost fullness of being, so the actual poem of "Kubla Khan" does not record the vision but only the allegory of love and the desire for recovery: "Could I revive within me / Her symphony and song" (ll.42–43). Recording loss, and separation of the sign from being, allegory is necessarily melancholy.

As we have seen, de Man defines post-Romantic allegory, following Benjamin, as the sequential presentation of signs that always point to anterior signs, so that the essence of the allegorical sign is "pure anteriority," and this rather strikingly calls to mind Tennyson's composition of *Maud* "as it were, *backwards.*" As Tucker describes it, *Maud* "situates its hero reactively, his phase of passion having been prompted by some action anterior to the text" (*Tennyson,* 413). The poem seems almost uncannily to mesh with Benjamin's account of "the heart of the allegorical way of seeing, of the baroque, secular explanation of history as the Passion of the world; its importance resides solely in the stations of its decline" (*Origin,* 166).

As allegory, *Maud* fits neatly into the series of late Romantic poems of melancholy quest discussed earlier. Like "Kubla Khan," *Alastor,* and *Endymion, Maud* is the account of a man seeking a projection of his own ego-ideal (the "blot" upon his brain, projected without), a woman who has never really existed. Ricks has described the poem in exactly these terms, noting that Maud appears "ghostlike, deathlike, half the night long / Growing and feeding and growing" in the speaker's dreams: "[T]his unsubstantiality . . . is the poem's peculiar regret. It is a poem about losing someone whom you have never really had. She is at first beautiful, but as a gem, as an epitome of womankind, as a phantasmal pulse, a dreamlike vision" (238). Similarly, as Culler notes, Tennyson pointed out that the "memory [presumably of the hero's betrothed in part i, section vii] is a phantasmal one which he cannot trace to its origin" (201).

Perhaps it should not be surprising that Tennyson's work resembles that of the baroque German dramatists, since his work was recognized as baroque in his own time. Walter Bagehot famously labeled Tennyson the foremost exemplar of the "ornate" poet. His interest in depicting madness, moreover, was bound to involve a representation that ostentatiously separated the language of poetry from "fullness of being," that abandoned the Romantic symbol for an allegorized mode that underscores the alienation of the speaker's mind from actuality. As has always been noted, *Maud* abounds with what Ruskin called the "pathetic fallacy," figurative language resulting from "violent feelings" that "produce in us a falseness in all our impressions of external things" (5: 205). For Ruskin such imagery is the product of a "morbid," deranged subjectivity, as it seems the natural language of madness. The sequence of pathetic fallacy in *Maud*, the sequence of morbid signs, produces a kind of morbid allegory, the perfect representation, perhaps, of melancholia.

The most obvious and most often noted pathetic fallacy in *Maud* occurs at the very outset, in the speaker's personification, or genitalization, of the blood-red lips of the "dreadful hollow" (i. 2). The allegorical significations in *Maud* may be read in a variety of ways, including, of course, as a sublimation of grief in the imperial work of the nation and as a working through in Freudian or Lacanian terms of the loss of the father emblematized by the hollow. The hollow is, of course, the "ghastly pit" (i. 5) in which the father's body was found, and its "blood-red" ledges suggest the female genitals as symbolic of death and burial in mother earth, as burial within the self, of birth and the loss of unity with the mother, and of the castrating wound that represents loss of the father and loss of the phallus as ego-ideal. The hollow is, in short, an explicit and overdetermined sign of absence and loss at the origin of the speaker's emotional life, of his desire, and of his quest. As everyone recognizes, however, the imposition of the speaker's consciousness on nature, the rampant excess of figurative meaning in the pathetic fallacy, is above all symptomatic of the speaker's morbid subjectivity, the kind of solipsistic alienation that afflicted the entrapped Mariana, the Lady of Shalott, the soul in "The Palace of Art," and, of course, the buried self hallucinated later in *Maud*, so the hollow must also be seen as an emblem of morbid solipsism itself, an emblem of melancholy.

The multivalent significance of this image and others makes it impossible or hopelessly reductive to read a single coherent allegorical plot in

Maud. Like Hamlet, the speaker thinks "too curiously," but his mad excess of meaning is itself the point. As Benjamin argues, "Overnaming [is] the linguistic being of melancholy" ("On Language," 122), and it is also the allegorical poetry of the melancholy sublime: "With every idea the moment of expression coincides with a veritable eruption of images, which gives rise to a chaotic mass of metaphors. This is how the sublime is presented in this style" (*Origin,* 173). For this reason, "the basic characteristic of allegory . . . is ambiguity, multiplicity of meaning" (*Origin,* 177). Still, something specific can be extracted from this sublime: clearly the "dreadful hollow," whatever else it may signify, is an allegorical emblem of death, and, coming at the very beginning of the poem, it positions all of the speaker's subsequent comments, like Hamlet's, as a gloomy contemplation of death. Further, the opening lines indicate that in the solipsistic brooding of the speaker, everything becomes an emblem of death: "And Echo, there, whatever is asked her, answers 'Death.'" As a further subtle implication that the answer "Death" is ventriloquized by the speaker, Echo answers "Death" conspicuously where the verse needs to echo, or rhyme with, "heath": the off-rhyme indicates the speaker's tendency to hear or understand nature in terms of his own imposition of allegorical meaning, just as when he variously hears the cawing of ravens once as "Keep watch and ward, keep watch and ward" (i. 247) and later as "Maud, Maud, Maud, Maud" (i. 414). As an emblem both of death and of the speaker's morbidly deranged perception and tendency to allegorize, the "dreadful hollow" is an overdetermined emblem of melancholy itself. In addition, if Walt Whitman's ear is to be trusted, the word "hollow" especially sounds Tennyson's depths: "Tennyson shows, more than any poet I know . . . how much there is in finest verbalism. There is a latent charm in mere words, and in the voice ringing them, which he has caught and brought out, beyond all others—as in the line, 'And hollow, hollow, hollow, all delight'" (quoted in Culler, 4–5).

The whole of *Maud,* in its incoherence, seems almost a parody of conventional allegory. Examples of morbid, deranged allegorization, ubiquitous in the poem, include the speaker's moralizing upon the "lovely shell" (ii. 49) found on the Breton coast as an ambiguous figure of either the speaker's passive fragility or his "force to withstand" (ii. 72). Another example is the whole of the famous lyric "Come into the garden, Maud" (i.xxii), with its seeming parody of courtly love allegory as the roses and lilies discourse beneath the "planet of Love" (i. 857). The effect of such imagery is to represent the pathological, hysterical structures of the speaker's emotions (Christ, 26–27). They represent an allegory of the speaker's own mind, as Tennyson more or less described *Maud:* "You must remember always, in reading it, what it is meant to be—a drama in lyrics. It shows the unfolding of a lonely, morbid soul, touched with inherited madness . . . The things which seem like faults belong not so much to the poem as to the character of the hero" (*Poems* 2: 517). Quite deliberately experimenting with genre, Tennyson produced an "allegory of his own mind," exactly the kind of unpoetic "multitudinousness" that Arnold deplored.

The distinctly modern Victorian quality of *Maud* is its description of the horrors of commodity culture as an especially vile form of civil war. The attack on commodity culture is overt and obvious, foregrounded at both the beginning and end of the poem with allusions to the contemporary scandals of infanticides for insurance fraud, "When a Mammonite mother kills her babe for a burial fee" (i. 45), and of food adulteration, "And chalk and alum and plaster are sold to the poor for bread, / And the spirit of murder works in the very means of life" (i. 39–40). The counterfeit representation of bread by "chalk and alum and plaster" in itself suggests a kind of anarchic materialized allegory displacing the semiotic system of material culture. The "wondrous Mother-age" and its spirit of progress had been a source of hope in "Locksley Hall," but in *Maud* it is just the reverse:

> But these are the days of advance, the works of the men of mind,
> When who but a fool would have faith in a tradesman's ware or his word?
> Is it peace or war? Civil war, as I think, and that of a kind
> The viler, as underhand, not openly bearing the sword.
> Sooner or later I too may passively take the print
> Of the golden age—why not? I have neither hope nor trust;
> May make my heart as a millstone, set my face as a flint,
> Cheat and be cheated, and die: who knows? we are ashes and dust. (i. 25–32)

It is because he *does* "passively take the print" of the age that *Maud* registers the pathology of the age in the melancholic psyche of the individual. The point is obvious, and universally accepted among Tennyson's readers, that *Maud* represents not only an individual person "but a condition—the condition of England" (Culler, 207): "The poem makes the laureate's principal contribution to the Condition of England question, by representing that condition and the condition of its deranged hero as utterly congruent and as reciprocally determined" (Tucker, *Tennyson*, 407).

The work's most profound contribution to the "Condition of England" question takes place not at the overt thematic level but in the ideologically inflected form. To a considerable extent the ideological content is imperialist and Orientalist, and perhaps, if we take an offhand comment of Culler's seriously, this is true at the level of form as well, since Culler describes the poem's incoherence, its leaps "from subject to subject and mood to mood" as a "wild Oriental manner" (196). The incoherence is better seen, however, as a consequence of a general loss of faith, hope, and trust in modern capitalist society. In a world emptied of the presence of God or any transcendental significance, faith is reduced to a foolish "faith in a tradesman's ware or his word," and the individual can have "neither hope nor trust." As Marx's analysis of the commodity powerfully demonstrates, the system of commodity exchange and money is, like all semiotic systems, like language itself, based on an unanchored system of exchange. The thematic references to capitalist economy point to a general loss of faith, hope, and the charity that would mitigate or eliminate the civil war of economic struggle. Loss of faith in the symbolic system of commodity culture, moreover, implies a similar loss of faith in the symbolic exchange of language, and the result is a breakdown of the connections between words and things, and between words and ideas, that deconstructs language to produce the pathetic fallacies of melancholy allegory.

Maud thus enacts, at the level of form, the close connections of melancholy with the systemic problems of a free market economy: "Such economies alienate workers from their products, efface for consumers the origin of their fetishized purchases, convert desire itself into an exchangeable commodity, and estrange human intelligence from a 'Nature' that at the close of the eighteenth century receded even as the mind mastered so many of its mysteries" (Batten, 1). It is perhaps an insight along these lines that leads Tennyson's speaker to idealize the suppression of desire, even if in a strongly Orientalist manner: "For not to desire or admire, if a man could learn it, were more / Than to walk all day like the sultan of old in a garden of spice" (i. 142–43). More important to Tennyson than the specific economic scandals he drew from Carlyle was Carlyle's proto-Marxist analysis of the dehumanizing cash nexus that takes the place of a stabilizing vision of truth in capitalism. Consequently, it is not surprising that, even without the help of Marx, Tennyson was able to see the end result of economic civil war as the reification of human life, with individuals reduced to wooden automatons moved only by Adam Smith's "invisible hand."

Tennyson consequently anticipates both Robert Browning and Edward Fitzgerald in characterizing the modern alienated subject as a puppet: "We are puppets. Man in his pride, and Beauty fair in her flower; / Do we move ourselves, or are moved by an unseen hand at a game / That pushes us off from the board, and others ever succeed?" (i. 126–28). *Maud* is the greatest and fullest expression of Victorian melancholy both because it thematizes the sources of melancholy in Victorian culture and, even more, because it reveals the content of Victorian ideology in its allegorical form.

Tennyson's poetry overtly illustrates both Victorian melancholy and its sublimation in imperial conquest, but it also illustrates the sublimation of melancholy in aesthetic form by demonstrating the manic pleasures of allegory. Because allegory enables the melancholic simultaneously to fill the hollow of loss with figuration and to expose the truth of history in his own terms, says Benjamin, "the only pleasure the melancholic permits himself, and it is a powerful one, is allegory" (*Origin*, 185). Strangely, Benjamin describes the pleasures of sublimation in allegory in terms particularly appropriate to my argument about Tennyson's Orientalism: "The wealth of ciphers which the allegorist discovered . . . may not accord with the authority of nature; but the voluptuousness with which significance rules, like a stern sultan in the harem of objects, is without equal in giving expression to nature" (184). It is, perhaps, only by chance that Benjamin's simile so propitiously fits my argument, but his general point about the pleasure of allegorization points to a fundamental connection between melancholy and aestheticism that characterizes Tennyson's poems from "Mariana" through *Maud* and that further illuminates the close connection in the later nineteenth century between melancholy and aestheticism.

Although the poetry of sensation led others into aestheticism, however, Tennyson was appalled when "he was attacked with the cry of 'Art for Art's sake'" and composed an epigram referring to the movement as "truest Lord of Hell!" (Hallam Tennyson, *Memoir*, 2: 91–92). At the same time that Tennyson was working on *Idylls of the King*, Walter Pater, Swinburne, Morris, and D. G. Rossetti were using medieval themes and sources to explore the meeting of the pagan world with Christianity, making what Pater called a "deliberate choice between Christ and a rival lover" (191), in which the poets of the "aesthetic school" all sided with the rival lover, with pagan sensuality, in order to write an uninhibited poetry of sensation. Tennyson, also using medieval material for the *Idylls*, pointedly separated himself from "Art with poisonous honey stolen from France" ("To the Queen," 1.56). Far from abandoning the theme and mode of melancholy, however, Tennyson wrote the *Idylls* as an allegory of melancholy, a tale "shadowing Sense at war with Soul" ("To the Queen," 1.37). Though he did not like to be pinned down by too dogmatic allegorical readings, or, as he put it, "tied down to say '*This* means *that*,'" he acknowledged that "there is an allegorical or perhaps rather a parabolic drift in the poem" (Hallam Tennyson, *Memoir*, 2: 127). In fact, Tennyson evidently conceived of the *Idylls* as early as 1833 as an allegory in which Arthur would symbolize "Religious Faith," Merlin would symbolize "Science," Mordred would be "the skeptical understanding," and so on. The poem underwent many changes over the decades of its composition, and symbolic meanings tended to shift, but in the finished *Idylls*, "Sense at war with Soul" plainly meant the sensuality of the flesh (Guinevere, Ettarre, Vivien) at war with conscience (Arthur).[7] The dialectic of personal desire at war with conscience, of course, constitutes melancholy itself, and the whole of the *Idylls* quite evidently allegorizes that dialectic. Ultimately, in this allegory, sensation triumphs and sins of the flesh unseat the conscience so that man rolls back into the beast. Still, Tennyson leaves no doubt that failure to obey the dictates of conscience is destructive at both the personal and social level. Gladstone was undoubtedly correct in saying that "Wherever [Arthur] appears, it is as the great pillar of the moral order" (quoted in Hallam Tennyson, *Memoir*, 130). As Gladstone's comment indicates, the conscience in this allegory is very obviously the internalized moral order of the age, and most obviously it rages against the perceived moral decay of the time. Unfortunately, the great pillar of the moral order inevitably sounds priggish to an almost inhuman extent, but the very severity of Arthur's repudiation of Guinevere may be regarded as the rage of the superego against the ego—the maiming rage that Freud would find to be the necessary but painful condition of civilization. Such a reading of the *Idylls* undoubtedly states the case too baldly: Tennyson himself allegorized his allegory in an attempt to ward off such readings: "Poetry is like shot-silk with many glancing colours. Every reader must find his own interpretation" (Hallam Tennyson, *Memoir*, 2: 127). For my purposes, however, it is not necessary to examine the subtleties of Tennyson's painted veil but simply to note that the *Idylls* presents both of the "two Tennysons," the spokesman of Victorian values and the poet of sensation, and that this dialogue of the mind with itself dramatizes the disastrous results when the conscience loses control but, as poetry, also illustrates the disastrous results if the conscience triumphs too fully: in Arthur's extraordinary rebuke to the groveling Guinevere, Tennyson's poetry is reduced to a smug moral superiority—the voice of a pillar, not a poet. As I will argue in the next chapter, the triumph of conscience, or superego, is damaging to the poetry of melancholy because it short-circuits dialectic and leaves the poet little more than a spokesperson for official culture.

CHAPTER THREE

Elizabeth Barrett and the Emotion of the Trapped

Consideration of Elizabeth Barrett as a melancholy poet raises the immediate question of whether women *can* be melancholic, even though the limited female poetic tradition available to Barrett emphasized women's supposed greater capacity to feel, and specifically to feel sad. Barrett's most immediate female antecedent, L. E. L. (Letitia Landon), for example, claimed "My power is but a woman's power, / Of softness and of sadness made" ("The Golden Violet," 3. 525–26), and Barrett herself was characteristically described by reviewers as writing in what the *Monthly Review* called "a melancholy, but not a morbid vein" (*Correspondence*, 9: 320[1]). Similarly, the *Athenaeum* said that "Much of her verse is profoundly, some of it passionately melancholy, but it is never morbid" (9. 320), and *The League* praised her "divine melancholy" (9: 378). Despite the praise of Barrett's melancholy, however, contemporaries still saw it as a relatively disempowered *female* malady, as well characterized by the term "depression": according to *The Westminster Review*, her poems expressed the "pressure of strong thought and intense emotion, that gives, occasionally, a shade too deep, and an aspect of life too depressing" (9: 377). The reviewers also, to Barrett's distress, frequently compared her to Tennyson and placed her firmly in the "school of Tennyson," but ironically, although she is easily seen as a Tennysonian symbol of melancholy like Mariana or the Lady of Shalott, she was not fully granted the male, Tennysonian power of symbol making.

The traditional association of melancholia with specifically male genius, of course, goes back to Aristotle and through Renaissance neo-Platonism, but even in twentieth-century psychiatry there remain powerful arguments to deny women access to melancholy. In her cogent account of the matter, Juliana Schiesari points out the gendered bias of Freud's immensely influential discussion of melancholy: for Freud, melancholy is the critical attack by the overdeveloped superego on the ego, but women are characterized precisely by an "undeveloped" superego (53). In the still more recent psychiatric tradition, the superego is the internalization of patriarchal morality, the "Law of the Father," and identification with this law involves an exclusively male Oedipal relation with the Father. Not surprisingly, melancholia would seem to be an inherently sexist psychological state and an exclusively male cultural discourse.[2]

Within this discourse, Elizabeth Barrett would seem to have no access to the cultural authority of melancholy, though as a particular victim of patriarchy in the form of her father's unusually harsh version of the ubiquitous Law of the Father, she had every reason to be sad. Almost entirely confined to her own bedroom by her father's strict rules and her own invalidism, she was herself a virtual embodiment of symbolic melancholy—a Tennysonian Mariana. Though she was the signified, she could not be the signifier of melancholy. In fact, she has been more generally perceived as suffering from the female malady of hysteria, a diagnosis that "explains" her somewhat mysterious invalidism but offers absolutely no cultural validation for her poetry.

Barrett recognized her resemblance to Mariana but resisted the implications. She regretted her lack of experience of the world, which deprived her of the subject matter that might have enabled her to be what Robert Browning called an "objective" poet, "whose endeavour [was] to reproduce things external" (*Poems,* 1: 1001), but she found "compensation to a degree" in her virtual imprisonment: "I have had much of the inner life—& from the habit of selfconsciousness & selfanalysis, I make great guesses at human nature in the main" (*Correspondence,* 10: 133). She was, consequently, more like the "subjective" poet described by Browning, one who sees "Not what man sees, but what God sees—the *Ideas* of Plato, seeds of creation lying burningly on the Divine Hand . . . and he digs where he stands—preferring to seek them in his own soul as the nearest reflex of that absolute Mind" (*Poems,* 1: 1002). For the nineteenth century, the subjective poet would seem to be implicitly melancholy, since Browning's primary example was Shelley, the ultimate example of the melancholic poet for John Stuart Mill, Hallam, and others. Though theoretically excluded from the discursive power of melancholy and from the masculine poetic tradition generally, Barrett struggled to make poetic capital of her feelings as intensified by her virtual imprisonment, of "the emotion of the trapped."

Although Barrett accepted Victorian assumptions about gender, her poetry struggles to formulate a social position for the woman poet's separate will as well as her official sentiments, but she ends up in her early work reinscribing the accepted role of the female poet with an eloquence and creativity that highlights the fault lines separating the limits of creativity for women poets from those of men, and distinguishing between a female tradition of sentimental poetry and a male tradition of melancholy. As Antony Harrison has pointed out, "Analysis of her work from 1828 to 1844 would necessarily feature the struggle within it between an apparent acceptance of dominant institutionalized value systems (as these were embedded in the discourses of aestheticism, love, religion, and motherhood) and opposition to those systems" (79). To Harrison's list of embedded discourses, I add the deeply embedded discourses of melancholy and of the moral authority of melancholy as exclusively male in the powerful poetic tradition handed down most recently by Shelley and, especially, Byron.

One way in which Barrett's sentimental poetry can be understood as a powerful, socially committed poetry of sorrow is suggested in Isobel Armstrong's comments about Freudian melancholy and women's poetry of affect. As Armstrong puts it,

> Freud and the ever-open wound of melancholia seem to open a path to the inhibition of symbol formation . . . for this is just what happens to the melancholic. The economics of mourning and loss are attributed to the loss of a loved person, or the loss of some abstraction which has taken the place of one, such as one's country, liberty, an ideal, and so on. At the heart of the psychic, Freud opens up the social, which is always a presence in the poetry of affect. ("Msrepresentations," 21)

Armstrong's comments are made within an argument that nineteenth-century women's poetry of affect needs to be rescued from "the systematic and even cruel policing of affect" that has seen the "domestic language of the affections" as necessarily a vehicle of "conservative sentiment" (5), but despite her intellectual capacity for radical critique and her often passionate liberal politics, Barrett's poetry is in fact conservative in its sentimentality at least throughout her early career writing as a trapped "Mariana" figure in her father's house. This poetry does not achieve the authority of melancholy critique because Barrett was so completely interpellated as a submissive woman in Victorian domestic ideology, not because of any biological or essentialist imperative about who can or cannot be melancholy. As long as Barrett submitted entirely to the hegemonic social morality of her own particularly harsh "Law of the Father," she had, *pace* Freud, a conscience or superego that was not too weak, but was too strong to allow room for a genuine dialectic of inwardness: the voice of the separate ego, the individual will, was stifled by the social order, as internalized in conscience.

Barrett's poetry of this period is unquestionably sad but never "morbid," because it never eats away at the foundations of the hegemonic Victorian moral order to which it completely submits. As a result, Barrett was able to write with considerable ease and fluency because her sentiment perfectly fit the marketing niche for female sentimentality generated by the poetry annuals and their demand for socially comfortable verse: moving but not subversively disturbing. Arguing for a reevaluation of "the poetics of sensibility and sentiment," Jerome McGann has suggested that studying such poetry "gives one a specially clear view of how a language of affective meanings—of how language *as* affective thought—functions" (*Poetics*, 6); Barrett's poetry displays, I think, specifically how it functions when the affect is the affect of the age, in sentimental poetry, rather than the affect of the alienated individual, as in melancholy.

Writing at least half seriously about the sentimental poetry of Felicia Hemans, McGann suggests that her poetry "accepts from the start that these kinds of social dreams are the constructions not of the unconsciousness but of the consciousness, even of the super-ego" (*Poetics*, 191), and I will argue wholly seriously that this is the case with Barrett's poetry for as long as she wrote under her father's roof. The majority of Barrett's most recent critics have argued that even her early poetry is subtly subversive of conventional morality, but I think the subversive possibilities of self-assertion in her early work take the form of latent Byronic melancholy that is, in fact, always kept in check by the "cruel policing" of her orthodox Christian conscience. Paradoxically, it is only when she escapes the entrapment of patriarchal authority and finds happiness that Barrett is able to free her individual will sufficiently to enable a genuine dialectic with her conscience and to engage in a poetics of melancholy in the *Sonnets from the Portuguese*.

I. Poetry of the Superego

Even as a very young poet, Barrett enthusiastically believed in the loftiest Romantic ideals of poetry and the poetic imagination, but her Romantic enthusiasm was always at odds with her still stronger Christian faith and belief in self-effacing humility. From a very early age she was intent on rivaling the greatest poets of the ages, and though she learned to moderate her aspirations as she matured, she always aspired to a lofty ideal of the poet as a chosen spirit, a visionary in touch with transcendent truth and able to transmit that truth to the larger public. David has compellingly argued that her idealism was a specific legacy of her immediate Romantic predecessors, from whom she learned "that the poet was a gifted being, called to the practice of poetry . . . she consciously performed as a member of an aesthetically advantaged élite, mythologising herself as a member of that clerisy of poets described by Samuel Coleridge, whose poetic function is redefined in a secular community" (105–6). David's argument, however, neglects the ways in which Barrett's fervent dissenting Protestantism conflicted with the somewhat self-aggrandizing claims of Romanticism. Her attempt to achieve the lofty status of the poet-prophet was fraught with difficulty, partly because the Coleridgean assumptions involved an impossibly transcendent ideal of autonomous poetic creativity, partly because her age's ideal of selflessness in women was radically opposed to the celebration of self involved in the Romantic egotistical sublime, partly because her religious beliefs were diametrically opposed to the secularization of transcendent values implied in the ideal of a clerisy, and partly because her dissenting religious views were opposed to hierarchic structures of spiritual authority.

The religious limits set on Barrett's Romantic aspirations, to be sure, are not entirely separable from those set by gender. As Dorothy Mermin has argued, for Barrett as for other women, adopting the "traditional role of the religious poet" reinforced "the self-effacement and self-suppression that threaten their existence as writers" and involved a "ready submission to God the Father" that pushes "them back into the childishness that Victorian women artists had to fight their way out of in order to write at all" (*Barrett Browning,* 70). Barrett plainly saw that devotional feeling was particularly well suited to what she herself regarded as the infirmities of "woman—who from the weakness & softness of her nature should so feel the need & the beauty of that strength & surpassing tenderness found in the religion of Jesus Christ, & only there!" (*Correspondence,* 3: 288). Nevertheless, her Christian faith cannot be regarded as just another patriarchal obstacle to her high Romantic aspirations since, as her poetry and letters make abundantly clear, her highest aspirations were as a specifically and emphatically Christian poet. Like many other religious poets of her time, most conspicuously John Henry Newman and John Keble, she firmly believed that the highest and best poetry was necessarily religious.

Seemingly, Romantic aesthetics need not be at odds with Christian faith—Coleridge, after all, was the great theorist not only of Romanticism but also of nineteenth-century Christian poetics. For him the egotistical sublime leads directly to worship of God: "we begin with the I KNOW MYSELF, in order to end with the absolute I AM" (*Works,* 1: 283). By the time Barrett began writing, Wordsworth as well as Coleridge firmly believed in the Christian mission of poetry; indeed, the Christian poetics of Newman and Keble were heavily indebted to the criticism and practice of Wordsworth and Coleridge. But only certain versions of Romanticism and of Christianity were compatible, and only up to a point. In the first place, such writers as Newman and Keble accepted only limited elements of Romantic thought and were careful to exclude the open-ended, speculative spirit that could lead to heterodox opinions. Newman admired Coleridge's originality but noted that he "indulged a liberty of speculation which no Christian can tolerate, and advocated conclusions which were often heathen rather than Christian" (Fraser, 14). Also, both Newman and Keble were careful to distinguish between secular and sacred literature and to counter what Keble described as a tendency of the age to be "satisfied . . . with that poetry which is but a shadow" of the "higher wisdom of religious truth" (Fraser, 15). And finally, the ultramontane Newman and Keble were advocates of decorous reserve in both their limited Romanticism and their religion, whereas Barrett was an ardent emotionalist in both poetry and religion. Newman and Keble were modified "Lakers" in their Romanticism[3] and high churchmen in their religion, whereas the young Barrett was Byronic in her Romanticism and low church in her religion. And Byronism was an obvious problem for a Christian woman: as Leighton understatedly remarks, "the idea of the poet as warrior, criminal, libertine and religious sceptic . . . seems expressly at odds with the domestic and religious faith required of Victorian women" (*Women Poets*, 81).

Early autobiographical fragments show Barrett sensing, yet resisting, the conflict between her religious and literary impulses, and aware of the need to restrain herself in *both*. She saw the need for Christian restraint from her impulse to revel in Byronic "turmoil of conflicting passions" and "an almost proud consciousness of independance [*sic*]." Similarly, she struggled to choose between "the deep persuasion of the mild Christian," which she evidently believed was the proper feeling, and "the wild visions of the enthusiast," which she saw as intrinsic to her nature (*Correspondence*, 1: 353, 355, 351). She recognized a need to exercise "command of my self," but she believed that her essential "self," her "inmost heart," was characterized by rebellious and tumultuous "violent inclinations" (*Correspondence*, 1: 353). In general, she collapsed emotional religious transports with a passionate love of poetry:

> My religion is I fear not so ardent but perhaps more reasonable than formerly and yet I must ever regret those enthusiastic visions of what may be called fanaticism which exalted my soul on the wings of fancy to the contemplation of the Deity—My admiration of literature especially of poetic literature can never be subdued nor can it be extinguished but with life. (*Correspondence*, 1: 353)

As her ambivalence reveals, the conflation of poetry and religion is problematic—poetry seems somewhat at odds with religion, or at least with "reasonable" religion. Not surprisingly, Barrett's Byronic self-characterization leads her into a Byronic contempt for the "tranquillity" that mild Christianity ought to bring about: "The energy or perhaps impetuosity of my character allows me not to be tranquil and I look upon that tranquillity which I cannot enjoy with a feeling rather like contempt as precluding in great measure the intellectual faculties of the human mind!" (*Correspondence*, 1: 353).

Though she eventually came to rank Wordsworth as the greatest poet of the age, Barrett's early Romantic enthusiasm for Byron, the leader of the "Satanic school," inevitably clashed with her Christianity. In a literal suppression of Byronic melancholy by the "Law of the Father," her outraged father laid down the law at her apparent endeavor to out-Byron Byron:

> The broodings of your hero are the broodings of a madman—& his egotism is insufferable. Lord Byron lets you look into his melancholy mind, but by glimpses only. There never *was* such a character as your Theon's.... I cannot read any more—I would not read over again what I *have* read, for fifty pounds—really not for *ten*. I advise you to burn the wretched thing. (*Correspondence*, 1: 359)

She never outgrew her admiration of Byron, but in future she was careful to "speak of the passion & sublimity of Ld. Byron's genius, not of his moral & pious characteristics" (*Correspondence*, 2: 112).[4] The fundamental difficulty Barrett faced, then, was to reconcile her religious faith, which called for self-restraint and even self-effacement, with a version of Romanticism committed to individual, even egotistical self-expression. This difficulty, fully internalized, might well have issued in the melancholy dialectic of ego and conscience, and perhaps does lead to occasional lyrics of melancholy when she seems to have given vent to her deepest feelings, as in the very early "The Tempest: A Fragment," which probably expresses "the poet's mingled exhilaration and terror at her Promethean or Satanic impulses" (Mermin, *Barrett Browning*, 51). Most characteristically, however, the early Barrett did not attempt to express the depths of her interiority but chose instead to write morally edifying verse as a conscientious and rigorous Christian.

Attempting to repudiate the notion that the poetry of affect is necessarily conservative, Armstrong concisely summarizes the opposing view:

> A long tradition, passing through eighteenth-century sensibility and the Burkean category of the beautiful, which endowed the non-rational, affective feminine with the pathology of hysterical symptoms—the

> limp, lisp, and stutter of disfunctional language—gradates into senti-
> mental poetry. Here, the story goes, a domestic language of the affec-
> tions, valorizing home and country as forms of one another, rests on
> conservative sentiment. ("Msrepresentations," 5)

Barrett can be acquitted, of course, of limping, lisping, or stuttering, but the traditional "story" of sentimental verse seems to fit her case. Two poems about the young Queen Victoria, whose accession was contemporaneous with Barrett's public emergence as a poet, almost seem deliberately emblematic of the conservatism of sentimental poetry. The feminist recuperation of Victorian women's poetry has, not surprisingly, seen even these poems as politically progressive, as in Helen Cooper's comments on "The Young Queen":

> Barrett suggests that token women who attain public prominence
> feel ambivalent about their status. As she reveals her own anxiety as
> a woman measuring her feet inside the shoes of her dead literary
> fathers, so she imagines Victoria to be similarly unnerved at her sud-
> den power. In "The Young Queen," she delineates how "Her palace
> walls enring / The dust that was a king—/ And very cold beneath her
> feet, she feels her father's grave." At fourteen Barrett had felt some
> comfort in walking in Homer's footsteps and not striking out a path
> for herself; now she imagines in chilling terms a severance from the
> father as a woman appropriates power traditionally reserved for him.
> Instead of guiding her feet, the precursor now numbs them with
> cold. It is a statement of loss; but it also determines the daughter to
> walk her own path. (44–45)

The poem, however, seems instead to alleviate any public anxiety about the accession of a woman to the symbolic head of patriarchal power. "The Young Queen" downplays Victoria's ascension to power, focusing instead on England's loss of a king and Victoria's loss of a father, and assuaging grief and anxiety with the balm of women's tears. In "The Young Queen" Victoria becomes a figure not of commanding authority but of domestic sympathy: "A nation looks to thee / For steadfast sympathy: / Make room within thy bright clear eyes for all its gathered tears" (46–48).

The most remarkable element of "Victoria's Tears" is the sleight of hand in which the nation's mourning for its king and Victoria's for her father are collapsed. Though no one could have been deceived by it, the poem strongly implies that Victoria weeps to ascend the throne left vacant by her father. The dead king, William IV, of course, was not Victoria's father nor even emotionally close to her, but the pretense of orphaned grief enables the poem to assuage the country's supposed grief for the loss of a dubiously "loved one," and to mix in the presumably genuine domestic grief of William's widow and of women in general to displace with manageable mourning the possible anxiety or melancholy over the loss of an "abstract ideal":

> The palace sounds with wail—
>   The courtly dames are pale—
> A widow o'er the purple bows, and weeps its splendour dim:
>   And we who hold the boon,
>   A king for freedom won,
> Do feel eternity rise up between our thanks and him.
>   And while all things express
>   All glory's nothingness,
> A royal maiden treadeth firm where *that* departed trod!
>   The deathly scented crown
>   Weighs her shining ringlets down;
> But calm she lifts her trusting face, and calleth upon God. ("The Young Queen," 13–24)

Most significantly, in what turns out to be a characteristic move of Barrett's sentimental poetry, the actual substitution of a queen for a king is displaced, not by the symbol making of melancholy but by an eschatological shift across the divide of matter and spirit: authority remains fully patriarchal and even spiritualized as the dead king is replaced by the ever-living King of kings, as Victoria is enjoined to meekly bow "While the King of kings shall bless thee by the British peoples' voice" (63).

Even in poems with much less evident social purposes, Barrett's early poetry raised concerns about the prevailing gender ideology only to soothe them over with an affect of tender sentiment. Her most popular poems, those that she characteristically wrote to order for literary annuals, are ballads that displace contemporary concerns to a mythic past. "The Romaunt of the Page," for example, written for *Finden's Tableaux of the Affections: A Series of Picturesque Illustrations of the Womanly Virtues* (1839), displaces Barrett's own desire to apprentice herself to the poetic tradition of Byron[5] with a chivalric legend of a bride who follows her lord to the Crusades as his page and sacrifices her life to spare his. The transgressive gender switch perhaps suggests a desire for female empowerment and a critique of the male code of chivalry, but if so, it is subsumed in the womanly virtue of self-sacrifice and assuaged by the emotional affect of grief for the dead wife.[6]

A more explicit rejection of the Byronic tradition of melancholy is offered in another ballad, "The Poet's Vow," which is not set in any specific era, though its gothic setting suggests a legendary past. The poet of the title, with his lordly scorn and pride, however, is clearly the type of the contemporary Byronic poet that Barrett was in many ways tempted to become. The Poet turns away from the social world, vowing "his blood of brotherhood / To a stagnant place apart" (ll.53–54). The Poet is characterized mainly by his soul-destroying introspection, as his melancholy brooding is described: "His steadfast eye burnt inwardly, / As burning out his soul" (ll.29–30). His "distant, sinful heart," of course, is explicitly condemned within the Christian scheme of the poem that, characteristically, replaces the possible moral authority of the man of melancholy with the supernatural moral authority of the anagogically substituted Man of sorrow. Certainly this is a poem of the superego: the Christian admonition against poetic pride is made in part by contrasting the haughty, sinful poet not only with Christ himself but also with "three Christians [who] wended by to prayers" and an account of a wedding that goes by without the Poet's blessing.

"The Poet's Vow" echoes Coleridge's "Rime of the Ancient Mariner" in its ballad form and its moral imperative to love all of God's creatures and even in its representation of a wedding,[7] but by substituting the arrogant Poet for the hapless mariner, Barrett's poem becomes a much more explicit repudiation of poetic self-sufficiency and of Romantic melancholy. Unlike the mariner's glittering eyes, the Poet's are turned inward in self-destructive melancholy and in his egotism, he vows to forego "man's sympathies" (1.92) and, like Byron's various heroes, to live apart in splendid isolation from the debased human species he declines to be a part of. Like Byron's Manfred, the Poet "wore the form" of human existence but "had no sympathy with breathing flesh," with the "Creatures of Clay that girded" him (*Manfred*, ii. 56–58). Apparently unconscious that his pride repeats the primal sin, Barrett's Poet proclaims his exemption from the fallenness of human nature in the universal curse: "*our* curse! do *I* partake / The desiccating sin? / Have *I* the apple at my lips?" (ll.80–82). Rejecting all human ties, he spurns his "plighted bride" (1.136) Rosalind, whose loving innocence is far wiser than the Poet's cold wisdom: she thought, she says, "The teachings of the heaven and earth / Should keep us soft and low" (ll.167–68).

But Rosalind's words have no effect on the Poet, and neither do the words of his friend Sir Roland, who castigates him for his "sinful heart / That climbest up so high" (ll.203–4) in a reversal of Christ's love, which descended to earth in divinely human sympathy. The narrator spells out the very obvious moral:

> The self-poised God may dwell alone
>   With inward glorying,
> But God's chief angel waiteth for
>   A brother's voice, to sing;
> And a lonely creature of sinful nature
>   It is an awful thing. (ll.270–75)

In his sublime egotism, the Poet has forgotten the duties of the creature and presumed to take the place of the Creator. But far from achieving even the sublimity of the Satanic antihero, he becomes merely "A lonely man, a feeble man" (l.278).

"The Poet's Vow" repudiates the excessive claims of Byronic Romanticism, but it generates more questions than answers about the proper role of the poet. At first glance Rosalind might seem to offer a female alternative to male pride—her humility, love, and suffering evidently show far more Christian and poetic feeling than the Poet's arrogance. But Rosalind is not a poet. She merely dwindles away in grief—ultimately she is less a subjective source of poetry than a subject for poetry, a mournful lady like Tennyson's roughly contemporaneous Lady of Shalott, Mariana, or Oenone.[8] In fact, before she has any influence at all, Rosalind is reduced literally to an object, a corpse, and presented to the Poet:

> It lay before him, humanlike,
>   Yet so unlike a thing!
> More awful in its shrouded pomp
>   Than any crownèd king:
> All calm and cold, as it did hold
>   Some secret, glorying. (ll.403–8)

In death, the beautiful woman may become "the most poetical topic in the world," but she hardly becomes a poet herself unless we take seriously the disturbing implication that true poetry is only to be found after death. And that, perhaps, is just the "secret" in which the corpse glories. Strangely, the dead Rosalind does seem to achieve what the Poet had only vainly aspired to. The Poet in his hall had been "As silent as its ancient lords / In the coffined place of stone" (ll.21–22). He had been too calm and too cold and had worn a face as still as those "Beneath the cerement's roll" (l.26). The Poet had rejected "his humanness" (l.266), and Rosalind had left her humanity behind in the merely "humanlike" husk (l.403). The implication of this unsettling fable is that the aspiration to a poetic power that transcends ordinary human limitations is sinful, but more, that it is fatal. Becoming a corpse, Rosalind has also become the perfect image of the poet removed from the debased human world to embody an enigmatic wisdom. Like other dead women in Victorian literature, Rosalind's

> cadaverous presence simultaneously occupies two places, the here and the nowhere. Neither of this world nor entirely absent from it, the corpse stages a relation between these two incompatible positions. Strangeness emerges because the corpse, resembling the deceased person, is in a sense doubled. It has no relation to the world in which it appears except that of an image.... The corpse pre-eminently marks an instance of resemblance, a moment of reduplication that turns back on itself to sever all links to any exterior world. (Bronfen, 104)

Rosalind's soul, perhaps, occupies a point mediating between God and his creation, but this poet as angel is not to be seen or heard. The corpse, on the other hand, is a visible emblem of the poet cut off from her kind without bringing evidence of a higher life, only unassailable evidence of death and the mystery that lies beyond. The closest the poem comes to transcendence is in Rosalind's "secret, glorying." But the secret is incommunicable to fallen mortals: in the end, the Poet, confronted by the absolute silence of Rosalind's corpse, is reduced to a "wailing human creature" and to feminized, sentimental poetry.

As my comments on some of the poems in Barrett's first major collection suggest, her sentimental poetry is significantly different from the poetry of melancholy both in its ultimate Christian aspiration and in its figural language. The expression of melancholy is inhibited not by any deep psychic mechanism but by the entirely conscious rejection of poetic figures that turn inward, away from domestic and Christian duties to morbid introspection. The poems in *The Seraphim and Other Poems* (1838) repeatedly insist that the melancholy poet is a dissonance in God's creation, a person to be explicitly contrasted with the Christian. As I have discussed at length elsewhere ("The Poet as Angel"), the ambitious title poem is only one of many poems in the volume to make the case that mortal poetry is necessarily fallen and incomplete, so that fully adequate poetry is possible only after death, to disembodied spirits or angels. The highest utterance a mortal woman can achieve, *The Seraphim* suggests, is akin to the weeping of Mary, mourning at the foot of the cross, "With a spasm, not a speech" (1.481). The epilogue to *The Seraphim* characterized the speech of the drama as a kind of hybrid, mixing the heavenly perspective of the angels with the "hoarse music" of the mortal speaker, "Cold with the weeping which mine earth inherits" (ll.1038–39). But this "cadence ... / Of sin and sorrow" (ll.1040–41) would seem to be the highest song imaginable, mixing the visionary sublime of angels with the passionate Christian love and devotion of the mortal woman.

Still, weeping is not poetry, and with the happy ending of Christian eschatology always in sight, weeping is not melancholy but sentimental. The drama ends up asserting that the human song can only be fulfilled after death, when the poet actually will join the chorus of angels and, as one of the angels anticipates, the music of angels and human souls will "mix the adoring breath / And breathe the full thanksgiving" (ll.663–64). Not surprisingly, then, the poem ends with the speaker longing to be translated to heaven to hear the "most sweet music's miracle" (1.1046) of the heavenly choir. The poem ends, that is, in a desire for death—if Barrett killed the "angel in the house," as Virginia Woolf contended, in this early verse it was only in order to translate her to heaven. Adopting the poetic persona of an angel empowers the woman poet, but only in the next world.

Characteristically, Barrett's sentimental poetry aspires to the condition of breathless rapture beyond language but is compelled to settle for "hoarse weeping." Trying to transcend fallen mortality, however, the poet looks beyond the earthly veil to last things and the truths of eternity, but Barrett's poetry differs from that of melancholy and the imagination penetrative because its figurative language gestures not toward mortal remains like the death's head but toward pure spirit. It is not allegorical but anagogical, and its characteristic figure is not the symbol or metaphor, finding analogies among earthly things, but is typological, substituting the spiritual meanings of earthly words for their material meanings: the heavenly King for the temporal king, the divine MAN for the fallen man, the seraphic angel for the domestic angel.

As Barrett realized from the beginning, her poetry, like any self-expressive poetry, needed to find language to represent unspeakable inwardness, but since her struggle was to express conscious thought rather than inchoate and possibly rebellious feeling, her concerns, as expressed in the juvenile *Essay on Mind*, are rather different from those of melancholy poets. As the *Essay on Mind* makes clear, for Barrett language is necessary to thought as well as expression, but as a part of fallen nature it cannot rise to heaven:

> For thoughts uncloth'd by language are, at best,
> Obscure; while grossness injures those exprest—
> Through words,—in whose analysis, we find
> Th'analogies of Matter, not of Mind. (ll.631–34)

Within the fallen world, "no freedom, Learning's search affords, / Of soul from body, or of thought from words" (ll.669–70). If thought could be freed from language, the escape from earthly bounds would not be Genius but madness—once freed from language, we would be freed from "The gravitating power of Common-sense" only to be "Through all the depths of space with Phaeton hurl'd, / T'impair our reason, as he scorch'd our world" (ll.672–74). Direct expression of "what passes show," in other words, would only be madness, but more, the association with Phaeton, coupled with an earlier allusion to Icarus, suggests that attempts to soar into God's heaven are presumptuous and smack of the sin of pride. The allusion to Phaeton takes on still more significance in light of Barrett's early analysis of the need to keep her passionate nature under "habitual restraint," lest she "again be hurled with Phaeton far from every thing Human . . . every thing reasonable!" (*Correspondence*, 1: 353).

Emphasizing disembodied reason, or thought, as opposed to emotion as defining the "human," Barrett seems to rule out the allegorical clothing of thought as corrupt "analogies of matter" and to choose eschatological figures as analogies of "Mind," but such a choice would hardly seem to lead to a poetry of the feelings. Another passage from the *Essay on Mind*, however, introduces feeling but only, it seems, the feeling of the superego, "moral feeling":

> Poesy's whole essence, when defined,
> Is elevation of the reasoning mind,
> When inward sense from Fancy's page is taught,
> And moral feeling ministers to Thought.
> And hence, the natural passions all agree
> In seeking Nature's language—poetry. (ll.944–49)

As long as Barrett remained committed to the belief that the "natural passions" of women corresponded to "moral feeling," as official culture taught, the affect of her poetry, its sentimentality, would refer beyond material sense to spiritual essence.

The sentimental poetry of moral feeling elevates poetry to its highest earthly possibility, but as Barrett's poem upon the death of Felicia Hemans makes clear, even the best sentimental poetry is necessarily limited. Barrett does full justice to her fellow poet's "mystic breath which breathed in all her breathing, / Which drew, from rocky earth and man, abstractions high and moving, / Beauty, if not the beautiful, and love, if not the loving" (ll.22–24). The qualifications are conspicuous—the earthly poet can communicate only high abstractions, but these earthly visions cannot communicate the highest truth: "Such visionings have paled in sight" (1.25) for Hemans, who has now met her Savior in heaven, where "learneth she the sweet 'new song' she will not mourn in knowing" (ll.27–28). Mortal song, especially for the woman poet, is mournful and incomplete—the true singers are the redeemed souls and angels in the heavenly choir. The best poet is the dead poet. Barrett's poem, addressed to another poet, Letitia Landon, concludes with the advice to accept mortal limitations and to recognize that her greatest poetic achievement will be her death. At her death, England will say of Landon what it is now saying of Hemans: "Albeit softly in our ears her silver song was ringing, / The foot-fall of her parting soul is softer than her singing" (ll.31–32).

The repeated paradox in Barrett's various comments about poets and poetry is that poets achieve their highest song only when they are silenced to earthly ears. The reason for this is apparent in a letter of 1836:

> How happy—even here—when those, who in the midst of this beautiful earth feel more sensitively than the very beauty, the sin & suffering & infirmity,—are able with hearts moistened & freshened by the blood & tears of Jesus, to look towards that calm & blessed & perpetual place beside His pierced feet, "reserved in the Heavens" for believers. Oh what an unspeakable poetry there is in Christ's religion! But like the poetry of inferior things, men look at it coldly because without understanding, & do not even cry aloud for an interpreter. (*Correspondence*, 3: 179)

Barrett was lamenting, in part, that her increasingly secularized contemporary culture was intolerant of devotional poetry because public displays of religious fervor seemed in bad taste; as Barrett complained elsewhere, "Because Christ died for me, I must love HIM—but it is very wrong of me to say it, & very improper—& above all things very unpoetical!" (*Correspondence*, 4: 182). But a still greater problem is that even apart from social constraints, the full poetry of Christ's religion is genuinely "unspeakable," because the full realization of human life is outside of human life, "reserved in the Heavens." Yet the passage also clearly implies Barrett's desire for a kind of poetry that would (in the phrase of Browning's Fra Lippo Lippi) "interpret God to all of you!" The Christian poet, like the Romantic, mediates between the transcendent Truth and fallen human society. But for Barrett, at least in the 1830s, the Romantic idealization of human genius as quasi-divine could only be blasphemous, and she was able to see transcendence of ordinary mortal limitations as possible only in death, or in the guise of an angel.

One obvious problem with this perspective was that it might seem literally insane. As one American reviewer (quite possibly Poe) put it, "We do not believe there is a poetical soul embodied in this world, that—as a centre of thought—sees further out, toward the periphery permitted to angels, than Miss Barrett. Yet you would get a verdict of insanity upon her from any jury in Christendom" (*Correspondence,* 9: 378). The categories of Romantic genius and Christian angel tended to collapse in the figure of the dying woman-as-angel, but this collapse only reaffirmed the marginality of living women within the contemporary world.

In the years following publication of *The Seraphim and Other Poems* Barrett came increasingly to accept the Romantic ideal of a secular (but still spiritual) clerisy, but in her early confrontation with Romanticism, her evangelical religion left her with no earthly standing ground for her poetic ambitions. Nevertheless, though some early reviewers were inclined to deplore the religious fervor of her verse, others were willing to grant her something like the angelic status she seemed to seek. She was praised for her "devotional glow, an almost seraph-like enthusiasm" (*Correspondence,* 4: 383) and was described as a mystic oracle rising "to glory in the spirit" (*Correspondence,* 4: 400). The most enthusiastic of reviewers, taking literally the phrases in other reviews, referred to Barrett as "the Seraphic Poet" (*Correspondence,* 4: 399) and hinted at the sublime danger in her passionate "moral feeling": "A smouldering fire is consuming her, which, if it do not quickly blaze into radiance, will slay her in the flesh, that, uncontrolled, she may rise to glory in the spirit." In effect, the critic upped the ante on her, urging her to become "the Perfect Poet and the Perfect Christian" and to rise in visionary power akin to that of the "Sainted JOHN"—the ultimate anagogical writer (*Correspondence,* 4: 400).

Despite her critical success as a seraphic singer, by the early 1840s Barrett was becoming convinced that full self-expression involved more than "moral feelings" and religious fervor, and she was attempting to move beyond the sentimental poetry of the superego. As a passing comment on Spenser made clear, by 1842 Barrett had come to regard the figure of the angel as inadequate for the expression of human actualities—Spenser's poetry, she said, "is like the singing of an angel in a dream: it has not enough of contrary for waking music" (*The Greek Christian Poets,* 138). Arguably the same was true of her own poetry to this point—her more rebellious passions were so entirely excluded that there had been no "contrary" to the dictates of social morality in the conscience, and consequently no "dialogue of the mind with itself," no genuine dialectic of inwardness. Responding to criticism, she agreed that "a cold mystical poetry strikes & falls from us like the hail," and she aimed in future to "make my access to human feelings *through* human feelings" (*Correspondence,* 5: 59).

She did not, however, repudiate her angelic stance entirely but rather qualified it. In her 1842 essays on *The English Poets,* she argued that the true poet may achieve a transcendent vision, but not without reflecting the flesh and blood of the fallen, material world: somewhat like the angelic speakers of *The Seraphim,* "the poetic temperament" is suspended "halfway between the light of the ideal and the darkness of the real," but unlike the angels, the poet is "Unable, without a struggle, to pass out clear and calm into either, [and] bears the impress of the necessary conflict in dust and blood" (*The Greek Christian Poets,* 135). The conflict between the ideal and the real, fully internalized as a dialogue of the mind with itself, is a version of the dialectic of inwardness that I have characterized as Victorian melancholy, so it is evident that Barrett was attempting in the early 1840s to move from the poetry of the superego to something more like the poetry of melancholy. Barrett's reasoning in the early 1840s reconciled Romantic self-expression with Christian humility or self-effacement and enabled her to insist confidently on the all-importance of individuality, originality, and sincerity in poetry: "to express the truth of his inward soul, *is* the business—& approves the original faculty of every true poet" (*Correspondence,* 8: 16). By 1844 she seemed confident in her Romantic-Christian aesthetic and in her ability to write sincere, morally earnest, original poetry. She believed that her own poetry had value precisely because she had replaced merely conventional writing with sincere self-expression: the difference between her past and present poetry was not merely "the difference between immaturity & maturity" but "the difference between the dead & the living . . . between a copy & individuality; between what is myself and what is not myself" (*Correspondence,* 9: 81). The "not myself" can, perhaps, be understood as the moral perspective of the contemporary ideology represented in her earlier poetry, but the distinction between the dead and the living and between a copy and an individuality is not as clear as Barrett's language suggests; rather, the "copy" is internalized and becomes part of the individuality, so that the "myself" exists as a conflict, or dialectic, of ideology as conscience and the inchoate feeling of flesh and blood. That is, it exists as melancholy.

Expressing her confidence in the *Poems* of 1844, she wrote that "The present volumes have, I hope & believe, some further advance of life & strength in them. Poetry is more to me than ever . . . & dearer . . . & (in an earthly sense) it is a vital organ left me to breathe with" (*Correspondence,* 9: 66). As her confidence in the aesthetics of full self-expression grew, Barrett began to rank poetry as at least the moral equal of religion. As her reliance on the external forms of religion decreased, she felt more able to draw from her own interiority with confidence that the resulting poetry, though melancholy, would be "vital" as well as morally purposeful—she was beginning to justify the poetry of melancholy that she had previously eschewed on religious grounds, and to find a poetic mode in which sorrow was not sentimentality and moral purposefulness not a lifeless copy of ideology. Her letters of this period are far less religious in tone than previously, and they tend increasingly to present poetry as the highest good: poetry, she writes, has been to her "the Life-light of existence" (*Correspondence*, 9: 67). And again, evidently neglecting religion for the moment, she comments that "All the life & strength which are in me, seem to have passed into my poetry. It is my POU STOO [the place Archimedes sought for his lever] . . . not to move the world, . . . but to live on in" (*Correspondence*, 9: 66).

The danger in Romantic idealization of poetry was that it might displace the worship of God with an idolization of human "genius," and, in fact, Barrett frequently referred to herself as a Carlylean "hero-worshipper" and observed that "it is difficult, nay, impossible for me to believe that the hero, the true genius, is not morally greater, more generous, more fruitful, more tender-hearted than the troop of vulgar men" (*Correspondence*, 6: 50). As a hero-worshipper, she was a devotee of "the religion of genius, or you will say *superstition*" (*Correspondence*, 4: 185). But even in this admission, significantly, the faith in poetry is qualified by a nagging doubt, a nagging fear of falling into idolatry and superstition. Further, some of her most emphatic comments about the importance of originality and individuality suggest at least a latent possibility that the self-singing of the poet may result in separation from rather than unity with God's creation: poetic "power," she argued, consisted precisely of "originality, which is *individuality*—the sign of the separate mind" (*Correspondence*, 5: 120).[9]

Like Coleridge and Carlyle, she believed that the full expression of the mind of "genius"—the mind of a Shakespeare or a Wordsworth—would be necessarily religious, necessarily in harmony with divine truth. But as Marjorie Stone has shown, she was also much influenced by Byron, whose melancholy self-expression of a less than full and deep genius was morally dangerous. Despite his greatness, Byron failed as a poet to the extent that he, too, simply identified "poetry and passion. Poetry ought to be the revelation of the complete man—and Byron's manhood having no completion nor entirety, his poems discovered not a heart, but the wound of a heart; not humanity, but disease; not a life, but a crisis" (*The Greek Christian Poets*, 197). The implications are troubling for a woman poet within an ideology where the woman was assumed to have a great capacity for feeling but was in other respects regarded as something less than—or at the very least other than—"the complete man." Even for a man, assuming the capacity of "genius" in order to justify self-expression might smack of spiritual pride, but for a woman the danger was especially obvious. Consequently, even the praise of "divine melancholy" (*Correspondence*, 9: 378) in the strong reviews of *Poems* in 1844 did not remove Barrett's poetry from the stigma of being something less than the utterance of a "complete man."

The Wordsworthian and Coleridgean version of Romanticism fit well with Barrett's Christian principles, but as a woman she appeared to lack Wordsworthian wholeness of being, and her poetry of sorrow obviously lacked the validating authority of "joy." In her conflation of Romantic egotism and Christian worship Barrett invariably praised Wordsworth as "a philosophical & Christian poet, with depths in his soul to which poor Byron could never reach" (*Correspondence*, 6: 127), but she nevertheless remained powerfully attracted to Byron as "a great and wonderful poet" with "more passion & intensity" than Wordsworth could muster (*Correspondence*, 6: 171, 8: 123). She was powerfully drawn, in short, to a Romantic "religion of genius" in which genius ought always to express Christian truth, but she was also uncomfortably aware that in a fallen world imperfect genius might instead represent only melancholy discontent, a diseased version of human nature. Nevertheless, in her *Poems* of 1844, she expressed confidence that Romantic self-expression and Christian praise could be one and the same. The point is emphatic in the closing stanza of "The Dead Pan," a poem she valued highly and insisted on placing at the end of the collection as a kind of manifesto:

> O brave poets, keep back nothing,
> Nor mix falsehood with the whole!
> Look up Godward; speak the truth in
> Worthy song from earnest soul:
> Hold, in high poetic duty,
> Truest Truth the fairest Beauty! (ll.267–72)

The poet who expresses innermost personal being, or soul, looks not only inward but "Godward" and sings in praise of God, not of self.

Less ostentatiously programmatic poems in the volume, however, indicate that Barrett was in fact not following the path of Christian Romanticism but that of second-generation Romantic melancholy. Even in the preface to the collection she insisted on the sorrow and suffering necessary to the poet, and she quoted from Shelley's "Julian and Maddalo" to clinch her argument that "we learn in suffering what we teach in song." An aesthetic of suffering is not, quite obviously, at odds with Christianity, but it does complicate Barrett's Romanticism by associating it, at least in part, with the rebellious "Satanic school" rather than with the pious Lake poets.

A series of sonnets explores Barrett's thought on the implications of her mixed Romantic and Christian beliefs and her concerns that, for example, mortal singers cannot understand the harmonies of God's will but are troubled by thoughts of mortality that, as in Keats's "Ode to a Nightingale," call us back from visionary fancies:

> deathly colds
> Fall on us while we hear, and countermand
> Our sanguine heart back from the fancyland
> With nightingales in visionary wolds. ("Perplexed Music,"ll.5–8)

And in this poem suffering is not a source of poetic power but a sign that the earthly poet is far below the seraph, who hears and understands immortal harmonies. Another sonnet suggests that sentimental sorrow, deepened by Romantic melancholy, takes the form of inexpressible dejection or depression:

> I tell you, hopeless grief is passionless;
> That only men incredulous of despair,
> Half-taught in anguish, through the midnight air
> Beat upward to God's throne in loud access
> Of shrieking and reproach. ("Grief,"ll.1–5)

Within these sonnets Barrett faces the familiar Victorian difficulty of finding ways to represent inwardness beyond the reach of conscious thought and language. In "The Soul's Expression," the octave describes the extreme difficulty of the "struggle to deliver right / That music of my nature" (ll.3–4), and the sestet asserts that reaching the impossible goal of self-expression would lift her out of mortal existence altogether:

> This song of soul I struggle to outbear
> Through portals of the sense, sublime and whole,
> And utter all myself into the air:
> But if I did it,—as the thunder-roll
> Breaks its own cloud, my flesh would perish there,
> Before that dread apocalypse of soul. (ll.9–14)

As in the poems of *The Seraphim* volume, earthly song is necessarily inadequate—the full song of self-revelation can only come from the disembodied soul when life is completed by death. "Insufficiency," similarly, describes the struggle to "utter forth in verse / Some inward thought" (ll.1–2) and the impossibility of bringing together the truth of the individual and the universe "In consummation of right harmony" (1.6). As in Arnold's "The Buried Life," satisfactory communication is impossible in fallen life: "The effluence of each is false to all, / And what we best conceive we fail to speak" (ll.10–11). But unlike the agnostic Arnold, Barrett avoids despair by displacing Romantic hopes with Christian faith in an afterlife of full self-knowledge: "Wait, soul, until thine ashen garments fall. / And then resume thy broken strains, and seek / Fit peroration without let or thrall" (ll.12–14). Unfortunately, of course, the religious consolation only emphasizes the impossibility of genuinely uttering forth the earthly self. As in the earlier work, poetry is fully realized only after death.

In the major poems of the 1844 volume Barrett ambitiously explores the possibilities and limits of sentimental religious poetry, the extent to which her poetry could be original and self-expressive, even melancholy, without falling into sinful morbidity. "A Vision of Poets" is a dream poem akin to Keats's "The Fall of Hyperion," which, as Stone remarks, it "uncannily resembles" even though Keats's poem was not yet published in 1844 (52, 85). Barrett's description of her poem could almost be a description of Keats's:

> I have attempted to indicate the necessary relations of genius to suffering and self-sacrifice. . . . I have attempted to express in this poem, my view of the mission of the poet, of the self-abnegation implied in it, of the great work involved in it, of the duty and glory of what Balzac has beautifully and truly called "la patience angélique du genie." (*Works*, 2: 147)

In both "The Fall of Hyperion" and "A Vision of Poets" a poet experiences a dream vision in which a powerful figure compels him to experience the utmost agonies of human existence in order to qualify as a genuine poet. But the differences between the two poems are significant. "The Fall of Hyperion" is spoken in the first person and uses the machinery of Greek myth. "A Vision of Poets" is spoken in the third person about a specifically male poet—and so is doubly distanced from the actual poet, Elizabeth Barrett, who consequently cannot be said to be making any claims for her own inward sublime. And "A Vision of Poets" uses Christian symbolism. Keats's speaker had ascended the steps of an ancient temple, but Barrett's ascends to a vast celestial church, with an altar presided over by an angel and a flock of dead poets, from Homer and Aeschylus to Shelley, Byron, and Coleridge (Wordsworth, of course, was still alive). Through suffering, evidently, the poet of genius will eventually become a poet-priest—but even in this ambitious celebration of poetry, the great poets of the Western tradition are imagined as fulfilling their song only after death, in heaven. The truly authoritative presence in the poem is not the protagonist Poet, or any of the dead earthly poets, but the "chief angel." Further, though the poets have given their hearts to swell the cosmic harmony, they can hardly be said to be singers—their hearts have been literally removed, formed into a giant clavier to be played upon by the angel. The poets are reified as things, like the mere mechanical strings of the many versions of Romantic aeolian harps. The individual hearts of the mortal poets can produce only "undertones / Of perplext chords" (ll.493–94) until the angel blends them into Harmony. Even though Barrett plainly saw her somewhat confused allegory as celebrating the great poets, her Christian argument undermines her Romantic worship of genius by reducing the work of even the greatest poets to "perplext chords." As in *The Seraphim,* human song is reduced to inarticulate wail, and the ideal poetic persona is an earthly impossibility—an angel. Even at her most visionary, and when she most closely resembles her Romantic predecessors, she is unable to find an earthly standing point for the poetry to which she aspires.

The difficulties of achieving an authoritatively self-assertive yet humbly self-abnegating Christian, female voice are especially evident in *A Drama of Exile,* the most ambitious of Barrett's *Poems* of 1844. A closet drama depicting the events immediately following the expulsion from Eden, *A Drama of Exile* represents cosmic history not only from the fallen perspective of Adam and Eve but also from the visionary perspectives of fallen and unfallen angels, of various Spirits of Earth, and even of God himself in the person of Christ. The work is reminiscent of *The Seraphim,* but in this case the setting is at least brought down to earth, brought down from just outside the gates of heaven to just outside the gates of Eden. Nevertheless, Barrett is still attempting to write with the more than human authority of angels, though the presence of Adam and Eve affords "access to human feelings *through* human feelings," and especially, as Barrett saw it, to women's feelings. Her account of the subject indicates that she was self-consciously attempting to find scope for a thoroughly ambitious yet specifically female poetry:

> My subject was the new and strange experience of the fallen humanity, as it went forth from Paradise into the wilderness; with a peculiar reference to Eve's allotted grief, which, considering that self-sacrifice belonged to her womanhood, and the consciousness of originating the Fall to her offence,—appeared to me imperfectly apprehended hitherto, and more expressible by a woman than a man. There was room, at least, for lyrical emotion in those first steps into the wilderness,—in that first sense of desolation after wrath,—in that first audible gathering of the recriminating "groan of the whole creation"—in that first darkening of the hills from the recoiling feet of angels—and in that first silence of the voice of God. (*Works,* 2: 143–44)

Dorothy Mermin, among others, has argued that Barrett "redefines Milton's subject by focussing on Eve's guilt and repentance and redefines the role of the poet by asserting that suffering is a source of knowledge— a source to which even those who lack a classical education or the authority of male experience may have access" (*Barrett Browning*, 87).[10] But the authority of suffering is problematic for a woman in the Romantic tradition. Even as Barrett attempts to empower herself as a female poet, she accepts the repressive ideology that disables her as a woman—the original guilt of woman compels her to a perpetual martyrdom of self-sacrifice.

Barrett wanted to believe that in true poetic inspiration the poet's word echoes the divine creative Word, yet she seems to assert here that the poetry of fallen humanity, the poetry of exile, must take place in the "silence of the voice of God." Consequently, despite the very obvious visionary ambition of the poem itself, the preface reduces her claims to the mere utterance of the "lyrical emotion" of grief and loss—and the poetry of lamentation had long been recognized as the appropriate province of the poetess, who was, as a woman, expected to have more feeling than intellect. The Christian dispensation leaves little room for a woman's authoritative voice because, despite the preface, the "voice of God" is not "silent" within the drama but is present in Christ's words and even, as we shall see, in Adam's. Because Christianity is overwhelmingly patriarchal, anagogical poetry always points to ultimate masculine authority, and the earthly figures of that authority are masculine as well.

Wherever Barrett looked, exclusively masculine authority was thoroughly and, in her view, justly entrenched in a lineage leading all the way back to God the Father. Not surprisingly, as the preface continued, she acknowledged a fear that she had not, after all, found a distinctively female space within the Christian tradition:

> But when all was done, I felt afraid . . . of my position. I had promised my own prudence to shut close the gates of Eden between Milton and myself, so that none might say I dared to walk in his footsteps. He should be within, I thought, with his Adam and Eve unfallen or falling,—and I, without, with my EXILES—*I* also an exile! It would not do. The subject and his glory covering it, swept through the gates, and I stood full in it against my will, and contrary to my vow. (*Works*, 2: 144)

These comments could easily be seen as representing what Harold Bloom calls the "anxiety of influence," the fear that a poetic father is, in Bloom's apt words, a "covering cherub" blocking access to the divine vision. But in this case the attempt to achieve an independent vision is evidently perverse. The space Barrett had allotted to herself was the space of exile, yet the whole tendency of her Christian life was to seek *return* to the Father, and the recurrent themes of her earlier poetry are the quest to *re-enter* the gates of Eden and the desire to join rather than to resist the angelic hosts.[11] The only possible space for a genuinely original or genuinely female visionary poetry would be as an exile from God and from the prophetic and literary tradition. But for Barrett this would mean an exile from Truth—an independent position, perhaps, but, for her, an utterly false one.

Barrett's declared intention as she began work on the poem was to emphasize Eve's role as "*first & deepest in the sorrow*" (*Correspondence*, 8: 117; original emphasis), but as she neared completion she saw the poem as more about the male figures of exile: "It refers to Lucifer's exile, and to That other mystical exile of the Divine Being, which was the means of the return homewards of Adam & Eve" (*Correspondence*, 8: 267). She must, perforce, submit to the male tradition and allow her own voice to be subsumed by it. How else, indeed, could her voice swell the harmony of Christian praise rather than strike the jarring, dissonant note of individual pride? And worse, to the extent that the anagogical referent of exile is Lucifer, the poem suggests that the eschatological end of woman, Eve, is not the domestic angel, or the heavenly seraph, but the fallen angel.

Barrett clearly was not endorsing the conclusions of the "Satanic school" that Lucifer's Prometheanism was admirable: the self-evidently mistaken, damnable, and damned character of Lucifer parodically reveals the error of Byronic autonomy and defiance simply by proclaiming it:

> I CHOSE this ruin; I elected it
> Of my will, not of service. What I do,
> I do volitient, not obedient,
> And overtop thy crown with my despair.
> My sorrow crowns me. (ll.90–94)

Throughout the drama, Lucifer continues to rant, though at times his agony of despair seems almost remorseful—but he resolutely denies any repentance, and in doing so seems perfectly to characterize the error of melancholy Byronism.

Barrett felt empowered to write this ambitious work because of her affinity with Eve, but of course the Christian story, especially the Miltonic version, represents selfless female love as powerlessly submissive to masculine authority. Eve presents herself within the Miltonic scheme: "He for God only; she for God in him." For her, "the shadow on [Adam's] face" is "awfuller" (1.415) than the light of the "angelic hosts" (1.405), and her repentant posture is that of a literally fallen woman, abased and prostrate: "*I*, also, after tempting, writhe on the ground, / And I would feed on ashes from thine hand, / As suits me, O my tempted" (ll.436–38). But though she likens herself to the serpent in her prostration, Eve is in some respects empowered by this posture. As the drama makes clear, in the lapsarian state, the highest and holiest apprehension of divinity is felt through grief for sin, a notion that confirms, perhaps, that the highest kind of poetry available to fallen humankind is the poetry of the superego, the sentimental poetry she had been writing all along.

Though Eve is consistently represented as less wise than Adam, she is also represented as more fully humbled by grief, more conciliatory, and perhaps more loving. She fully accepts her role within patriarchy and within the Victorian ideology that claimed to exalt women precisely by humbling them: "Only my humbleness shall make me great, / My humbleness exalt me" (ll.1278–79). In confronting a fallen and hostile nature, Adam is proud and defiant, but Eve is meek and yielding. Adam even seems to retain a taint of Lucifer's pride. Shortly after Lucifer has proclaimed himself "Self-orphaned by my will, and self-elect / To kingship of resistant agony," Adam (echoing Byron's "Prometheus" as well as Lucifer) defies the spirit of earth:

> By my free will that chose sin,
> By mine agony within
> Round the passage of the fire,
>   By the pinings which disclose
> That my native soul is higher
>   Than what it chose,
> We are yet too high, O Spirits, for your disdain! (ll.1505–11)

Eve, on the other hand, pleads for love and reconciliation. Within the Christian scheme, her humility is ultimately more powerful for human good than Adam's pride as, presumably, female sentimental poetry is more powerful for good than male melancholia. When Christ intercedes to subdue nature to humankind, it is in response to Eve's appeal for God's pity, not Adam's appeal for God's power.

Barrett's empowerment of the female in this respect, however, can hardly be affirmed as a feminist gesture since it simply reinforces the prevalent gender ideology. Eve's only power, evidently, is that of the vessel of male seed, the maternal power that will enable her (as generic Woman) to be the mother of Christ. Her prayer is to Christ as the "mystic Seed that shalt be!" (1.1749)—her prayer is one of submission to a divine order, but also to a male line. She prays to the Son who is also the Father, and she submits to the authority of her own male progeny. When Christ intercedes, his charge to the spirits of nature may be taken as a charge also to women to be domestic angels:

> Be ye to man as angels are to God,
> Servants in pleasure, singers of delight,
> Suggesters to his soul of higher things
> Than any of your highest! (ll.1802–5)

Both Eve and, apparently, Barrett accept the gratifications of serving God by serving Man as sufficient recompense, and even as Woman's high calling:

> I accept
> For me and for my daughters this high part
> Which lowly shall be counted. Noble work
> Shall hold me in the place of garden-rest,
> And in the place of Eden's lost delight
> Worthy endurance of permitted pain. (ll.1897–1902)

Eve accepts, in short, the role of domestic angel. As Adam's speech makes explicit, she is to be a substitute for the angels lost to the service of man by her transgression:

> thou shalt go forth
> An angel of the woe thou didst achieve
> Found acceptable to the world instead
> Of others of that name, of whose bright steps
> Thy deed stripped bare the hills. (ll.1852–56)

But to be empowered as an angel in this context is scarcely to be empowered at all. In her representations of the woman poet's aspiration toward angelic song, Barrett had envisioned the poet serving God directly and mediating between God and humanity, but in this case the mere mortal is only a substitute angel, serving Man directly as Man mediates between her and God. As David has pointed out, Christ and Adam discipline Eve to accept a subservient role, so that the "poem inspired by Barrett Browning's desire to give utterance to Eve's (and woman's) 'peculiar anguish,' becomes a silencing of Eve's expressive voice" (109). It becomes a revelation of how inevitably, for Barrett, women's sentimental poetry returns to the "domestic language of the affections" and ends in "conservative sentiment."

Her representation of divine song in *A Drama of Exile* is once again that of a chorus of angels, whose praises of God reverberate through the cosmos and may be distantly apprehended by fallen mortals. But since it is impossible for a mortal to sing in the angelic chorus, perhaps the next best thing is to be an earthly substitute. Within the cosmic scheme set forth in this drama, the apotheosis of Barrett's anagogical mode, this kind of substitution is revealed as the very essence of God's economy. Lucifer, the Angel of the Morning Star, has been lost, but he is replaced by Christ, the "Bright and Morning-Star" ever present from the dawn of redemptive time. Further, in this poem about exile, Lucifer's pride is to be the ultimate exile, the king of exiles, but even in this, he learns, he is displaced by the incarnate Christ, self-exiled from heaven: "He will be an exile from his heaven, / To lead those exiles homeward" (ll.2223–24). Within this typological scheme, then, the things of fallen time take upon themselves a very different sense seen from the aspect of eternity—the ultimate mortal exile is God Himself, and by the same token, the domestic angel, from the perspective of eternity, may be a veritable heavenly angel. From God's perspective, the substitutions are not metaphors but truths. As Christ puts it,

> Eternity stands alway fronting God;
> A stern colossal image, with blind eyes
> And grand dim lips that murmur evermore
> God! God! God! (ll.1934–37)

All of the sounds of the universe are, as in Coleridge's theology, echoes of the all-creative Word of God, and this Word, moreover, is precisely the burden of the angelic chorus; it is the "WORD innumerous angels straightway lift / Wide on celestial altitudes of song / And choral adoration" (ll.1947–49). The ultimate WORD, however, is not sung by the angels but spoken by a mortal at the moment of death—it is a word empowered by despair. As in *The Seraphim*, the focus of providential time is on the moment of Christ's fullest humanity in his momentary despair on the cross:

> in the noon of time
> Eternity shall wax as dumb as Death,
> While a new voice beneath the spheres shall cry,
> "God! why hast thou forsaken me, my God?"
> And not a voice in Heaven shall answer it.
> [*The transfiguration is complete in sadness.*] (ll.1951–56)

Evidently the highest utterance is a human one after all, and further, it is an apotheosis of human sadness that fulfills the Atonement and restores humanity to God. Consequently, it is not surprising that the highest visionary power available to mortals is achieved through "the passion of our grief." And arguably, precisely because the burden of the curse is placed most emphatically on Eve until Christ comes to lift it, it is she—or Woman generally—whose passion of grief and consequent empowerment is greatest. In this way, perhaps, the Christian Woman displaces the melancholy "Satanic" Man as the highest visionary.

But there are evident problems with this logic. In the first place, Christ's words are spoken as the culmination of mortal despair—they express the agony of exile rather than the serenity of submission (Barrett chose not to quote Christ's final words, as she had done in *The Seraphim*: "FATHER! MY SPIRIT TO THINE HANDS IS GIVEN"). Even Christ's words lead, in mortal terms, to a continuing acceptance of tyranny, a sense of empowerment through martyrdom. In addition, the poem's logic might be said to repeat rather than repeal the logic of Satanic self-singing. Arguably the domestic angel, the mortal angel, is not simply a substitute for the heavenly angel—she might just as reasonably be described as a fallen angel. Her claims for power through humility are closely akin to Lucifer's claim that because he is the most agonized and fallen of sinners, he is the most empowered. Her own comments in the preface seem to concede this point: "I took pleasure in driving in, like a pile, stroke upon stroke, the Idea of EXILE,—admitting Lucifer as an extreme Adam, to represent the ultimate tendencies of sin and loss—that it might be strong to bear up the contrary idea of the Heavenly love and purity" (*Works,* 2:144). Within the drama this Luciferian logic is echoed without irony by Christ, as he castigates the Spirits of Earth for opposing themselves to fallen humanity: "Which of you disdains / These sinners who in falling proved their height / Above you by their liberty to fall?" (ll.1774–76). Despite earlier comments in the preface implying that the poetry of exile is the peculiar province of women, it becomes clear that even the experience of exile is essentially masculine, most fully known to "Lucifer as an extreme Adam," not to Eve. But of course Lucifer (and by implication, Adam) cultivates defiance rather than remorse in grief, precisely the attitude that, for Barrett, spiritually crippled the melancholy poets of the Satanic school. Yet her poetry seems dependent upon the melancholy she rejects, if only in the form adopted as appropriate to the theme of exile—the closet drama of mortals and supernatural beings inevitably reminded contemporaries of Byron's *Manfred* and *Cain* and, to a lesser extent, Shelley's *Prometheus Unbound.* Immediately upon finishing the drama, in fact, Barrett sensed that its strength was primarily in the depiction of Lucifer's lot; at one point, she said, "I determined to make one or two extracts from Lucifer's speeches & mix them up into a monodram[a] which I might call 'Lucifer'" (*Correspondence,* 8: 271). But her stronger impulse was to throw the whole manuscript into the fire—as perhaps the best place for Lucifer (she was dissuaded by John Kenyon's praise of the poem).

Even without deconstructing the poem's logic to show the similitude of Eve's grief with Satan's eternally doomed rebellion, it is clear that the preservation of traditional gender hierarchy leaves Man, not Woman, both in temporal power and in the spiritual authority of speaking with the primal Word of God's breath. The dominant idea, the idea to which Eve's or Satan's voice can only offer a counterpoint, is represented as emphatically masculine since the Christian drama necessarily finds the incarnation and apotheosis of "heavenly love and pity" in the masculine figure of Christ. Not only is Lucifer more a type for Adam's exile than for Eve's, but Christ is more a type for Adam's love and pity than for Eve's.

A Drama of Exile makes powerful though traditional claims for the authority of Christian vision, but despite Barrett's evident desire to empower women's speech, it leaves women in the thoroughly subordinate role of subservient angel. The alternative, which Barrett at least half-recognized but wholly resisted, is the role of rebellious, fallen angel—or demon. In fact, like at least one other Romantic woman writer of her time, Barrett expressed some fear that inspiration itself might be morally compromising. Charlotte Brontë defended the passion of her writing by asserting that "When authors write best . . . an influence seems to waken in them, which becomes their master—which will have its own way—putting out of view all behests but its own" (quoted in Gaskell, 239–40). A man may submit himself to his muse without raising moral issues, but for a woman to allow a male master to "have its own way" with her begins to sound problematic. Barrett herself stated in 1844 that "I write from impulse & conviction of heart & mind—that my faculty, whether it be, angel or demon, rather possesses than is possessed by me" (*Correspondence,* 9: 154). Barrett's language is not, I think, merely figurative—she was, in fact, simultaneously fascinated and repulsed at this time by the idea of mesmerism, which she perceived as a kind of usurpation of the soul, closely akin to demonic possession.[12]

There can be little doubt, of course, that Barrett believed in the moral worthiness of her writing and that she saw her inspiration as angelic rather than demonic, though her fear of the latter possibility was quite genuine. Such a fear sounds almost comic to modern ears, but it is consistent with Barrett's interest in mesmerism, and contemporary critics entertained it as a possibility, especially in the more outspoken works that followed the 1844 *Poems.* W. E. Aytoun, commenting on *Poems before Congress,* explained Barrett's "poetic aberrations" by insisting that like a "Pythoness" "under the influence of her cacodaemon" she "had been seized with a . . . fit of insanity." Henry Chorley said that Barrett had taken "to its extremity the right of the 'insane prophet' to lose his head and to loose his tongue," and he also expressed his suspicion that the poet of *Casa Guidi Windows* "had been biologized by infernal spirits" (*Correspondence*, 12: 406–7). The critics were surely writing figuratively, but Barrett's writings persistently reveal at least a hint of uncertainty about the moral propriety of inspiration for women. The uncertainty surfaces emphatically in her mixed feelings of admiration and moral repulsion for George Sand, whom she regarded as "*shameless*," yet a "true woman of genius" and "eloquent as a fallen angel" (*Correspondence*, 6: 163). Her two sonnets addressed to George Sand in the 1844 *Poems* express both admiration and censure—both sonnets call upon Sand to be less defiant, more womanly. But most significantly, neither sonnet can imagine Sand as a fully realized woman and author. In both, Barrett can only envision a redemption from fallen angel to heavenly angel. In the first, she hopes that Sand "to woman's claim / And man's, mightst join the angel's grace." In the second, the fulfillment of woman's creativity is once again deferred until death, "Till God unsex thee on the heavenly shore / Where unincarnate spirits purely aspire!"

Barrett's *Poems* of 1844 are rightly viewed as a turning point in her career, a shift from the perspective of the meek Christian "poetess" to that of the outspoken Romantic prophet-bard—but the collection is especially interesting because it so clearly contrasts the claims of female sentimental poetry with Romantic melancholy. Still, despite her obvious desire to speak out her full personal being in the *Poems* of 1844, Barrett could not fully articulate a role for an inspired woman poet.

II. Melancholy Eros in *Sonnets from the Portuguese*

Until the relatively recent rehabilitation of *Aurora Leigh*, Barrett Browning's position in the canon of Victorian poetry was secured almost exclusively by *Sonnets from the Portuguese*. As Tricia Lootens has demonstrated, in the early days of canon formation the sonnets not only secured Barrett's canonical status but constituted almost the entire "representation of her sex in the Victorian era" (136), and well into the 1970s the sonnets were still being described as Barrett's one clear claim to a "modest immortality" (117). But as Lootens has also convincingly shown, the effect of this emphasis was to efface not only Barrett's other poetry but even the genuine poetic achievement of the sonnets, displacing the poetry with the legend of the Brownings' immortal love. The sonnets were characteristically viewed as artless expressions of ideal female love, and in their representation of the feminine virtues of "abnegation, hope and Faith" they were a "testament to the indispensable 'relations of art and marriage, where the female genius is concerned'" (138). Not her poetry but her happy and fulfilled womanhood, "the apotheosis of womanhood," is her enduring achievement, with the paradoxical result that even as the poetry was canonized readers were encouraged not to study it, or read it with care, but only to look past it, "to read the truth through this slight veil, and to see the woman more than the poet" (133). The highly sexist effect of praising the sonnets on these grounds as "the definitive works of women's poetry altogether" is to encourage readers to look past, or overlook, "women's poetry altogether," to find poetry not in women's words but in their happy love for men. For the late Victorians,

> E. B. B.'s futile attempt at "competition with men" hence becomes a "glorious [if inadvertent] success, as a higher illustration than was ever otherwise afforded of what a woman is, and of what she may do in her own exalted and luminous sphere." A monument to True Womanhood glimmers behind Barrett Browning's verse, refuting the poet's own articulated feminism. (130)

By misreading or cursorily reading the sonnets, critics simultaneously canonized and disabled Barrett's poetry.

As her best critics now realize, the sonnets are not the artless outpouring of true womanhood but a complex introduction of a woman's voice into the exclusively male tradition of courtly love. The prolonged failure to read them in this light, perhaps, was caused both by a reticence to see pure womanhood sullied by erotic desire and by an inclination to see the speaker's self-abasement not as an expression of eroticism but as proper female submissiveness and even, as Mermin points out, as an "embarrassing" and, to modern ears, degrading submission to male superiority (*Barrett Browning*, 141). Such abasement, evidently melancholy in man, was seen as a source of happiness in a woman, so that even as astute and sympathetic a reader as Christina Rossetti could not see the sonnets as an effective intervention in the melancholy male tradition of courtly love. In a brief prefatory comment to her own intervention in the tradition, *Monna Innominata*, Rossetti lamented that none of the beloved women addressed by courtly lovers ever left a record of her own voice:

> Had such a lady spoken for herself, the portrait left us might have appeared more tender, if less dignified, than any drawn even by a devoted friend. Or had the Great Poetess of our own day and nation only been unhappy instead of happy, her circumstance would have invited

> her to bequeath to us, in lieu of the "Portuguese Sonnets," an inimitable "donna innominata" drawn not from fancy but from feeling, and worthy to occupy a niche beside Beatrice and Laura. (*Works*, 329)

There is some justification for this comment, to be sure, insofar as the "Portuguese" ends up with a satisfying exchange of love, a "happy ending," whereas masculine courtly love, from its beginnings in Ficino's *De Amore*, had been seen as an erotic desire seeking an impossible fulfillment, and ineluctably melancholy precisely because, as in *Alastor* and *Endymion*, the beloved has been internalized as an ego-ideal. As Giorgio Agamben lucidly describes the process, courtly love is necessarily unhappy since "Not an external body but an internal image, that is, the phantasm impressed on the phantastic spirits by the gaze, is the origin and object of falling in love" (23). Agamben's comments on courtly love and melancholy are well worth quoting at some length as a way of approaching both Barrett's difficult enterprise in the sonnets and the long tradition of misreading them:

> The imaginary loss that so obsessively occupies the melancholic tendency has no real object, because its funereal strategy is directed to the impossible capture of the phantasm. The lost object is but the appearance that desire creates for its courting of the phantasm, and the introjection of the libido is only one of the facets of a process in which what is real loses its reality so that what is unreal may become real. . . . If the external world is in fact narcissistically denied to the melancholic as an object of love, the phantasm yet receives from this negation a reality principle that emerges from the mute interior crypt in order to enter a new and fundamental dimension. No longer a phantasm and not yet a sign, the unreal object of melancholy introjection opens . . . [an] intermediate epiphanic place, located in the no-man's land between narcissistic self-love and external object choice. The *locus severus* (austere place) of melancholy, which according to Aristotle signifies genius and prudence, is also the *lusus severus* (serious play) of the word and of the symbolic forms through which, according to Freud, man succeeds in "enjoying [his] own day-dreams without self-reproach or shame." The topology of the unreal that melancholy designs in its immobile dialectic is, at the same time, a topology of culture. (25–26)

According to Ficino,

> every love begins with sight [and internalizes the beloved in the visual phantasm held in the mind]. But the love of the contemplative

> [Saturnian, melancholy] man ascends from sight to intellect. That of the voluptuous man descends from sight to touch. That of the active man remains in sight . . . the love of the contemplative man is called divine; that of the active man, human; that of the voluptuous man, bestial. (*Commentary*, 119–20)

Evidently the difficulty of writing about fulfilled, happy love in the courtly tradition is that the shift from the melancholy inward dialectic of contemplation to fulfillment moves the lover from the high cultural plane of the divine, short-circuiting the poetic creativity of melancholy in the *locus severus* of genius and the *lusus severus* of the word. More drastically, it lowers the lover from the divine to the bestial, so it is not wholly surprising that Barrett's contemporaries, shocked by the scandal of the elopement and carnal consummation of the Brownings, were inclined to shy away from discussion of the sonnets. As Lootens puts it, for them "the general operating consensus seems to have been the less said about the whole business, the better" (126).

From our distant perspective, however, a closer look reveals that the sonnets, the last major book written by Elizabeth Barrett as opposed to Barrett Browning, intervene in the courtly love tradition precisely by dwelling in the melancholy of desire until ultimately Barrett adopts the woman's prerogative of crossing through the "no-man's land" between narcissistic self-love and external object choice, and so short-circuits the courtly love tradition and passes through melancholy to a more socially directed mode. As various critics have noted, with the *Sonnets from the Portuguese,* Barrett began to find a public voice very different from the sentimentality of her enclosed, "trapped" consciousness. She had, of course, previously intervened in the public sphere in such poems as "The Cry of the Children," but her general shift after the sonnets was sufficiently marked to justify Cora Kaplan's remark that "Elizabeth Barrett was a lyric poet with an interest in political and social questions; Elizabeth Barrett Browning was primarily a political poet" (71).

Before the external object choice is fully made, the sonnets represent melancholy as the "emotion of the trapped." The choice of the sonnet form is itself the choice of a confining form, and the choice of courtly love implied by the formal decision is the choice of a tradition of melancholy. Angela Leighton has noted that among the "old generic postures and conventions" of the amatory sonnet tradition is the figure of "the woman who waits" ("Stirring," 222) and that Barrett specifically compared herself to the most conspicuous contemporary figure of the melancholy waiting woman: she wrote to Browning that she was "Like Mariana in the moated grange and [would] sit listening too often to the mouse in the wainscot" (223). Leighton makes the point even more emphatically with reference to another letter to Browning: "'As for me,' Elizabeth writes at one point, 'I have done most of my talking by post of late years—as people shut up in dungeons, take up with scrawling mottos on the walls.' The scene of writing, for this woman poet, is the prison" (225). Like many of Barrett's self-characterizations in the letters, the sense of imprisoned isolation belongs also to the speaker of the sonnets, especially sonnet 4, which echoes the lonely moated grange, the "dreamy house" of Mariana waiting in desolation for her lover to come to her from his palace:

> Thou hast thy calling to some palace-floor,
> Most gracious singer of high poems! where
> The dancers will break footing, from the care
> Of watching up thy pregnant lips for more,
> And dost thou lift this house's latch too poor
> For hand of thine? and canst thou think and bear
> To let thy music drop here unaware
> In folds of golden fulness at my door?
> Look up and see the casement broken in,
> The bats and owlets builders in the roof!
> My cricket chirps against thy mandolin.
> Hush, call no echo up in further proof
> Of desolation! there's a voice within
> That weeps . . . as thou must sing . . . alone, aloof.

Unlike Mariana's, this speaker's lover will come, and does come, and the prisoner will eventually manage a prison break, but for much of the sequence she chirps, as here, in the melancholy isolation that provides at least a *locus severus* for her voice, even if only to weep, and maintaining the separation of the lovers enables them both to sing "alone, aloof." As Leighton points out, courtly love traditionally sets obstacles to sexual consummation, "constantly resists its material expenditure in either sexual satisfaction or social bonding. It is a sentiment, satisfied in the indefinite postponement of its final gratification. In that postponement, the lover finds time to speak" ("Stirring," 219–20).

From the beginning of the sequence obstacles to love are described, but described as providing a time for love to speak. In the second sonnet, for example, all separation, even to "heaven being rolled between us" (1.13), leads only to love's speech: "We should but vow the faster for the stars" (1.14). Further, the echoes of desolation in sonnet 4, like the "old voices" heard by Tennyson's Mariana, suggest a reverberation of the old voice of a poetic tradition belatedly entered. Reverberation suggests the possibility of belated song, but only as a re-verbing of what has already been sung. Despite the common misconception that Barrett's sonnets were the unmediated expression of her feeling, the insistent intertextuality of the poems (beginning with an explicit reference to Theocritus in the opening line of the sequence) indicates that Barrett herself was well aware that her language, coming so late in the tradition, would inevitably refer not to her unique feeling but to other texts, so that the language of her love operates like all emblems in melancholy allegory to refer, as de Man puts it, only to the sign that precedes it, so that the "meaning" of the words "can then consist only in the *repetition* . . . since it is in the essence of this previous sign to be pure anteriority."[13] Leighton makes a similar point about the echoing of old voices in the sonnets:

> The lover's discourse, according to Barthes, "proceeds from others, from the language, or from books." He concludes, "no love is original." The "dreamy house" is haunted by other voices. The text of feeling has been written already. This *déjà vu*, or rather, *déjà écrit*, inevitably turns the lover's passion into a pose; the lover's poem into another, older one. Feeling suffers the anxiety of having been preempted by literature. ("Stirring," 228)[14]

The sense of melancholy as the emotion of the trapped is perhaps overdetermined in the sonnets, by the sonnet form itself, the courtly love tradition, the distance from original feeling, and even the modern Nietzschean sense of language itself as a prison house, but entrapment also provides a place of safety, a refuge where love can rest in contemplation without risking descent into the actual:

> On me thou lookest with no doubting care,
> As on a bee shut in a crystalline;
> Since sorrow hath shut me safe in love's divine,
> And to spread wing and fly in the outer air
> Were most impossible failure, if I strove
> To fail so. (15. 5–10)

From the very first sonnet, the sequence begins an inward dialectic in which the speaker balances the promise of love against her long-held infatuation with death, with the visions of past years and past loved ones. Whichever way she turns, she is mastered, constrained, trapped in her own longing:

> I thought once how Theocritus had sung
> Of the sweet years, the dear and wished-for years,
> Who each one in a gracious hand appears
> To bear a gift for mortals, old or young:

> And, as I mused it in his antique tongue,
> I saw, in gradual vision through my tears,
> The sweet, sad years, the melancholy years,
> Those of my own life, who by turns had flung
> A shadow across me. Straightway I was 'ware,
> So weeping, how a mystic Shape did move
> Behind me, and drew me backward by the hair;
> And a voice said in mastery, while I strove,—
> "Guess now who holds thee?"—"Death," I said. But, there,
> The silver answer rang,—"Not Death, but Love."

Love presents itself not as an alternative to the sweet, sad immobility of melancholy but as another form of it. The sonnet anticipates the process of the entire sequence, in which the speaker will exchange the familiar, poetically enabling melancholy in which she lived "with visions for my company" (26. 1) for a love that puts at risk the poetic safety of melancholy enclosure. Eventually love triumphs to draw her forth from the prison of melancholy interiority, but for much of the sequence this escape from "vision" to an external world of "men and women" (26. 2) is deferred to make a space for language. Startled from her security in sonnet 1, the speaker immediately retreats behind God's interdiction in sonnet 2: "God . . . laid the curse / So darkly on my eyelids, as to amerce / My sight from seeing you" (4–6).[15] The gradual shift from infatuation with Death to Love can occur only when Love displaces the "visions" with a phantasm of its own. Rather than leave the solipsistic security of her isolated inner world, the speaker, after the proper Ficinian method, draws the lover into her inner world as a phantasmal image of himself. The process by which she fends off the threat of actuality by internalizing the lover is described with surprising precision in sonnet 6:

> Go from me. Yet I feel that I shall stand
> Henceforward in thy shadow. Nevermore
> Alone upon the threshold of my door
> Of individual life, I shall command
> The uses of my soul, nor lift my hand
> Serenely in the sunshine as before,
> Without the sense of that which I forebore—
> Thy touch upon the palm. The widest land
> Doom takes to part us, leaves thy heart in mine
> With pulses that beat double. What I do
> And what I dream include thee, as the wine
> Must taste of its own grapes. And when I sue

> God for myself, He hears that name of thine,
> And sees within my eyes the tears of two.

The external, physical figure of the lover is banished so that the immaterial image may be internalized, not compelling the speaker out of her solitary contemplation—curtailing dialogue, perhaps, but enabling a dialectic of inwardness as the speaker communes with her phantasmal lover. In Ficino's terms this is the highest love, divine love, and in poetic terms it is a new inspiration as the speaker is "taught the whole / Of life in a new rhythm" (7. 6–7). Breaking from the neo-Platonic tradition, however, the speaker not only contemplates the divine love but incarnates love—the physical transformation in sonnet 6 is soon seen in audacious religious language not just as a transformation but as a "transfiguration" (sonnet 10). Unlike neo-Platonic love, which can only raise its sights to heaven, the speaker's Christian love, in a bold "imitatio Christi," can bring the divine love into the actual:

> I stand transfigured, glorified aright,
> With conscience of the new rays that proceed
> Out of my face toward thine. There's nothing low
> In love, when love the lowest: meanest creatures
> Who love God, God accepts while loving so.
> And what I *feel*, across the inferior features
> Of what I *am*, doth flash itself, and show
> How that great work of Love enhances Nature's. (10. 7–14)

The incarnation of love as Christ sets the example of the sanctifying incarnation of love in the flesh, justifying even erotic physical love as divine, not bestial. Dismissing any spiritual presumptions of love by insisting on materialist criteria, Iago says of Desdemona that "The wine she drinks is made of grapes" (*Othello*, II.i.251–52), but the speaker of *Sonnets from the Portuguese* accepts that "the wine / Must taste of its own grapes" (6. 12–13), conceiving spiritual distillation not as transcendence but as transfiguration of the body. The speaker consequently moves from God's law, the "Law of the Father," to God's love, the incarnate love of the Son. Ironically, it is only when Barrett has moved beyond conventional asceticism to embrace erotic love that she is able to figure in her eschatological scheme of things as a figura for Christ. In biographical terms it is easy enough to see that the Christian allegory submerged in the sonnets constitutes a reasoned and devout justification of Barrett's ultimate denial of the prohibitions of her own father and her choice of erotic love, and in the sonnets it provides a newfound sense of worthiness to love and to be loved.

The image of love as fire indicates the extent to which this Christian reasoning liberates the demure, modest speaker into erotic passion:

> Yet, love, mere love, is beautiful indeed
> And worthy of acceptation. Fire is bright,
> Let temple burn, or flax; an equal light
> Leaps in the flame from cedar-plank or weed:
> And love is fire. And when I say at need
> *I love thee* . . . mark! . . . *I love thee*, in thy sight
> I stand transfigured. . . . (10. 1–7)

Leighton, Mermin, and Cooper have all argued that the utterance, *I love thee*, from a woman speaker transforms the courtly love tradition by switching the amatory gender roles of lover and beloved, and for the first time makes a woman the subject rather than merely the object of loving. In her excellent reading of the sequence Mermin fully demonstrates the extent to which Barrett renovated the traditional sonnet sequence by making room for two subjectivities (rather than the traditional male subject and female object) and consequently emphasized the reciprocity of love (*Browning*, 130). I want only to emphasize here that the lovers' exchanges all follow from the exchange of divine contemplation for earthly love. This is a choice to leave melancholy behind, and it is reiterated many times in the sonnets:

> my soul, instead
> Of dreams of death, resumes life's lower range
> . . .
> I yield the grave for thy sake, and exchange
> My near sweet view of heaven, for earth with thee! (23. 8–9, 13–14)

Similarly, she chooses "men and women" instead of "visions for [her] company" because "God's gifts put man's best dreams to shame" (26. 14). In effect, she exchanges a dialectic of inwardness for the outward exchange of dialogue, and even insists on the almost sordid social world of exchange in the tit for tat of "What can I give thee back?" (8. 1). The exchanges of locks of hair, of "I love yous," and of poems for flowers are all put in the extreme social context of exchange as the marketing of merchandise. Referring pointedly (for Browning) back to Browning's description of selling his intellectual efforts on "the Rialto where verse-merchants most do congregate," she leaves solitary contemplation, at least metaphorically, for the busy world, "The soul's Rialto [which] hath its merchandise" (19. 1). The exchange, like all barter, moreover, must be on equal terms—for the sweet melancholy that she gives up, she must receive equal value: "If I leave all for thee, wilt thou exchange / And be all to me? (35. 1–2). The exchange of her inner world of visions, thoughts, and images for the real presence of her lover is shown most clearly in sonnet 30, where she contrasts the internalized, imaged lover with the corporeal presence: "I see thine image through my tears to-night, / And yet to-day I saw thee smiling. How / Refer the cause?" (1–3). Working through the problem, she remains sad, but the description of her tears as "hot and real" (14) suggests a tentative entry into actuality and physical expression. Ultimately what the lovers exchange is a melancholy eros in which the lover is possessed only as a neo-Platonic phantasm, for a physical eros in which he is seen as himself, an external and autonomous individual. The process is metaphorically described in sonnet 29:

> I think of thee!—my thoughts do twine and bud
> About thee, as wild vines, about a tree,
> Put out broad leaves, and soon there's nought to see
> Except the straggling green which hides the wood.
> Yet, O my palm-tree, be it understood
> I will not have my thoughts instead of thee
> Who art dearer, better! Rather, instantly
> Renew thy presence; as a strong tree should,
> Rustle thy boughs and set thy trunk all bare,
> And let these bands of greenery which insphere thee
> Drop heavily down,—burst, shattered, everywhere!
> Because, in this deep joy to see and hear thee
> And breathe within thy shadow a new air,
> I do not think of thee—I am too near.

Leaving her isolated, contemplative life, the speaker gives up her poetic prerogative of a green thought in a green shade, replacing her fantasy for the actual lover, imagined in strikingly phallic terms as she reveals the hard wood usually hidden behind the veil of poetic idealization. Further, the green vine has a biographical significance for Barrett, calling to mind the ivy that grew in her bedroom window, more deeply closing her into the imprisoning cocoon of her solitary life. Ultimately, in the final poem of the sequence, the vine is seen to figure not only the speaker's thoughts but also the poems produced from melancholy. In the exchange for his flowers the speaker offers her lover the vine, the eglantine and ivy which have grown in her "heart's ground" (44. 8, 10–11).

Accepting Browning as her lover and breaking from the prison of her melancholy isolation under her father's roof, Barrett passed up a source of melancholia in her own poetry, though she gave it up in fair exchange for life with real "men and women" and with the "Men and Women" of Browning's poetry. All of this, of course, contributes to the most famous of the sonnets, sonnet 43, the sonnet by which Barrett is best known, though *mis*known as a writer of sentimental pap:

> How do I love thee? Let me count the ways.
> I love thee to the depth and breadth and height
> My soul can reach, when feeling out of sight
> For the ends of Being and ideal Grace.
> I love thee to the level of everyday's
> Most quiet need, by sun and candle-light.
> I love thee freely, as men strive for Right;
> I love thee purely, as they turn from Praise.
> I love thee with the passion put to use
> In my old griefs, and with my childhood's faith.
> I love thee with a love I seemed to lose
> With my lost saints,—I love thee with the breath,
> Smiles, tears, of all my life!—and, if God choose,
> I shall but love thee better after death.

The opening quatrain is a Pauline allusion that integrates the beloved into the Christian faith that has enabled the speaker's acceptance of incarnate love. The allusion, in fact, leads to the image of the heart's ground in the next and final poem: Paul prays "that Christ may dwell in your hearts by faith; that ye, being rooted and grounded in love, may be able to comprehend with all saints what is the breadth and length, and depth and height; and to know the love of Christ, which passeth knowledge, that ye might be filled with all the fulness of God" (Ephesians 3:17–18).

What is surprising about the sonnet is its acquiescence in the actual and earthly. While leaving the transcendent idealism of the courtly love tradition to pursue the infinite ideal that "passeth knowledge" "out of sight," the earthly love is rooted in and is replete with the measurable "depth and breadth and height" of the actuality that is apparent in terrestrial light. In a sense Barrett is accepting a poetic role somewhat diminished from the possibly vainglorious desire of the 1844 sonnets to "utter all myself into the air" and so speak the "dread apocalypse of soul" that would discard the fleshly tabernacle of the body, but she is embodying the highest earthly poetic role instead of aspiring futilely to express the "ends of Being and ideal Grace" only available to the disembodied spirit. The love and passion invoked are not the infinite, mortally impossible ideals of courtly love but are drawn from what might be called the earthly idealism of "everyday's" use and need. An infinite love may come after death, but for the purposes of life, the bodily realities of breath, smiles, and tears are sufficient.

Far from being the simple unmediated effusion it is generally taken for, the sonnet is heavily mediated by both the literary and religious traditions, and it offers the complicated exchange of the speaker's safe and familiar melancholy for the world and human love. In effect, the lover's melancholy is cast off when the prolonged grieving for lost saints, Barrett's mother and brother, is resolved as normal mourning and its emotional depths are transferred to erotic love. Finally, it seems, Barrett had found a way through melancholy to an affirmative poetic voice, negotiating a subjectivity of her own grounded in both Christian teaching and erotic human love.

From a feminist perspective it might at first seem tempting to think that Barrett was a greater poet before meeting Browning, that her acceptance of patriarchal marriage was destructive of her autonomous poetic gift. Such a view seems preferable, at any rate, to the late Victorian view that her greatest poetic achievement was turning herself into a wife and mother, the "apotheosis of womanhood." The truth, however. is that her most outspoken feminist works were written after her marriage. It is not that her marriage *qua* marriage was liberating, but her affirmation of an autonomous selfhood grounded in erotic love did coincide with a decided change in her poetic practice.

Several critics have, in recent decades, affirmed that Barrett first established a poetic voice of her own in *Sonnets from the Portuguese,* and that thereafter she wrote in a confidently public, often political and occasionally inflammatory voice in *Casa Guidi Windows, Aurora Leigh, Poems before Congress,* and *Last Poems.* When she adopted and worked through the poetics of melancholy by working through the dialectic of the *Sonnets,* she finally worked her way through the influence of the second-generation Romantics and also overcame the prevailing female tradition of poetry grounded in submissive sorrow. Like Carlyle, she shut up her Byron and took up not Goethe but the Carlylean mode of heroic utterance to which she had been attracted throughout the 1840s. In *Casa Guidi Windows,* she explicitly rejected melancholy as an adequate response to the "stress of conscience," calling for poets to lead rather than indolently "To gaze long / On mournful masks and sad effigies" (i. 45–47). She set aside the sorrowful voice of the woman poet and of melancholy to raise, in part I, a voice of exultant prophecy, refusing to align herself with "rhymers sonneteering in their sleep, / And archaists mumbling dry bones up the land, / And sketchers lauding ruined towns a-heap,—" (i. 148–50). Rather, she made a point of separating herself from sentimentalists who would

> Sigh for Italy with some safe sigh
> Cooped up in music 'twixt an oh and ah,—
> Nay, hand in hand with that young child will I
> Go singing rather "*Bella libertà*,"
> Than, with those poets, croon the dead or cry
> "*Se tu men bella fossi, Italia!*" (i. 163–68)

Still, after the bitter disappointment of her hopes for Italian liberty, in part II her anger draws on the stuff of melancholy for a sense of solemnity:

> If I speak
> These bitter things against the jugglery
> Of days that . . . proved blind and weak,
> It is that tears are bitter. When we see
> The brown skulls grin at death in the churchyards bleak,
> We do not cry "This Yorick is too light,"
> For death grows deathlier with the mouth he makes.
> So with my mocking: bitter things I write
> Because my soul is bitter for your sake,
> O freedom! O my Florence! (ii. 185–94)

In her most ambitious poem, *Aurora Leigh*, Barrett Browning emphatically sought to write of the actualities of her

> live, throbbing age,
> That brawls, cheats, maddens, calculates, aspires,
> And spends more passion, more heroic heat,
> Betwixt the mirrors of its drawing-rooms,
> Than Roland with his knights at Roncesvalles. (v. 203–7)

In representing the growth of a woman poet's mind, she indicates that the conventional passive sentimentality of women poets is inadequate, that Aurora must grow beyond the popular sentimental ballads of women's poetry and direct her art outward, to actions, because "Passion is / But something suffered after all" (v. 364–65). Crucially, however, she affirms that the artist's lifeblood is her passionate interiority. The poet must work though the depths of melancholy, as Barrett had done, before turning to the world of actualities and action:

> The artist's part is both to be and do,
> Transfixing with a special, central power

> The flat experience of the common man,
> And turning outward, with a sudden wrench,
> Half agony, half ecstasy, the thing
> He feels the inmost. (v. 367–72)

The passionate interiority, moreover, is experienced precisely as a melancholy dialogue of the mind with itself, a dialectic between a severe conscience and an inner personal life:

> Does a torch less burn
> For burning next reflectors of blue steel,
> That *he* should be the colder for his place
> 'Twixt two incessant fires,—his personal life's
> And that intense refraction which burns back
> Perpetually against him from the round
> Of crystal conscience he was born into
> If artist born? O sorrowful great gift
> Conferred on poets, of a twofold life,
> When one life has been found enough for pain! (v. 373–82)

For Barrett Browning, of course, the conscience is not simply the contemporary moral ideology but the voice of God, the "universal" truth. Still, the universal is embodied in the vesture of the age, the "times we live in" (v. 182), so that her poetry, or Aurora's, is grounded in the melancholy dialectic of the personal and the internalized social order.

Chapter Four

"Filthy Rags of Speech": Browning's Melancholy Optimism

> As image, the corpse concentrates into a dialectical unity the subjection of the human spirit to the creaturely, to the consignment of all things to ruin. The corpse is the most graphic representation of subject turned object. But at the extreme limit of allegorical reflection, the corpse is also the hope for redemption encoded into the most physical and most profane of all possible images. (Pensky, 180)

I. Confused Multitudinousness: Browning's Early Poetry

Robert Browning might seem an odd poet to characterize as in any sense melancholy. In his own day he was famous for his optimism, and G. K. Chesterton even went so far as to call him "something far more convincing, far more comforting, far more religiously significant than an optimist: he is a happy man" (186). Certainly he is poles apart from the lugubrious, passive melancholy of Tennyson's Mariana or Lotos-Eaters—reading his vigorously energetic rhythms, it is difficult not to imagine Browning as Hopkins did, "bouncing up from table with his mouth full of bread and cheese and saying he meant to stand no blasted nonsense" (*Letters,* 157). Still, as such poems as "A Toccata of Galuppi" and "The Last Ride Together" clearly show, jaunty rhythms may accompany melancholy themes, and as Loy Martin has demonstrated, the tension between poetic form and content is one of many indications in Browning of an overarching concern about the modern "divided self" (115–22).

One reason why the early Browning societies saw Browning as a reassuring optimist was that unlike Tennyson, he evidently had a firm Christian faith and a confident hope in an eternal afterlife, yet in poem after poem, Browning's characters struggle with the conviction that full achievement is only possible in heaven, that the earthly fate of the subject is to strive for the impossible infinite but, like Elizabeth Barrett's poet-figures, to recognize that all earthly effort falls short of our aspirations. In the most famous of Browning's affirmations, the most melancholy of his characters, Andrea del Sarto, observes that "a man's reach should exceed his grasp, / Or what's a heaven for?" (11.97–98). But Andrea's problem, and the human problem generally as Browning saw it, is that, in Christina Rossetti's words, the human condition is to be "Hopeless on earth, and heaven is out of view" (*Monna Innominata*, xi. 8). Still, I do not want to argue that Browning is not an optimist, but only that his optimism is consonant with melancholy, and its particular forms and affirmations are generated from an engagement with the melancholy of his age. He shares with Carlyle the view that earthly life may be sorrowful and dark, but it is always darkest before dawn. The ambivalence of Browning's thought is summed up by Herbert Tucker:

> In Browning's temporal economy the anticipation of something yet to be is no mere compensation for present dissatisfaction; his thirst for the future is so strong that the apparent compensation in effect pre-pays and insures the loss. The imperative of expectation demands that the present always be found wanting. If there is to be something to look forward to—and for Browning there must be that at all costs—then there must be something missing now. (*Browning's Beginnings*, 5)

Tucker's stress here falls on the optimism of Browning's assurance of reward, but I will emphasize not the "pre-payment" but the something wanted, the melancholy lack that drives the poetry toward the promise of fulfillment without the possibility of ever finding it in earthly terms or in the finite forms of language. Browning's optimistic melancholy has strong affinities with Kierkegaard's Christian melancholy. In *The Sickness unto Death*, a work that Walter Lowrie (Translator's Introduction, 138) has aptly characterized as an Anatomy of Melancholy, the condition of the self always aspiring to the infinite is almost a definition of "despair": "[A] self every instant it exists, is in process of becoming, for the self . . . does not actually exist, it is only that which it is to become. In so far as the self does not become itself, it is not its own self; but not to be one's self is despair" (163).

Another reason why early readers were able to see Browning as an uncomplicated optimist is that they, perhaps justly, tended to neglect the ambitious but formidably difficult early poems in which Browning most extensively explored the melancholy, divided sensibilities of the post-Romantic subject. Browning's earliest major poem, *Pauline,* was famously described by John Stuart Mill as the product of a writer "possessed with a more intense and morbid self-consciousness than I ever knew in any sane human being" (quoted in Irvine, 40). Browning more or less disowned the poem until he was forced by the appearance of corrupt pirated editions to publish it apologetically in 1867, so Chesterton and others could easily dismiss *Pauline* as a boyish aberration, not at all typical of the mature poet. Later readers, however, have recognized that, whether or not it is a successful poem in itself, *Pauline* was a poetic experiment of the greatest importance in the development of Browning's mature poetry.

Setting the keynote for Browning's poetry of melancholy, *Pauline* is modeled on prior Romantic texts, particularly Shelley's *Alastor*, and it both imitates and parodies the claims of the Romantic subject.[1] Most obviously, it parodies the claims of what Shelley called alternately "imagination" or "love" and what Hallam called "sympathy," to encounter and absorb other subjectivities. At his most grandiose, the *Pauline* poet makes extraordinary claims for the Romantic self, "a most clear idea of consciousness" (1.269):

> linked, in me, to self-supremacy,
> Existing as a centre to all things,
> Most potent to create and rule and call
> Upon all things to minister to it;
> And to a principle of restlessness
> Which would be all, have, see, know, taste, feel, all—
> This is myself. (ll.273–79)

Such a fully unified self would embody the whole of a subjectivity made in the image of God and would have infinite depth and range of power, successfully achieving the desire to fit the infinite into the finite mortal self and the Kierkegaardian desire fully to become the infinite self. But even beyond the obvious hubris of the *Pauline* poet's claim there are worrying implications in his ebullient self-aggrandizement. First, the definition of a "self" distinct from all of its qualities may shelter the self from possible contamination, but a buffer separates the self from the world in a solipsistic isolation that would make poetic communication impossible and that the rest of the passage seems at pains to deny. Second, counter to this centripetal force is a centrifugal force that gives the self empire over all but simultaneously seems to involve a dispersal of the self. As the poet remarks later, "A mind like this must dissipate itself" (1.291). In addition, the introversion of the poem (the continuous returns upon the self that provide the content of melancholy and the subject of the poem) and the absence of any real audience indicate that no escape from the self has been achieved. The same problem arises even more clearly in the celebration of

> an imagination which
> Has been a very angel, coming not
> In fitful visions but beside me ever
> And never failing me.... (ll.284–87)

The lines exult in the constancy of the Romantic imagination, but at the same time the metaphor of the imagination as a visiting angel indicates that imagination is not intrinsic to the self but a thing apart. The mind is divided and the self, or soul, remains sheltered and apart from both the material world of the senses and even, "confined to clay," from the angel of inspiration. The angel, always near but always apart, is as elusive, haunting, and debilitating as the Poet's vision in *Alastor*. In *Pauline* as in *Alastor* the vision is both enticing and tormenting, evidence, in its beauty, of election as a poet and, in its evasiveness, of the poet's isolation, solipsism, and irremediable melancholy. Both poems seem almost to model a fundamental stage that we have noted in Butler's analysis of melancholy, the moment of "recognition that the subject produced as continuous, visible, and located is nevertheless haunted by an inassimilable remainder, a melancholia that marks the limits of subjectivation" (29). There is much of Browning himself in this characterization of the ambitiously aspiring Romantic poet, but he was not being disingenuous when he claimed that *Pauline* was the expression of a constructed persona, for the poet of *Pauline* is plainly the logical Romantic successor of Wordsworth and Shelley, if such a successor were possible.

Browning's insight was that the infinite subjectivity aspired to by Romanticism is impossible to fit into the "limits of subjectivation," the finite forms of representation, and that if it could be so presented it would be tyrannical in its domination of other subjects. *Pauline,* however, is not "morbid" for its extravagant Romantic claims but for its consciousness of failure to achieve the unified self predicated by Romantic aspirations: bound to trust "All feelings equally, to hear all sides: / How can my life indulge them? yet they live, / Referring to some state of life unknown" (ll.598–600). Such a fractured, discontinuous subjectivity can obviously not dominate or absorb other subjectivities into itself, because it has no coherent self. The restlessness described here is a primary indication of melancholia as understood since Ficino's influential analysis of melancholy as the tormented homelessness and wandering of genius exiled from unity with God. The "form of life unknown" seems to correspond remarkably well with Butler's description of "an inassimilable remainder." In

Browning's later work this is generally described as the heaven that lies beyond our grasp, the unity with God that we seek futilely on earth, even if our striving will eventually be rewarded after death.

Because of the similarity of Browning's and Kierkegaard's aspiration for the infinitude of self, Kierkegaard's philosophy and writing practices provide a somewhat surprising gloss on Browning's. Throughout his writings, Kierkegaard too was concerned with the extreme difficulty of defining the infinite and infinitely complex self, and like Browning's, his approach was generally dramatic in form, though based on introspection. In *The Concept of Dread* Kierkegaard, or rather his pseudonymous speaker, Vigilius Haufniensis, argued for a "psychological-poetic authority" based on the psychological observer's ability to "insinuate himself under the skin of other people" (49), but he also argued that this dramatic capability was grounded in introspection: "If only one pays attention to oneself, an observer will with five men, five women, and ten children have enough for the discovery of all possible states of the human soul" (112). From this perspective the kind of multitudinous, disjunctive self apparent to introspection might provide the sources for a multitude of "possible states of the human soul," most especially for an "aesthetic" personality such as the author of the first part of *Either/Or*, who is accused in part 2 of "hovering above yourself, but the ether, the fine sublimate into which you are volatilized, is the nullity of despair, and beneath you you behold a multiplicity of subjects for learning, information, study, observation, which for you, indeed, have no reality, but which you capriciously combine and employ to adorn as tastefully as possible the palace of the mind's luxurious delight" (2: 203). The passage seems better to describe the Tennyson of "The Palace of Art" than Browning, but the objects in this palace of art are reified subjects, like the many speakers of Browning's works. Kierkegaard's melancholy young aesthete, like the speakers of *Pauline* and *Paracelsus*, typifies the dangers of melancholy and poetic vanity. Further, as David Shaw has argued, many of the speakers of Browning's most famous monologues are evidently stunted in their spiritual growth: like Kierkegaard's young aesthete they have failed to move on to the higher ethical and religious stages of subjectivity.[2] As Browning's first experiment with the lifelong poetic desire that he described to Ruskin, to fit the infinite into the finite, the *Pauline* poet's infinite and unappeasable aspirations anticipate the melancholy later pithily expressed in "Two in the Campagna": "infinite passion, and the pain / Of finite hearts that yearn." The voraciousness of the *Pauline* poet's appetite to "be immortal, taste all joy" (1.810) resembles the exorbitant excess of the Byronic imagination as parodied by Carlyle in *Sartor Resartus*, in the figure of the unhappy Shoeblack, who "has a Soul quite other than his stomach, and would require, if you consider it, for his permanent satisfaction and saturation, simply this allotment, no more and no less: *God's infinite Universe altogether to himself,* therein to enjoy infinitely, and fill every wish as fast as it rose" (*Works,* 1: 152). The Shoeblack illustrates the difficulty faced by both Kierkegaard and the *Pauline* poet: "Man's Unhappiness . . . comes of his Greatness; it is because there is an Infinite in him, which with all his cunning he cannot quite bury under the Finite" (1: 151–52). The poet's desire perfectly fits this model of melancholy: "my hunger for / All pleasure, howsoe'er minute, grows pain" (ll.602–3).

The *Pauline* poet finds that for him even the unified though melancholy imagination of Shelley and Byron has become, as for Arnold in "Stanzas from the Grande Chartreuse," an "outworn theme." Browning's returns to Shelley and especially his quest for the angel/demon of late Romanticism keep open the poetic possibilities of Romantic melancholy only *as* melancholia. As Tucker argues, the "impossibility" of fully becoming a Romantic poet in Browning's generation leaves Browning with the open-ended quest that provides the very possibility of his characteristic striving for the unattainable infinite (*Browning's Beginnings,* 31). Browning's early examination of the melancholy imagination led him, as early as *Pauline,* to a very Victorian, Carlylean critique of morbid introspection. *Pauline* was the first in a series of works to present the extraordinarily complex implications of a poetic effort to unite the unlimited infinite self to an equally unlimited infinite of an other. To do so, one or both of the subjects would have to be reduced to a limited object, capable of being grasped and assimilated. Browning's faith in an infinite worth striving for may be described as optimism, but it is an optimism best seen as resistance to melancholy.

Since Browning suppressed *Pauline* after its first, anonymous publication in 1833, his next publication, the ambitious *Paracelsus,* constituted his entrance into the post-Romantic literary world in 1835. Chesterton was able to maintain his belief in Browning's optimism and genuine happiness in the face of the undeniably morbid *Pauline,* which he dismissed as a boyish aberration, but he saw *Paracelsus* as Browning's first truly characteristic work, as the first expression of the concerns that preoccupied the mature poet. Chesterton's opinion has been widely supported: according to William O. Meredith, "practically all of the leading and controlling ideas of [Browning's] poetry are present in *Paracelsus*" (156). Yet although *Paracelsus* may lack the "morbidity" of *Pauline,* it is another trial of Shelleyan imagination (the historical Paracelsus was a particular favorite both of Shelley and of the young Frankenstein), and it firmly situates Browning's early poetry within the melancholy modern condition deplored by Arnold. As a character, Paracelsus is manifestly like Faust,

Hamlet, and Byron's Manfred, so it is appropriate to place him within Arnold's account of the disease of modernity: "the dialogue of the mind with itself has commenced; modern problems have presented themselves; we have already the doubts, we witness the discouragement, of Hamlet and of Faust" (*Works*, 1: 1).

And now, of Paracelsus. Even more clearly than Hamlet or Faust, the overreaching alchemist Paracelsus epitomizes the beginning of what Schiesari refers to as "a great age of melancholia" (3). As represented by Browning, moreover, the career of Paracelsus seems remarkably consistent with Bradley's account of the special significance for the nineteenth century of *Hamlet*, which "must bring home to us at once the sense of the soul's infinity, and the sense of the doom which not only circumscribes that infinity but appears to be its offspring" (108).

Paracelsus may almost be regarded as Browning's version of Bradley's Hamlet:

> I was restless, nothing satisfied,
> Distrustful, most perplexed . . .
> . . . yet felt somehow
> A mighty power was brooding, taking shape
> Within me; and this lasted till one night
> When, as I sat revolving it more and more,
> A still voice from without said—"Seest thou not,
> Desponding child, whence spring defeat and loss?
> Even from thy strength." (i. 506–14)

Paracelsus's sufferings seem to epitomize what Wilhelm Dilthey diagnosed as the melancholic disease of the period: "It was clear that the eighteenth and nineteenth centuries, being the age of individualism, would bring forth a thoroughly pathological literature in which the individual's endeavours to engender the overall life of humankind, of the ideal, became a painful, fatal (!) disease" (quoted in Lepenies, 59). Like Bradley's Hamlet, Paracelsus sees the infinite within himself, so that his aspirations take on a quality of melancholy interiority:

> There is an inmost centre in us all,
> Where truth abides in fulness; and around,
> Wall upon wall, the gross flesh hems it in,
> This perfect, clear perception—which is truth.
> A baffling and perverting carnal mesh
> Binds it, and makes all error. (i. 728–33)

Paracelsus's aspiration for the infinite, an expression of the infinite desire of the soul locked in the limiting, finite borders of the body, is a variant of what Durkheim later labeled *anomie,* an "acute, even suicidal distress" caused by a "continuing sense of limits" set upon "boundless desire" (Herbert, 72). Paracelsus's sense of restlessness, disgust, perplexity, and self-loathing tallies almost exactly with Christopher Herbert's account of "the state of unappeasable cravings and its accompanying 'dejection and pessimism'": "that state known almost technically by now as 'restlessness': erratic, irregular, redundant, uncontrollably self-contradicting motion" (72). Not only *Paracelsus* but all of Browning's poetry from *Pauline* through *Sordello* (1840) startled contemporaries with an energetic but near incomprehensible "multitudinousness," an incoherence that seems to be the overflowing abundance of an exuberant imagination, the product of a buoyantly "happy" mind but more likely a paradoxical result of the strict policing of the self as character that leaves the curtailed self restlessly in search of its infinite remainder. Paracelsus's mind seems accurately described by Hegel's account of skeptical consciousness and Durkheim's account of anomie as "mind endlessly moving, a veritable kaleidoscope that changes from one moment to the next" (quoted in Herbert, 72). Browning's bumptious incoherence seems far removed from Mariana's listless stagnation or Elizabeth Barrett's brooding, but it might be seen as a kind of high-energy version of Mariana's hyperesthesia. Further, the search for an "inmost center" is almost definitive of melancholy as defined by Ficino:

> But it seems to be a natural principle that in the pursuit of especially abstruse patterns of intellectual inquiry the mind must be directed from outward matters to inward matters, from the circumference to the center as it were, and, while in pursuit of its speculations, should remain firmly established at the center of the individual, so to speak. But the mental activity of being drawn away from the periphery and becoming fixed at the center is the special characteristic of the mind to which melancholy is akin. (quoted in Benjamin, *Origin,* 153n)

The melancholy of the classical tradition, and of Browning's speaker, is also in this respect clearly akin to the "penetrating imagination" of Ruskin and Carlyle.

Browning saw the form of *Paracelsus* as sufficiently innovative to warrant prefatory explanation of it as

> an attempt, probably more novel than happy, to reverse the method usually adopted by writers whose aim it is to set forth any phenomenon of

> the mind or the passions, by the operation of persons and events; . . . instead of having recourse to an external machinery of incidents to create and evolve the crisis I desire to produce, I have ventured to display somewhat minutely the mood itself in its rise and progress. (*Poems*, 1: 1029)

Evidently Browning was interested in the representation of a mood like that which Arnold attempted in *Empedocles on Etna* and later called fundamentally unpoetic because "the suffering finds no vent in action." In this respect the preface is consistent with Browning's well-known comment about his failures as a dramatist—his interest was in "Action in Character, not Character in Action" (DeVane, 62). As a result, in the first third of his career, he was precisely the kind of poet deplored by Arnold, brooding on the intensity and idiosyncrasy of a stagnant "dialogue of the mind with itself" and guilty of a "confused multitudinousness" (*Letters*, 1: 128). Like *Maud*, in fact, *Paracelsus* is characterized by a superabundance of imagery much like that of the "spasmodic" poet Alexander Smith, whose work inspired Ludlow's adoption of the phrase "allegory of the state of one's own mind."

Despite moments of manic aspiration, the mood of *Paracelsus* remains melancholy throughout. Even when Paracelsus "attains," he sums up his life's work, and his life itself, as sound and fury, signifying nothing, "the whole / slipt in the blank spaces 'twixt an idiot's / And a mad lover's ditty" (ii. 34–35). *Paracelsus* was not a youthful aberration, but it anticipates later works, especially "Childe Roland to the Dark Tower Came" (Preyer, 159). Paracelsus himself anticipates ultimately behaving "like some knight traversing a wilderness" (i. 474), and the characteristic melancholy note in both poems is struck by Paracelsus's account of his life as a metaphoric landscape, a "tract, doomed to perpetual barrenness" (ii. 116).

While *Paracelsus* may have been the quest poem underlying "Childe Roland," the prior quest poem for *Paracelsus* itself is *Alastor*. Just as *Alastor* represents the desolate narcissism of a visionary quester who turns away from human community and love, Paracelsus was designed specifically around a castrated protagonist who would seek godlike knowledge without human love. Paracelsus's quest is for godlike knowledge, but like Shelley's Poet, he seeks it in the shape of a visionary female:

> I had just determined to become
> The greatest and most glorious man on earth.
> . . . life, death, light and shadow,
> The shows of the world, were bare receptacles
> Or indices of truth to be wrung thence,

> Not ministers of sorrow or delight;
> A wondrous natural robe in which she went.
> For some one truth would dimly beacon me
> From mountains rough with pines, and flit and wink
> O'er dazzling wastes of frozen snow, and tremble
> Into assured light in some branching mine
> Where ripens, swathed in fire, the liquid gold—
> And all the beauty, all the wonder fell
> On either side the truth, as its mere robe;
> I see the robe now—then I saw the form. (ii. 148–49, 157–68)

The passage more or less defines melancholy allegory: truth is hidden and unattainable, and the mind, at best, can perceive and represent only the bare allegorical markers, "indices of truth" or "A wondrous natural robe." The allegory is all but identical with the clothes philosophy of Carlyle's Teufelsdrockh in its efforts to perceive and communicate spiritual truths in material forms:

> The thing Visible, nay the thing Imagined, the thing in any way conceived as Visible, what is it but a Garment, a Clothing of the higher, celestial, Invisible, "unimaginable, formless, dark with excess of bright." Under which the point of view of the following passage, so strange in purport, so strange in phrase, seems characteristic enough: "The beginning of all Wisdom is to look fixedly on Clothes, or even with armed eyesight, till they become transparent." (*Works*, 1: 52)

In practice, the mystery or enigma produced by the fixed gaze on objects, so characteristic of the melancholic, is only communicable by representation of the objects themselves, the "indices of truth." In a very different context Donald Hair has noted the affinity of Browning's thought and method with "Carlyle's descendentalism, where one examines with intense scrutiny every minute particular of the appearance of this world. Such scrutiny will ultimately be revelatory (and hence, in Carlyle, the terms 'descendentalism' and 'transcendentalism' are paradoxically synonyms)" (146).

The allegorical quest of *Paracelsus* clearly derives from melancholy quest poems of second-generation Romanticism: even though Browning explicitly took up the challenge of writing about Paracelsus as a man who could not know the saving power of love, he represented him in Shelleyan terms as a man on a quest to complete himself with his own female ideal. *Paracelsus* resembles its precursors even in its Orientalist slant. Addressing "Persic Zoroaster" (v. 187), Paracelsus seeks knowledge from the exotic otherness of the Orient. As he lies dying and delirious in part v, he seems to recollect his visionary efforts as an erotic quest, but as in *Alastor*, the vision fades into the light of common day, and the failure of imagination is a failure of human love:

> Cruel! I seek her now—I kneel—I shriek—
> I clasp her vesture—but she fades, still fades;
> And she is gone; sweet human love is gone!
> 'Tis only when they spring to heaven that angels
> Reveal themselves to you. (v. 213–17)

Both in form and theme, *Paracelsus* is an account of the restless, melancholy poetic imagination, its protagonist absorbing all it encounters into the imperial selfhood but inevitably failing to absorb the infinite.

Paracelsus's desire for godlike power is obviously hubristic and a bit absurd:

> I must henceforth die
> Or elevate myself far, far above
> The gorgeous spectacle. I seemed to long
> At once to trample on, yet save mankind. (i. 458–61)

Even though Browning satirizes excessive ambition in Paracelsus, the poem is in some ways a self-portrait, as generations of readers have recognized. It represents the strenuous aspirations that always characterize Browning, and it even represents a kind of optimism as Paracelsus concludes the poem and his life with an enthusiastic view of man and the world evolving toward a higher perfection: "progress is / The law of life, man is not Man as yet" (v. 742–43). Paracelsus recognizes Aprile as the man that he aspires to be in the unattainable future, when man will have fully evolved to be Man: "Myself of after-time, my very self" (ii. 348). As Paracelsus broods on his past self and on his unattainable future, he is caught between two worlds, one dead, the other powerless to be born. He suffers from precisely the Kierkegaardian melancholy described by Lowrie and the similar melancholy that Hallam described in "On Sympathy," a sense of disconnection from both his past and future, a disconnected, alienated self. He can "attain" only if he ceases to aspire and accepts the limitations of a bounded self, so it is appropriate that only after the death of Aprile can he say, with grim irony and only provisionally, "I have attained, and now I may depart" (ii. 661).

Nevertheless, by the end of the play Paracelsus has learned the lesson urged by many of Browning's poems—aspiration for what is unattainable in the finite of this life lifts us toward a next, higher life:

> Truly there needs another life to come!
> If this be all—(I must tell Festus that)
> And other life await us not—for one,
> I say 'tis a poor cheat, a stupid bungle,
> A wretched failure. I for one, protest
> Against it, and I hurl it back with scorn. (v. 274–79)

Rather than settle into this Byronic defiance, however, Paracelsus resists his melancholy and lives up to the Browning credo to strive on, if rather gloomily: "Well, onward though alone!" (v. 280)

II. Melancholy Allegory

Though the monodrama is complex and obscure, the source of Paracelsus's difficulties is quite simple. Within the optimistic teleology that man evolves toward some ultimate good, the individual man is only teased out of his "proper joys and griefs" (v. 780) by "August anticipation, symbols, types / Of a dim splendour" (v. 775–76) that beckon him as the visionary maiden beckoned the Poet of *Alastor*. Paracelsus finds the world empty (the angels have fled to heaven and only the empty robe remains, like the abandoned "attire of the gods" in Benjamin's account of allegory) and allegorizes it, finding everywhere symbols and types, indices of truth, but only as ultimately empty signifiers—in the familiar metaphor, language is the clothing of thought, not of truth, and in *Paracelsus* it is the empty robe, not the embodied truth. Like Baudelaire as described by Benjamin, his genius, "which is fed on melancholy, is an allegorical genius" (*Reflections*, 156) in which the types and indices that ought to correspond to a higher truth instead gain their truth only structurally, as a more or less coherent system of signs that appear as the emptied robe or outward surface of a transcendent truth but only have meaning in themselves as an aesthetic surface, a phantasmagoria: like *Maud*, the work is a melancholy allegory. Paracelsus is "high-dowered but limited and vexed / By a divided and delusive aim, / A shadow mocking a reality" (v. 789–91). For all his strenuous aspiration, Paracelsus is left only with melancholy: "What wonder if I saw no way to shun / Despair? (v. 846–47). Like Barrett's idealized poets, his infinite aspirations cannot issue in action, but hope for fulfillment and culmination after death.

Finally, the optimism of *Paracelsus*, such as it is, is entirely in the evolutionary teleology ending the work, but this is represented less as Paracelsus's conclusion than as "God's message" (v. 462) voiced by Paracelsus. The distinction perhaps seems minor, but it confirms Aprile's dying words that "God is the perfect poet" (ii. 648), a good Christian sentiment, but a confirmation of the futility of human poetic aspirations to the infinite, to perfection. Further, though it is comforting Christian doctrine to affirm that we are in God's hands, Browning's succeeding works increasingly insist on the lack of human agency if we are not autonomous selves but merely instruments of God. To anticipate the language of *Pippa Passes* and *Sordello,* Paracelsus in the end is God's puppet, and his relation to his maker, speaking "God's message," is disturbingly analogous to his relation to his more immediate maker, Robert Browning.

The doctrinal conclusion to *Paracelsus* is disturbing not because the doctrine is particularly sinister but because it abandons the monodrama's attempt to study a "mood . . . in its rise and progress" (*Poems,* 1: 1029), and so in effect it abandons Paracelsus as a subject. By making him the mouthpiece of a fairly standard doctrine of Victorian Christian teleology, Browning also makes him wooden, no longer a subject but an object. Because of its comforting message, *Paracelsus* can be called an optimistic work, but the optimism comes not from working through the "mood" of post-Romantic subjectivity but by reverting to a worldview involving what Charles Taylor calls an "ontic logos," in which the subject is not alienated but is comfortably fitted into a "meaningful order" where the individual self and its self-representation in thought and language are at one with the "self-manifesting reality" of "Reason, Goodness" and, "in the theological variant, the Wisdom of God" (160–61). This makes historical sense for Paracelsus at the end of the Middle Ages, but it evades the difficulties faced by the modern self, which, as Taylor argues, evolved in the thought of Locke and the Enlightenment as disengaged from the welter of perception in a cosmos increasingly viewed as mechanistic. The only circumstance in which the experiential self corresponds with the self represented by reason (and reason's instrument, language) is when it exists within an "ontic logos" that continues to be the ideological order of Christian teleology but no longer represents the cosmic order or disorder perceived and experienced by consciousness. Simply put, doctrine and ideology, like "character," are constituted by language for the modern subject, but perception and experience are not, and the only time language is adequate to the representation of the self without alienation is when the self experiences the world as ideology. Like the concluding speech of *Paracelsus,* which finally coalesces the thought and being of the protagonist in Christian ideology, Browning's famous optimism displaces the experiential self with the false consciousness of ideology: it is poetry of the superego, spoken by a subject reduced to an object, a mere mouthpiece. Such rhetorical set-pieces as "Rabbi Ben Ezra," "Abt Vogler," and "A Death in the Desert" fail as what Robert Langbaum calls "poetry of experience" because the speakers fit so perfectly with their ideological message that there is no sense of a subject coming to terms with experience but only of the terms themselves, the finished product, of ideology. Even David in "Saul" speaks the language of Judeo-Christian teleology so much as a set speech as to seem no more than a puppet, even to himself:

> I, a work of God's hand for that purpose, received in my brain
> And pronounced on the rest of his handwork—returned him again
> His creation's approval or censure: I spoke as I saw:
> I report, as a man may of God's work—all's love yet all's law.
> (ll.239–42)

As a prophet, David is appropriately the mouthpiece of God, but as a mouthpiece, he is "God's puppet," made "for that purpose." Even David seems aware of his merely instrumental character as he hopes "to discover some province, some gift of my own" (1.256). In "Saul" as elsewhere Browning's "optimism" is rhetorically powerful, but it erases the modern subject and its difficulties. W. David Shaw, who sees "Saul" as transcending the Kierkegaardian aesthetic stage to reach the ethical and religious (*Dialectical Temper*, 222), argues that the poem "affords a rare pleasure, which we cannot experience to the same degree in any of Browning's other works, of seeing the poet, like his speaker, soar magnificently to the 'pure white light'" (232). If so, one might say (paraphrasing Browning's lines on Shakespeare), "did Browning? If so, the less Browning he." Shaw himself acknowledges that "to appreciate 'Saul' it is not necessary to agree that Browning's true genius lay in visionary writing" (232). When Browning transcends the "aesthetic" to teach ethical or religious truths, he becomes the Victorian sage admired by the Browning societies, but in leaving behind the aesthetic realm appropriate to the poet he also leaves behind his attempt to explore the developments in the growth of a soul. "Saul" does dramatize the conflict between self and conscience, ego and superego, since David's song is attempting to ease Saul's melancholy, but there is no true dialectic since only David's voice is heard, and his eschatological vision, however magnificent, issues in poetry of the superego in which, as in Elizabeth Barrett's early poetry, the speaking self is at one with the ideology he voices.

Ironically, however, when Browning attempted to explore the modern self, what Charles Taylor calls the "punctual self," he encountered an analogous dilemma. The punctual self disengages thought (and therefore language) from experience, reifying the self as an object to be scrutinized. Descartes and, even more radically, Locke call on the modern self to "stop living 'in' or 'through' the experience, to treat itself as an object, or what is the same thing, as an experience which could just as well have been someone else's" (162)."

For this reason, to get a grasp on experience, to control it, "Locke *reifies* the mind to an extraordinary degree" (166; Taylor's emphasis). Browning's problem, then, is that whether he examines experience within an anachronistic Christian teleology or from a more modern empirical perspective, he is likely to reify the mind, taking it not as an experiencing subject but as an object. In *Sordello* and *Pippa Passes,* the ambitious works following *Paracelsus,* Browning both formally and thematically explores the project of representing subjects in language without reducing them to objects, puppets rather than people, finite "characters" rather than infinite "selves."

Not surprisingly, poststructuralist critics have noted that Browning deconstructs the ontic logos in *Sordello* by representing the impossibility of "a poetry of presence and wholeness" (Tucker, *Browning's Beginnings,* 94). As Browning says of Sordello, because language and thought are not commensurate with experience,

> Because perceptions whole, like that he sought
> To clothe, reject so pure a work of thought
> As language: thought may take perception's place
> But hardly co-exist in any case,
> Being its mere presentment—of the whole
> By parts, the simultaneous and the sole
> By the successive and the many. (ii. 589–95)

The metaphor of language as clothing, here as in *Paracelsus,* suggests that at best language can represent the outward show of reality but not the truth that "passeth show" behind the clothing. Language is allegorical because it is "the veil that those who live call Life" (Shelley, "Lift Not the Painted Veil") and only presents emblems of the infinite depths below. The clothing imagery constitutes an unusually economic and accessible explanation of why Sordello, and Browning writing *Sordello,* cannot incarnate in poetry the jumble of sensory perception that constitutes experience. They also indicate why Ezra Pound was wrong in castigating Browning: "Hang it all, Robert Browning! / There can be but the one 'Sordello.' / But Sordello, and my Sordello?" (*Cantos,* ii. 1–3). One problem facing Browning was precisely that there could not be only one Sordello: the Sordello represented in language could not be the same as the real, living, breathing, experiencing Sordello. The represented self is inevitably different from the experiencing self, as an object is different from a subject. The written self, whether written by Sordello or by

Browning, can only be "the stuff / That held the imaged thing" (ii. 570–71)—language is an object on the same material level as "stuff," and the self, still more bluntly, is reified as a "thing." The represented self is finite and material, at best an emblem of the infinite and spiritual soul.

Like Browning as a writer of dramas and, later, of dramatic monologues, Sordello attempts by a kind of negative capability to imagine himself into the consciousness of his characters and reproduce it in words, and so—God-like—to create a "creature" rather than merely cobbling together a character, a thing: he took "An action with its actors, quite forsook / Himself to live in each, returned anon / With the result—a creature" (ii. 582–84). He soon realizes his failure, however, partly on the grounds that language cannot capture "perceptions whole," so that his representation is only at best the vesture of thought: in this case a suit of armor is the analogy, and the various parts of the armor are a more or less coherent set of metaphors, a melancholy allegory gesturing toward the wholeness of perception. But he also fails because, like Browning's in *Paracelsus,* his language must be completed by the reader's "intelligence and sympathy" (*Poems,* 1:1030), the "co-operating fancy" that would reconstitute thought and language into perception and experience. As Sordello puts it elsewhere,

> what I supplied yourselves suggest,
> What I leave loose yourselves can now invest.
> . . . Leave the mere rude
> Explicit details! 'tis but brother's speech
> We need, speech where an accent's change gives each
> The other's soul—(v. 623–24, 634–37)

But of course "brother's speech" cannot be presented on the printed page, only writing, the signs of speech. Though the subject, in its vitality and wholeness, cannot exist on the written page, it can exist in the infinite reaches of the poet's mind and, Browning hoped, could be reproduced in the reader's mind if the reader's imaginative sympathy were sufficient to recreate the wholeness of the poet's perception from the fragments of thought and writing he has produced in the effort to represent it. Readers would have to become allegorists of the same order as the poet, brooding over the material signifiers of the printed page as the poet broods on the ruins of history, discovering the intention in the poet's creation as the poet discovers the intention of God in the abandoned and emptied fragments of Creation. As Browning saw it, the only way to transmit the wholeness of perception was to share "brother's speech" with a sympathetic, creatively collaborative audience, but he had not found such an audience for his early works—even a brother poet, Matthew Arnold, saw only fragmentation, a "confused multitudinousness" (*Letters*, 1:28) in Browning's work. Browning assigns Sordello the same fate:

> His auditory recognized no jot
> As he intended, and, mistaking not
> Him for his meanest hero, ne'er was dunce
> Sufficient to believe him—(ii. 623–26)

The description of Sordello's failure to find believers underscores the sad irony of Browning's opening lines to *Sordello:* "Who will, may hear Sordello's story told: / His story? Who believes me shall behold / The man" (i. 1–3), an assertion that Tennyson called a lie. Sordello's failure is represented as a process of melancholy "internal struggles to be one, / Which frittered him incessantly piecemeal" (ii. 694–95): he struggled even to experience a unified self, let alone to represent it, or communicate it to the minds of an auditory in which each individual probably lacked unity of being, and in which, certainly, the multitudinous readership would not share a unified perception of his work (ii. 690–702).

In an 1845 letter to Elizabeth Barrett, Browning expressed a melancholy very like Sordello's:

> you *do* what I always wanted, hoped, to do, and only seem now likely to do for the first time—you speak out, *you*—I only make men and women speak—give you the truth broken into prismatic hues, and fear the pure white light, even if it is in me: but I am going to try . . . so it will be no small matter to have your company just now,—seeing that when you have your men and women aforesaid, you are busy with them, whereas it seems bleak, melancholy work, this talking to the wind. (*Correspondence*, 10: 22)

Despite the energy of his verse, Browning seems in the mid-1840s to have been genuinely melancholy about the possibilities of effective poetic communication or even of escaping what Walter Pater called "the narrow chamber" of his own mind—what Tennyson called the "abyss of personality." His correspondence with Elizabeth Barrett, though full of enthusiasm, is frequently a record of hypochondria, of being "unwell" and even "weary in [his] soul" (*Correspondence*, 10: 42). Another comment in 1845 indicates that he conceptualized writing as necessarily insufficient to grasp the infinite of the soul and express it adequately even to the most sympathetic possible reader: "writing to you—all is helpless and sorrowful work by the side of what is in my soul to say and write—or is it not the natural consequence? if these vehicles of feeling sufficed—*there* would be the end!—and that my feelings for you should *end!*—For the rest, the headache which kept away while I sate with you, made itself amends afterward" (*Correspondence,* 11: 226–27). Here once again is the philosophic optimism of infinite possibility, but this fundamental tenet of Browning's optimism is presented as the anodyne for the experiential melancholy of entrapment within the self, of the inevitable failure to communicate the self adequately in language. The anodyne, that is, would correspond to the song of David to cure the melancholy of Saul, but as we have seen, such an anodyne, eliminating melancholy, would take Browning away from his "true genius."

Browning's attempt in *Sordello* to fit infinite subjectivity into the communicable form of the finite poem resulted inevitably, as he was well aware, in the reduction of infinite selves to the finite forms of puppets: the poet's art reduces subjects to objects, reifies human beings, and makes lifeless things available to contemplation. In the poem's opening meditation on poetry, Browning first imagines a purely dramatic method like that used in *Paracelsus:* "making speak, myself left out of view / The very man as he was wont to do, / And leaving you to say the rest for him" (i. 15–17). Rather than this, however, he chooses a specifically allegorical method for its greater clarity:

> it seems
> Your setters-forth of unexampled themes,
> Makers of quite new men, producing them,
> Would best chalk broadly on each vesture's hem
> The wearer's quality; or take their stand,
> Motley on back and pointing-pole in hand,
> Beside him. (i. 25–31)

As the narrator admits, however, producing labeled allegorical clothing is not the same as making "quite new men," and the narrator as showman can only "play [his] puppets" (i. 72). Ironically, late in the poem the puppet labeled "poet," Sordello, suggests the limitations of the allegorical method as he considers his own poetic possibilities:

> What shall I unlock
> By song? behold me prompt, whate'er it be,
> To minister: how much can mortals see
> Of Life? No more than so? I take the task
> And marshal you Life's elemental masque,
> Show Men, on evil or on good lay stress,

> This light, this shade make prominent, suppress
> All ordinary hues that softening blend
> Such natures with the level. Apprehend
> Which sinner is, which saint. (v. 580–89)

To clarify the allegorical roles still more clearly, Sordello suggests that he will station his characters in specific regions of heaven and hell, unconscious of course that Dante's allegory would station him as a guide in Purgatory. Realizing the reductiveness of the allegorical morality play, Sordello reaches beyond the grasp of his narrator to apprehend Browning's own more ambitious method:

> "Next age—what's to do?
> The men and women stationed hitherto
> Will I unstation, good and bad, conduct
> Each nature to its farthest, or abstract
> At soonest, in the world: light, thwarted, breaks
> A limpid purity to rainbow flakes,
> Or shadow, massed, freezes to gloom: behold
> How such, with fit assistance to unfold,
> Or obstacles to crush them, disengage
> Their forms, love, hate, hope, fear, peace make, war wage,
> In presence of you all! Myself, implied
> Superior now, as, by the platform's side,
> I bade them do and suffer,—would last content
> The world . . . no—that's too far! I circumvent
> A few, my masque contented, and to these,
> Offer unveil the last of mysteries—
> Man's inmost life shall have yet freer play:
> Once more I cast external things away,
> And nature composite, so decompose
> That" . . . Why, he writes *Sordello!* (v. 601–20)

Evidently the poet-puppet anticipates becoming Browning, not only writing *Sordello* but also representing real "men and women" by breaking the truth "into prismatic hues." Insofar as Sordello seems to become Browning, at least in poetic aspiration, the "confused multitudinousness" of the poem resolves itself into an allegory of the poet's own mind.

The representation of allegory in *Sordello* indicates clearly that Browning shared the Romantic sense of the mode's limitations and reductiveness, and that he shared his age's preference for psychological realism, but it also indicates that he found his way to the psychological realism of the dramatic monologue through experiments in allegory. As Theresa Kelley has recently argued, Browning's attempts to present abstract ideals in finite material forms remained allegorical, though a new kind of allegory "at the peripheries where Victorian realism gives way" (218). To "unveil the last of mysteries / Man's inmost life," Browning would have to shed the material vesture of language, but in fact his subsequent poetry immerses his subjects increasingly deeply in the "stuff" of language and material objects as he continued in a style most often described as grotesque. As Kelley says, Browning's "grotesque figures persistently mark the difficulties of getting from particulars to ideas" (219)—that is, from the finite and material to the infinite and spiritual. Further, "though his contemporaries hardly praised him for it, they recognized that Browning's figures and syntax are intriguingly (or idiotically) adhesive to the visual or material vehicle for a given allegorical tenor. . . . Browning's poetic experiments in grotesquerie force allegory to a material limit" (220). Walter Bagehot, whose 1864 essay forever linked Browning to the grotesque, attributes this characteristic to his being "the most of a realist, and the least of an idealist of any poet we know" (1033). Yet Bagehot also noted that Browning's realism was in the interest of presenting the ideal in material terms: "He must *see* his religion, he must have an 'object-lesson' in believing . . . the great but vague faith, the unutterable tenets—seem to him worthless, visionary: they are not enough 'immersed in matter'" (1033–34).[3] If only by accident, another of Bagehot's comments links Browning's grotesque to both Matthew Arnold's evocation of the great difficulty of finding language to represent the inner self and to medieval allegory: "A *buried* life like the spiritual medieval was Mr. Browning's natural element, and he was right to be attracted by it" (1033).

The grotesque also has affinities with specifically melancholy allegory since, as Benjamin notes, it is associated with the melancholy tendency to contemplate the ruins of history, to look beneath the surfaces of things to "buried ruins and catacombs. The word is not derived from *grotta* in the literal sense, but from the 'burial' in the sense of concealment" (*Origin*,171). Bagehot's version of Browning's grotesque is almost uncannily akin to both Benjamin's account of melancholy allegory and to Carlyle's and Ruskin's accounts of the penetrating imagination: it deals with "the vestiges of ancient civilizations, the germs of modern civilization . . . buried under a cumbrous mass of barbarism and cruelty. Good elements hidden in horrid accompaniments are the special themes of grotesque art" (1033). Further, because of its unblinking acceptance of the reality of death and its enigmatic remains at the archaeological foundations of human history, the grotesque is profoundly historical and, as Bagehot concedes, closely connected to realism in its unflinching representation of actualities:

> It deals, to use the language of science, not with normal types but with abnormal specimens; to use the language of old philosophy, not with what nature is striving to be, but with some lapse what she has happened to become . . . it shows you what ought to be by what ought not to be; when complete it reminds you of the perfect image by showing you the distorted and imperfect image. (1032)

No doubt it was for reasons very much like what Bagehot suggests that Browning, as what Chesterton called "a kind of cosmic detective," searched the "thieves' kitchens and dark corners of history" to contemplate the "abnormal specimens" found in his dramatic monologues, the "evil men on which," according to Chesterton, "the poet was to pour out so much of his imaginative wealth—Djabal, Fra Lippo, Bishop Blougram, Sludge, Prince Hohenstiel-Schwangau, and the hero of *Fifine at the Fair*" (51).

III. The Dramatic Monologues

As a cosmic detective, Browning clearly resembles Kierkegaard, whose "works prove that he was an acute observer and did not vainly describe himself as a 'police detective'" (*Concept of Dread*, 97). Browning's greatest works, his dramatic monologues and *The Ring and the Book,* generally avoid the confused multitudinousness of the early works, though they may be said to originate in a Kierkegaardian aesthetic "hovering" over the infinite multiplicity of subjects in the poet's mind. Each monologue focuses on just one of the diverse subject-possibilities, realizing that state of self and achieving "psychological-poetic authority" over it as the poet shows himself "more agile than a tightrope walker in order to be able to insinuate himself under the skin of other people and to imitate their attitudes" (*The Concept of Dread*, 49). Browning's "How It Strikes a Contemporary," one of his many self-reflective studies of his own art of impersonation, describes a poet very much like the Kierkegaardian observer, who

> is so well oriented in human life and his glance is so inquisitorially sharp that he knows where he should seek and easily discover some individual or another who would be successful for his experiment. . . . To this end he imitates in his own person every mood, every psychic state, which he discovers in another. Thereupon he sees if he cannot delude the other by his imitation, whether he can draw him into further development which is his own creation. . . . Thus if one would observe a passion, one has to choose one's individual. (49–50)

The seemingly sinister usurpation of various people and personae to incorporate states of the poet's own subjectivity, as I suggested in chapter 1, is also akin to the somewhat sinister "secret violation of the self" described by Nietzsche, "this artist's cruelty, this urge to impose on recalcitrant matter a form, a will, a distinction. . . . this sinister task of a soul divided against itself" (221). This "artist's cruelty" would seem to be the imposition of the conscience raging against the ego, finding in it types to be fully delineated and punished with irony. Such a model is in perfect accord with familiar perspectives on the dramatic monologues, most particularly with Robert Langbaum's influential view of their dialectic of sympathy and judgment, since sympathy is necessary to experience and recreate the imitated psychic state, and judgment is the goal of the punitive conscience. Browning's selection and incarnation of diverse possibilities of the self, and his disciplining of them by reducing them to the finite and chastening them with dramatic irony, becomes a drama of melancholy. Browning's gallery of villains, murderous dukes and counts, whoring monks, adulterers, and other assorted knaves represent forbidden forms of reality, but the necessary irony subverts Browning's complicity with the speakers. Of course the balance of sympathy and judgment varies in Browning's diverse works, but those that compel strict judgment invoke a disciplinary conscience and enact the policing of a self characteristic of melancholy. The gallery of characters is also a gallery of Browning's own "psychic states" and therefore constitutes exactly what Arnold deplored: an allegory of his own mind.

From this perspective, the most suggestive of all the monologues is "Childe Roland to the Dark Tower Came," a kind of allegory of Browning's allegorizing (Bloom, *Ringers*, 166). Roland hardly seems to be an "evil man," but when he shuts his eyes and turns them on his heart he sees only the criminal pasts of his former comrades, whom he seeks to imitate, if only "just to fail as they" (1.41). W. David Shaw, who sees the poem as a dialectical advance that "enacts the very process of spiritual growth" from the aesthetic to the ethical (*Dialectical Temper*, 126), observes that "nobody, including the reader, is quite sure what Childe Roland's 'guilt' is" (133), but his penitential pilgrimage implies both guilt and the desire to purge it, implying a dialectic of conscience and ego.

As many critics have recognized, the nightmare quest in "Childe Roland" brings into sharp focus the melancholy hopelessness of the Shelleyan quest themes of *Pauline* and *Paracelsus*, and so as Harold Bloom argues, it becomes his most incisive effort to establish a poetic authority by putting his poetic predecessors behind him. Critics have disagreed about whether "Childe Roland" is a celebratory poem, affirming that "he who endureth to the end will be saved" (to which Browning laconically responded that it was "just about that" [DeVane, 231]), or whether, as Bloom calls it, it is the "darkest" of all Browning's poems, the expression of "that variety of poetic melancholy that issues from the terrible strength of post-Enlightenment tradition" (*Ringers*, 166). Most readers agree, however, that whether it affirms damnation or salvation, it is a mysterious allegory in which "Writing in a dream Browning expressed the innermost pattern of his mind" (DeVane, 231–32). Like *Maud*, "Childe Roland" becomes an allegory by virtue of relentless and excessive pathetic fallacy, indicating everywhere that the landscape expresses primarily the state of the speaker's crazed subjectivity. And also like *Maud*, the allegory is very much of the kind described by Benjamin. The landscape is not merely personified by pathetic fallacy but as a dying, diseased body, even as a corpse: "starved," leprous, "like a distorted mouth that splits its rim / Gaping at death, and dies while it recoils" (ll.155–56). In his most definitive comments on melancholy allegory, Benjamin remarked that "it is precisely visions of the frenzy of destruction, in which all earthly things collapse into a heap of ruin, which reveal the limit set upon allegorical contemplation" (*Origin*, 232). In fact, as Benjamin elaborates the allegorical significance of landscapes like that of "Childe Roland" he arrives at a Kierkegaardian meditation that expresses the profound significance of the melancholy inwardness of such works. Man fell by accepting Satan's offer of a knowledge of good and evil, but since the creation in which Adam and Eve had lived was declared very good by God, they knew good from experience in the world, while evil was to be found only in themselves, by contemplation of their own subjectivities. As David Shaw rightly observes, the objects in the poem's landscape have no objective existence at all: instead of registering an externally real landscape Roland projects a landscape of the mind "as a focus for his inner nature" (*Dialectical Temper*, 129). A projection of his own interiority, Roland's landscape epitomizes the connection of allegory with the fallen knowledge of good and evil as described by Benjamin: "Related as it is to the depths of the subjective, it is basically only knowledge of evil. It is 'nonsense' in the profound sense in which Kierkegaard conceived the word. This knowledge, the triumph of subjectivity and the onset of arbitrary rule over things, is the origin of all allegorical contemplation" (*Origin*, 233). Browning, of course, denied any allegorical intention, and he probably would not have wanted to hear the poem called "nonsense," but the title, "Childe Roland to the Dark Tower Came," is drawn from the nonsense of Edgar's mad act in *King Lear*, and Roland's final blast on the "slughorn" only returns to the nonsense in which he began. Like "Kubla Khan," the poem came upon the poet "as a kind of dream" with an accompanying compulsion to put it in writing (DeVane, 229). It is not surprising, then, that the poem is deeply enigmatic, profound "nonsense," so that readers have been able to see in it both assurance of salvation and the despair of damnation and failure. Paradoxically, the hideousness and horror of the allegorical landscape can lead to a triumph in the ultimate realization of melancholy. According to Benjamin,

> this is the essence of melancholy immersion: that its ultimate objects, in which it believes it can most fully secure for itself that which is vile, turn into allegories, and that these allegories fill out and deny the void in which they are represented, just as, ultimately, the intention does not faithfully rest in the contemplation of bones, but faithlessly leaps forward to the idea of resurrection. (222–23)

Browning said that he did not know what the poem "meant," and he would have been unlikely to accept an abstruse metaphysical explanation, but the interpretation through melancholy does account for the paradoxical sense of profundity in "nonsense," and it does reconcile the bleakness of the poem with the readings of Browning as "optimist."

Though the corpus of Browning's monologues, taken as a whole, may not approach the bleak melancholy of "Childe Roland," it does represent an allegory of the poet's own mind, with frequent symbolic reference to the disquieting effects of reification of the subject under capitalism, and, with surprising frequency, it returns to the symbolic representation of Browning's own artistic practice of reducing speakers and audiences to puppets, or even corpses, and to his regrets at the failure of even love to gain full access to the infinite of subjectivity.

Browning's best and most characteristic poems are the dramatic lyrics and monologues published in *Dramatic Lyrics* (1842), *Dramatic Romances and Lyrics* (1845), *Men and Women* (1855), and *Dramatis Personae* (1864). The representation of reification is evident even in the very first of these poems: "Porphyria" (later "Porphyria's Lover") and "Johannes Agricola" (later "Johannes Agricola in Meditation"), published in 1836, both reflect Browning's concerns about poetic representation of subjectivity by attempting to represent subjects, particularly his concerns about making puppets of people.

"Porphyria's Lover," most obviously, discloses this concern in two ways. First, the speaker himself attempts to enter into the consciousness of another, Porphyria, but his appropriation of her consciousness reduces her to a mere puppet, figuratively at first, and then literally as he props up her murdered body and takes possession of her "will": "The smiling rosy little head, / So glad it has its utmost will" (ll.52–53). The clear implication is that such utter appropriation of another's consciousness, such desire to speak for another, is insane, so it is not surprising that Browning should have published this poem (along with "Johannes Agricola in Meditation") in 1842 under the title "Madhouse Cells." Browning could not be unaware that he himself, claiming to speak from within the consciousness of the lunatic, was performing a similar act. As Richard Stein has pointed out, the dramatic genre here devised "gives us access to a world otherwise closed, not just to the rooms in which these men are confined but to the innermost 'cells' of their beings, to what Pater would call 'the narrow chamber of the individual mind.'" And Stein adds that "the fixity and depth of this gaze" suggests observation akin to "the model proposed by Michel Foucault; if we feel as if we are within the cell, we also seem to be peering into it with the intensity of a keeper" (33). Browning had dismissed the sideshow barker, pointing pole in hand, and let his characters speak, but the exhibitor is still there, in this case in the form that implies a keeper, and in nearly all cases in the irony that implies a moral judge just outside the frame of the picture. In fact, though he keeps himself and his pointing pole just outside the frame of the pictures and declines to write allegorical labels on the vesture of his characters, Browning's "abnormal specimens" are characteristically judged, to use Langbaum's term, by the poet's irony, an unspoken appeal to "normal," conventional values, to the moral ideology that would constitute conscience in higher natures. Irony is the sign of the dialectic of the fallen, sensual self and conscience in Browning's monologues.

Browning himself was evidently conscious of the moral implications of the kind of penetrating, appropriative gaze that Foucault has made a concern in our own age—throughout his career, those of his characters who claim to speak for others, to appropriate and control their consciousness, come in for harsh treatment. Moreover, as Stein has pointed out, Browning's later publication of the poems as "Madhouse Cells" in *Dramatic Lyrics* implies the subjection of the speakers to the surveillance of both poet and reader and so hints at what we now recognize as a disciplinary technique involved in the making of the modern and postmodern subject. This should not be surprising: Browning was well aware that in his dramatic poetry he was not so much devising speeches as examining "action in character," particularly in the character of subject formation. For my purposes it is important to stress that Foucault's model of character formation by disciplinary surveillance may be seen as a social equivalent of the psychic disciplining of the ego by the superego, since the superego or conscience is the psychic medium that instantiates the moral policing of the social order. Foucault's project was to show how the policing of the self became the function of social surveillance in the eighteenth and nineteenth centuries, and it would seem that to the degree that such policing seemed too harsh, melancholy came to be the mode and mood not just of the individual body but of the social body. The perfect fit of Browning's ironic allegory with Foucault's thought, in fact, may be taken to suggest that Foucault's analysis of disciplinary regimes in the social order is itself an allegorizing of the disciplinary dialectics of self and society, sense and conscience, sympathy and judgment.

Whereas "Porphyria's Lover" represents the moral difficulty of appropriating another subjectivity, "Johannes Agricola" examines what subject formation would look like if God's presence filled the world and men and women fully conceived of themselves as "God's puppets."[4] Agricola, based on the historical antinomian, sees himself as entirely predestined by God, fully conceived and formed from the beginning of time:

> I lie where I have always lain,
>   God smiles as he has always smiled;
> Ere suns and moons could wax and wane,
>   Ere stars were thundergirt, or piled
>   The heavens, God thought on me his child;
> Ordained a life for me, arrayed
>   Its circumstances every one
> To the minutest; ay, God said
>   This head this hand should rest upon
>   Thus, ere he fashioned star or sun.
> And having thus created me,
>   Thus rooted me, he bade me grow,
> Guiltless for ever, like a tree
>   That buds and blooms, nor seeks to know
>   The law by which it prospers so. (ll. 11–25)

Clearly Johannes has no human agency—his very posture is dictated by how God pulls and holds the strings of his mechanism. At best he is like a tree, growing by laws beyond his awareness—he has no self-consciousness at all, no subjectivity in any meaningful sense of the word. Further, not only is the puppet reduced to an insentient object in this scheme of things, but by putting words into God's mouth ("He said"), the puppet is reversing the terms on the puppet-master, making a puppet of God. There is no dialectic of self and other, not even a dialogue of the mind with itself, or even the time in which such a dialectic or dialogue would occur, since time itself is collapsed into the "always" in which God has smiled and Johannes has lain. Quite obviously, if Pippa were right that "God's puppets, best and worst, / are we" (*Pippa Passes*, "Introduction," 195–96), we could not also be human beings conscious of ourselves.

Like "Porphyria's Lover" and "Johannes Agricola in Meditation," many of Browning's dramatic poems are not only implicitly about the disciplinary, shaping power of surveillance but explicitly about exercises of power that enable or disable agency, the autonomous exercise of subjectivity. In poem after poem Browning establishes a relation of speaker to auditor as of puppet-master to puppet, implicating within the poem the relation of poet to poetic subject. The result is that the speaker engages in a "dialogue of the mind with itself," using others not for reciprocal communication but only as ventriloquist's dummies that enable the speaker to turn inward upon himself in another voice—to internalize the dialectic of self and conscience. Almost always the poems involve what Butler describes as "the figure of consciousness turned back upon itself" that characterizes Hegel's "unhappy consciousness" and prefigures Nietzsche's account "of how repression and regulation form the overlapping phenomena of conscience and bad conscience, but also of how the latter become essential to the formation, persistence, and continuity of the subject" (3).

The turnings of consciousness are more than doubled in Browning's poems, since the relation of speaker to auditor is reflected in the relation of poet to speaker and again in that of poet to reader. Inevitably, then, Browning's experiments in subject formation entail crucial issues concerning the poet's relation to his public and his ability to speak for, or represent, a particular subject.

In "Porphyria's Lover" the speaker kills Porphyria and manipulates her body like a meat puppet, but only after he has already spoken for her and as her by representing her thoughts within his own internal dialogue: she is

> Too weak, for all her heart's endeavour,
> To set its struggling passion free
>   From pride, and vainer ties dissever,
>   And give herself to me for ever.
> But passion sometimes would prevail,
>   Nor could tonight's gay feast restrain
> A sudden thought of one so pale
>   For love of her, and all in vain:
>   So, she was come through wind and rain.
> Be sure I looked up at her eyes
>   Happy and proud; at last I knew
>   Porphyria worshipped me. (ll.22–33)

The danger inherent in representing the subject is obvious—the speaker achieves autonomous agency, but only because he has *not* been able to form himself as a responsible subject, to subject himself to reciprocity in a genuine exchange of recognition with another. In addition, of course, the poet manipulates the speaker's thoughts and speech just as the speaker had manipulated Porphyria's. First-time readers of the poem are usually surprised, even shocked, by the speaker's sudden strangulation of Porphyria, but experienced readers of Browning see that the reader, like Porphyria, has been set up from the beginning. As many critics have recognized, Browning often achieves his ironic effects, his critical distance from the speaker, by playing poetic form against the speaker's syntax. Though the absence of breaks between the stanzas obscures the form, "Porphyria's Lover" is written in five-line stanzas and, at first, the speaker's syntax is controlled and contained within the stanzaic form:

> The rain set early in tonight,
>   The sullen wind was soon awake,
> It tore the elm-tops down for spite,
>   And did its worst to vex the lake:
> I listened with heart fit to break. (ll.1–5)

The excess of pathetic fallacy in personification indicates the speaker's lunacy, but the lines are all end-stopped, the final couplet is climactic, and the stanza is entirely self-contained as the poet constrains the speaker's thoughts within his own prosodic forms. In the following lines, however, with the entrance of Porphyria, the speaker's thoughts overflow the lines and stanzas as his syntax loses connection with the stanza form and even the rhythm, but though Browning seems to cede agency of sorts to the speaker, the passage characterizes him as a puppet, manipulated by Porphyria:

> When glided in Porphyria; straight
>   She shut the cold out and the storm,
> And kneeled and made the cheerless grate
>   Blaze up, and all the cottage warm;
>   Which done, she rose, and from her form
> Withdrew the dripping cloak and shawl,
>   And laid her soiled gloves by, untied
> Her hat and let the damp hair fall,
>   And, last, she sat down by my side
>   And called me. When no voice replied,
> She put my arm about her waist,
>   And made her smooth white shoulder bare,
> And all her yellow hair displaced,

> And, stooping, made my cheek lie there,
> And spread, o'er all, her yellow hair,
> Murmuring how she loved me—(ll.6–21)

Everything in the passage objectifies the speaker, most obviously Porphyria's control of his body, but also his alienation from his own voice and the grammatical connections, the glut of simple conjunctive "ands" that merely link the most simpleminded, passive registering of facts, with no controlling thought. The point is obvious, of course, that Browning controls the symmetry of the poem by first presenting the speaker as Porphyria's puppet and then reversing the roles, with the murder making Porphyria the lover's puppet. As in *Sordello* the puppet turns on the puppet-master: the lover not only breaks free of Porphyria's control but even seems to break free of the poet's as he bursts through the constraints of form.

Porphyria treats the speaker as, at best, half alive, and the speaker turns Porphyria into an inanimate object. The poem dramatizes *in extremis* the failure of dialogue to communicate; from both subject positions of mastery and subordination, the result is reification as the people become not subjects but objects, things. Most obviously, Porphyria is made an object and Browning's original title of the poem, "Porphyria," called attention to the corpse as the object of the poet's and reader's gaze. The subsequent publication as "Porphyria's Lover" does not necessarily refer to the lover's ability to speak his own consciousness, to realize his subjectivity, but rather points to him as another object to be observed, as seems obviously to be the point in publishing the poem as a "Madhouse Cell." Browning's construction of these poetic characters as objects rather than subjects thematizes the relation between masterful speakers and their auditors and thus stages his anxieties about his relation as a maker of poems, or persons, to a reading and purchasing public.

Like other Victorian artists, Browning worried about the changed relation of the artist to the public in a purely commercial age, and he worried particularly that he was producing poems as mere commodities. Writing to Elizabeth Barrett, he expressed these concerns under a thin veil of flippancy:

> [O]f course I must, if for merely scientific purposes, know all about this 1845, its ways and doings, and something I do know, as that for a dozen cabbages, if I pleased to grow them in the market here, I might demand, say, a dozen pence at Covent Garden Market,— and that for a dozen scenes, of the average goodness, I may challenge as many plaudits at the theatre close by; and a dozen pages of

verse, brought to the Rialto where verse-merchants most do congregate, ought to bring a fair proportion of the Reviewers' gold-currency, seeing the other traders pouch their winnings, as I do see. (*Correspondence*, 10: 70)

For Browning the commodification of poetry was especially troubling in the sense that he was producing not merely poems but something very like reified men and women as commodities.

It might seem a far-fetched anxiety for Browning to worry about the morality of pimping his men and women "where verse-merchants most do congregate," but a conspicuous number of his poems, especially in his early collections, are concerned explicitly with the transformation of living subjects into works of art or with the ethics of selling art. In addition to Porphyria, who is presented as a rosy-cheeked simulacrum of a woman, "My Last Duchess" confronts the public as a framed work of art, and yet another poem from the 1842 *Dramatic Lyrics*, "The Pied Piper of Hamelin," is a fable about the sale of art for public use and the vexed relations between artist and audience and artist and public. In Browning's next volume, the 1845 *Dramatic Romances and Lyrics*, "The Bishop Orders His Tomb at Saint Praxed's Church" is explicitly about the reification of life to art, and both "Pictor Ignotus" and "The Lost Leader" are about "selling out," the exchange of art for payment. The displacement of life by art in these works indicates the extent to which Browning's sense of alienation and reification in the commodity culture fed his melancholy fixation on what Shaw sees as the Kierkegaardian aesthetic stage and reveals why so many of Browning's abnormal specimens are artists, and vice versa.

The resemblance of "My Last Duchess" to "Porphyria's Lover" is obvious, though "My Last Duchess" is more complex due to its more fully developed dramatic situation. In both poems the masterful male reduces his "beloved" to a thing, though in "My Last Duchess" the thing is more clearly a work of art, the portrait of the Duchess who, like Porphyria, looks "as if she were alive." The Duke, however, not only reduces his Duchess to a thing but also transforms the auditor in the poem, the envoy from the *next* duchess, into a puppet. Everyone who sees the portrait is made to play the same role in the Duke's dialogue with himself, as he makes them seem "as they would ask me, if they durst, / How such a glance came there" (ll.11–12).

Further, the Duke effectively turns himself into a puppet, apparently playing over and over again the same role in his elaborate staging of the scene as he draws the curtain from the portrait and conducts both sides of the dialogue with his audience. As everyone knows, the Duke is a "control freak," scrupulous about maintaining the unruffled dignity of his "nine-hundred-years-old name," but Slinn has described the Duke's role and its consequences especially well:

> [T]he repetition of pulling the curtain before strangers suggests the continuing need to remake and reinforce the desired persona, his conscious mind acknowledges no other self, in himself or in others, and so he *is* the constructed persona, his own mask . . . just as he turns [the Duchess] into an artefact so he makes his own personality into an impressively controlled form, precisely and masterfully sustained, as if alive. (*Browning*, 41)

Because of the Duke's mastery in rendering himself inhuman, Erickson faults the poem for assuming "too great a knowledge of Browning's point of view by expecting the reader to be suspicious both of formal tidiness and of the absence of a struggle for significant self-discovery through the recognition of others" (*Robert Browning*, 84). Erickson is surely right about Browning's point of view, and his belief that "to see the self as a source of order in life leads to moral fascism" (84), but instead of finding fault with the poem for expecting too much of its readers, it seems reasonable to see the poem as Browning's staging of "salutary anxiety" about the construction of such "personae," such tidily packaged "selves," and as educating his public to read with due suspicion. The poem's evident irony at the expense of the Duke's performance of authoritatively packaging and interpreting the Duchess's spot of joy is, at the very least, a reminder of Browning's tendency to pass judgment on his own practices. In Benjamin's terms, the Duke has preserved the Duchess and the lover his perfect moment with Porphyria only as the corpses of the past, "souvenirs" of collectors who inventory the past as "dead possession" (Pensky, 181). Benjamin suggests that the ultimate emblem of seventeenth-century melancholy, resurrecting the intention of God as preserved in fallen nature, is the relic or corpse, while the ultimate image of nineteenth-century allegory, preserving the intention of the poet, is the souvenir. In the chilling images of Porphyria's corpse and the painted Duchess, Browning collapses the distinction, presenting the corpse as both relic and souvenir. Preserving dead lovers as souvenirs is, of course, grotesque in the extreme and so presents "the most graphic representation of subject turned object" and "the extreme limit of allegorical reflection" (Pensky, 180) in Browning's poetry.

It would be superfluous to attempt to analyze all of Browning's many poems about painters, musicians, and poets, but a brief glance at some of the most celebrated should make it clear that Browning's poems about art are characteristically grounded in concerns about the forbiddingly multitudinous possibilities of artistic representation and about the melancholy necessity of the artist to fall short of artistic perfection, to produce only commodities or souvenirs of once-vital experiences or intentions. As the unknown painter of "Pictor Ignotus" argues, even if the artist were able to produce perfect representations of his soul, his "gift / Of fire from God" (11.5–6), if he were to part with his gift to those who "buy and sell our pictures" (1.50), he and his art would blasphemously betray the gift and the Giver in a world corrupted to a "strange house of idols at its rites" (1.63). To be true to his art, to his gift from God, the painter must alienate himself from the world of getting and spending, retreating to where "no merchant traffics in [his] heart" (1.62), to a "sanctuary's gloom" (1.63) where he retains perfect integrity, wholeness of being, by refusing to sell, or even share, his devotional paintings. The result, of course, is that he paints only for himself in solipsistic isolation. Wholly removed from life, the painter and his works are devoted only to a sterile perfection that is also death or, at best, a buried life in mouldering catacombs where painter and paintings "surely, gently die" (1.69).

Similar alienation is evident in all of Browning's many poems about artists. In both "Fra Lippo Lippi" and "Andrea del Sarto" he evidently examines many of his own artistic beliefs and ambitions through insinuating himself under the skin of obviously flawed characters. A monk caught carousing where "sportive ladies leave their doors ajar" (1.6), Fra Lippo is obviously morally flawed, but his exuberance seems very much Browning's own, and his discourse on art is generally regarded as expressing Browning's own principles and practices in poetry: it may well have been for this reason that Browning chose this particular poem to read aloud to his fellow poets, Tennyson and D. G. Rossetti. An authentic Pre-Raphaelite in fact as well as name, Fra Lippo advocates a Ruskinian and Victorian Pre-Raphaelite eschewal of formal rules in art and a return to nature:

> God's works—paint anyone, and count it crime
> To let a truth slip. Don't object, "His works
> Are here already; nature is complete:
> Suppose you reproduce her"—(which you can't)
> "There's no advantage! you must beat her, then."
> For, don't you mark? we're made so that we love
> First when we see them painted, things we have passed
> Perhaps a hundred times nor cared to see;
> And so they are better, painted—better to us,
> Which is the same thing. Art was given for that;
> God uses us to help each other so,
> Lending our minds out. (ll.295–306)

As these lines suggest, Browning was able to be cheerful in a supposedly "unpoetic" age and to see abundant matter for poetry in a never belated Christian perspective (like the young Ruskin's), and in his sense of the "Beauty and the wonder and the power, / The shapes of things, their colours, lights, and shades, / Changes, surprises" (ll.283–85).

Evidently, "Fra Lippo Lippi" is neither melancholy nor allegorical, but it does exhibit what might be called Browning's allegorical realism in a particularly clear way in the confrontation of the prior's preference for allegory with Fra Lippo's vigorous realism. Lippo's, and presumably Browning's, rejection of allegory as defined by the prior could not be more convincing:

> What's here?
> Quite from the mark of painting, bless us all!
> Faces, arms, legs and bodies like the true
> As much as pea and pea! It's devil's game!
> Your business is not to catch men with show,
> With homage to the perishable clay,
> But lift them over it, ignore it all,
> Make them forget there's such a thing as flesh.
> Your business is to paint the souls of men—
> Man's soul, and it's a fire, smoke . . . no, it's not . . .
> It's vapour done up like a new-born babe—
> (In that shape when you die it leaves your mouth)
> It's . . . well, what matters talking, it's the soul!
> Give us no more of body than shows soul! (ll.175–88).

Browning evidently rejects the prior's version of allegory for the same reason Coleridge rejected allegory in general, because it is only "a translation of abstract nature into a picture-language, which is itself nothing but as an abstraction from objects of the senses; the principal being even more worthless than its phantom proxy, both alike unsubstantial, and the former shapeless to boot" (*The Statesman's Manual*, 30). The case against such an art is obvious in Lippo's distinction between his mimetic art and the presentation of the mere abstracted and unsubstantial sign:

> This world's no blot for us,
> Nor blank; it means intensely, and means good:
> To find its meaning is my meat and drink.
> "Ay, but you don't so instigate to prayer!"
> Strikes in the Prior: "When your meaning's plain
> It does not say to folk—remember matins,

> Or mind you fast next Friday! Why, for this
> What need of art at all? A skull and bones,
> Two bits of stick nailed crosswise, or what's best,
> A bell to chime the hour with, does as well." (ll.313–22).

Fra Lippo's art, like Browning's, is plainly not allegorical in the sense derided by Coleridge, but his realism is nevertheless symbolic in the sense that faithfully represented realities "are symbols also in some deeper way" than such "devious symbols" (Rossetti, 141) as the crucifix or the skull and bones. Because Lippo's paintings show body and show soul, they do not so much replace allegory with realism as fuse the two modes after the typological mode of "Scriptural history" that Coleridge contrasted with the emptiness of allegory, but that is more often understood as itself a form of allegory. For Fra Lippo, as for David in "Saul" and for Elizabeth Barrett such an unquestioningly Christian art is still ideal, but as we have seen, it was no longer adequate for the problems of a skeptical age that Browning sought to represent.

Even for someone who could adopt the early Christian aesthetics of Fra Lippo, to some extent the problem of multitudinousness remains, as do problems with the relation of art to its audience. At the outset of his career, Lippo's painting had been somewhat of a chaotic jumble: a shrewdly observant person, once Lippo had the opportunity to practice his imitative art, drawings poured forth profusely, but apparently with little purpose:

> my head being crammed, the walls a blank,
> Never was such prompt disemburdening.
> First, every sort of monk, the black and white,
> I drew them, fat and lean: then, folk at church. (ll.143–46)

Nothing in Lippo's monologue suggests that he ever developed a shaping vision of his own that would enable him to produce anything more than a kaleidoscope of more or less random images: he partially reproduces God's "mighty maze" but without a plan. The endless proliferation of aesthetic objects in the poem, as well as the account of God's works less in terms of their truth than of their shapes, colors, lights, and shades reveals his wholly aesthetic rather than moral response to God's creation, an aesthetic response that corresponds to his moral failures as a profligate monk, still subjected to the sense and sensuality that the moral conscience of the poem censures, not only through the stern judgment of "the prior and the learned" (1.174) but also by the irony of the poet, just out of the poem's frame with his pointing pole. No doubt Browning admired Lippi's mimetic art and prized the diversity of his representations, yet for all its undeniable exuberance, the poem at least hints at his anxiety about his art. Chesterton must certainly have seen Browning's severe conscience at work judging Lippi's life, since he included Fra Lippo, apparently a spokesman for Browning's own practices, on his short list of Browning's evil men.

Fra Lippo's unhappy conscience, moreover, is apparent within the poem in the bad faith production of pictures to satisfy rather than educate his audience. Lippo is able to resist the injunctions of "the prior and the learned" that he imitate his predecessors in order to paint soul and not merely body, but ultimately he continues to paint pictures according to the dictates of others—despite his own robust sensuality, his paintings seem to be mainly of ascetic martyrs, notably Saint Jerome and Saint Laurence, and he sees his art as a job undertaken to please his employers, or at least to satisfy the learned, who seem to know what they want:

> Don't you think they're the likeliest to know,
> They with their Latin? So, I swallow my rage,
> Clench my teeth, suck my lips in tight, and paint
> To please them. (ll.241–44)

Though Lippi's manifesto about art is expressive of many of Browning's most cherished ideas, the poem does not resolve the vexing problems of how to give shape to the multitudinousness of life, or even of how the artist should relate to his patrons. Unlike the unknown painter, Lippi attempts to share his gift, but as the unknown painter chastened himself, the "prior and the learned" chasten Fra Lippo: in both cases the artist is unable to be true to his own vision, to retain his artistic integrity as wholeness of being.

The melancholy Andrea del Sarto is represented as a failure, but he ironically speaks some of Browning's most famous lines, particularly the sentiment that Browning's readers have always seen as a pithy summation of the poet's own most cherished belief: "a man's reach should exceed his grasp, / Or what's a heaven for?" (ll.97–98). Browning's irony, of course, is that Andrea's reach does not exceed his grasp, that he has always settled for the mediocrity that is well within his grasp. Because he can easily do the limited amount he sets out to do, he earns the title Vasari and Browning concede him: the "faultless painter." His perfection, however, is the sign of his failure for the same reason that, according to Ruskin, perfection of execution is always a sign of failure: "while in all things that we see, or do, we are to desire perfection, and strive for it, we are nevertheless not to set the meaner thing, in its narrow accomplishment, above the nobler thing, in its mighty progress; . . . not to prefer mean victory to honourable defeat; not to lower the level of our aim, that we may the more surely enjoy the complacency of success" (*Works,* 10: 191).

As Browning saw it, the failure to strive after a goal beyond earthly possibility is a failure to grow into the highest reaches of human possibility. All aspiration, if worthy, must end in failure—in this respect it even makes sense for Childe Roland to aspire "just to fail as" his peers had failed. Andrea's contemptible failure as a person and artist is evident in the failure of aspiration to set its sights higher than earning a little money by producing a passable commodity, and so perhaps keeping his wife by his side for the sake of gain, if not love: "If you would sit thus by me every night / I should work better, do you comprehend? / I mean that I should earn more, give you more" (ll.205–7). As in so many of his other poems about artists, Browning is clearly concerned here with the problem of the artist's relation to his work as a commodity: he had the usual concern of the artist about selling his genius, but more than this, he knew that a person only becomes a "self," a fully realized human being, in relation to other people, so the possibility of relating to the social order only in the marketplace was inevitably a worrying one. Ideally the self should be formed in a dialectic of individual personality and conscience, which is for Browning the voice of God, so the dialectic of self and market evidently displaces God with the cash nexus, displaces Christianity with capitalism. Such a possibility is certainly realized in the figure of Andrea del Sarto, who reduces both art and interpersonal relationships to money—he has stolen money from the king of France, he has seen his parents die of want, and he even sees his love for Lucrezia as something to be bought and sold: "More gaming debts to pay? you smiled for that? / Well, let smiles buy me! have you more to spend?" (ll.222–23). Andrea merely wants to break even to the extent that "Men will excuse me" and that ultimately his account will balance with God:

> At the end
> God, I conclude, compensates, punishes.
> 'Tis safer for me, if the award be strict,
> That I am something underrated here. (ll.140–43)

Browning did not know Marx's arguments about the reification of people that results from the commodification of labor, but he was certainly aware of Carlyle's analogous argument about the dehumanizing effect of reducing all personal connection to the "cash nexus." He shows Andrea reducing both himself and Lucrezia to the status of objects: Lucrezia, as his model, is unsurprisingly treated as a lay figure ("Let my hands frame your face in your hair's gold" [l.175]), yet even in his most impassioned speech to her, Andrea describes her as an accumulation of beautiful parts, without a mind or soul to give:

> Nay, Love, you did give all I asked, I think—
> More than I merit, yes, by many times.
> But had you—oh, with the same perfect brow,
> And perfect eyes, and more than perfect mouth,
> And the low voice my soul hears, as a bird
> The fowler's pipe, and follows to the snare—
> Had you, with these the same, but brought a mind! (ll.120–26)

Further, like Johannes Agricola, Andrea sees himself not as an autonomous person but as God's puppet: "I might have done it for you. So it seems: / Perhaps not. All is as God over-rules" (ll.132–33). Andrea, of course, is not a spokesman for Browning's views, but quite to the contrary, in his submissive acceptance of melancholy, of his art and life "all in a twilight" (1.36), he is, as Tucker puts it, a "preemptive loser" (*Browning's Beginnings*, 198) whose monologue is an "intricate yet faultless accommodation of a need to fail" (196). Yet even as a negative expression of Browning's beliefs, Andrea offers a rationale about the inevitability of failure that is perhaps dangerously close to Browning's own—dangerous because by ventriloquizing Browning's ideas Andrea becomes a mere spokesman: even a puppet, after all, can be made to voice a doctrine, but the doctrine, even Browning's most cherished beliefs, becomes reified in the process. Like Paracelsus at the end of the play, David in "Saul," Rabbi Ben Ezra, and other cheerleaders for Browning's beliefs, Andrea is less a self than a character, but in this case the speaker's melancholy, utterly unlike the euphoric optimism of other puppets of Browningism, reveals the poet's own anxieties about his aesthetic creed.

Because of its consistency of mood, its harmonizing of emotional tones, "Andrea del Sarto" is certainly among the most beautiful and lyrical of Browning's poems, but the mood and tone are like Andrea's art in its harmonies of silver and gray, a sign of limitation, too contentedly perfect. The poem shows particularly clearly the tonal register and high degree of polish Browning could have given his poetry had he acquiesced in melancholia as Andrea did. Unlike Andrea's paintings, however, Browning's poems characteristically resist melancholic lassitude, striving for an impossible expression of the infinite. Expressing melancholy rather than optimism, the poem resists a tendency to the kind of sage literature valued by Browning societies, but the irony that severely judges Andrea's materialism implies both the doctrine of Christian optimism and the melancholy that makes that doctrine necessary to Browning: ideally, striving for the infinite should be a source of exuberant energy, but inevitable failure may well become a source of melancholy and lassitude. As Carlyle's Shoeblack shows, the source of man's unhappiness is that he has an infinite within himself that can never be wholly satisfied in a finite world, just as Browning can never expect to succeed in his poetic goal to put the infinite into finite form.

Still, Browning's characters do, on rare occasions, claim a kind of success in momentarily achieving the infinite. The best example, perhaps, is one of Browning's poems about a musician, "Abt Vogler." Vogler (and Browning) would have agreed with Walter Pater's judgment that all art aspires to the condition of music because music offers no definitive statement and can never be bounded as finite representation. Extemporizing upon "the musical instrument of his invention," Vogler's entirely spontaneous art seems wholly to express his infinite soul. It has occasionally been argued that "Abt Vogler," like other poems in *Dramatis Personae,* is more concerned with doctrine than with dramatizing a character, and that it consequently fails by achieving a static perfection, but Robert Langbaum may be right in seeing the poem as effectively dramatic in recording not only Vogler's transcendent moment of vision but also the melancholy recoil that necessarily succeeds it. Also, very obviously, in being privy to the direct word of God, Vogler is the rare exception in human life, as he himself recognizes:

> Sorrow is hard to bear, and doubt is slow to clear,
> Each sufferer says his say, his scheme of the weal and woe:
> But God has a few of us whom he whispers in the ear;
> The rest may reason and welcome: 'tis we musicians know.
> (ll.85–88)

Vogler's commentary on the meaning of his vision does, perhaps, serve as a dogmatic exposition of the optimism that Browning societies admired in their bard, but his concluding remarks are a reminder that despite, or even because of, the rare vision, earthly life is a period of melancholy probation in which Vogler must "soberly acquiesce" (1.90), "Surveying a while the heights I rolled from into the deep" (1.94). The sense of melancholy is deepened when Vogler contemplates the transience of his music, which is gone as soon as performed, but this melancholy is dissipated immediately as he affirms Browning's optimistic faith that man's imperfect and transient efforts will be perfected in heaven:

> Therefore to whom turn I but to thee, the ineffable Name?
>   Builder and maker, thou, of houses not made with hands!
> What, have fear of change from thee who art ever the same?

> Doubt that thy power can fill the heart that thy power expands?
> There shall never be one lost good! What was, shall live as before;
> The evil is null, is naught, is silence implying sound;
> What was good shall be good, with, for evil, so much good more;
> On the earth the broken arcs; in the heaven, a perfect round. (ll. 65–72)

The optimism of the stanza, however, is a reminder that man is "Hopeless on earth, and heaven is out of view." What one surveys on earth, in this case the broken arcs, is a field of ruins. Enduring construction of Vogler's palace of art could only be possible with something like the Coleridgean symbol that would share in the divine Word, "the ineffable name." But as Donald Hair reminds us, even Coleridge's rapt poet in "Kubla Khan" could not "build that dome in air" without being able to revive within himself the lost "symphony and song" of the "damsel with a dulcimer," and neither Vogler nor Browning can construct enduring "houses not made with hands" without recovering the "ineffable Name," lost in Eden and therefore always already lost in the fallen world.

Browning selected "Abt Vogler" as one of the two lyrics that he thought most truly represented him, but the poem does seem to represent his "philosophy" rather than his dramatic method, which is perhaps better represented by an analogous poem from *Men and Women*, "Master Hugues of Saxe-Gotha," also spoken by an organist building his music Orpheus-like into a palatial structure of sounds. The difference from "Abt Vogler," however, is that the organist is not improvising but performing and responding to the music of another, Master Hugues, and the building, far from reaching heaven, is a tower of Babel, a parody of a dialogue of the mind with itself. The five themes of the fugue, rather than toiling together to one end, produce discord and fail to communicate with any audience:

> *Est fuga, volvitur rota.*
> On we drift: where looms the dim port?
> One, Two, Three, Four, Five, contribute their quota;
> Something is gained, if one caught but the import—
> Show it us, Hugues of Saxe-Gotha!
> What with affirming, denying,
> Holding, risposting, subjoining,
> All's like . . . it's like . . . for an instance I'm trying . . .
> There! See our roof, its gilt moulding and groining
> Under those spider-webs lying! (ll.86–95)

Hugues's music is not ultimately like the gothic tracery of the roof, or even like the intricate spider's web, but is so multitudinous, so interwoven as to be simply opaque, "Blacked to the stoutest of tickens" (1.100). Unlike "Abt Vogler," "Master Hugues" is fully dramatized, and instead of representing the solipsism, however satisfying, of a musician playing his own thoughts to his own perfect comprehension, it describes the gaps between intention, expression, and execution, and the still more melancholy gap between expression and the comprehension of an auditor. As Tucker and Martin have both argued, a similar dynamic is at work in the melancholy "A Toccata of Galuppi's." Galuppi's light and deft touch-pieces apparently spoke to and of the gay Venetians of his day, but the speaker of the poem, playing Galuppi's music centuries later, provides a melancholy closure with the painful knowledge that the once gay music is now a souvenir, a memento mori: "Then they left you for their pleasure: till in due time, one by one, / Some with lives that came to nothing, some with deeds as well undone, / Death stepped tacitly and took them where they never see the sun" (ll.28–30).

For the speaker, then, the meaning of the toccata is simply "dust and ashes, dead and done with, Venice spent what Venice earned" (1.35). As Martin puts it, "the music of the toccata tells the speaker he will not die, just as it had the Venetians. But the message has been insidious; it has spoken as much of loss as of hope by recalling distant Venice" (1.20). From this perspective, even the most cheering music, far from expressing infinite subjectivity in finite form, speaks of "dust and ashes," the mortality implied in its temporal medium. Whatever it may have meant to its Venetian audience, Galuppi's commodity is for the speaker a melancholy reminder of the swift passage of life: "cold music" that makes him "creep through every nerve" (1.33). If history is a field of ruins, even the most light and cheerful work of art is a memento mori.

In Browning's poems about poetry, art, and music he repeatedly returns to the inability of all art forms to transcend the merely finite object, to express the infinite subject, but arguably, love poetry more than any other kind aspires to perfect sincerity, perfect accord between intention and expression, and between expression and comprehension as two minds strive to break down the finite barriers of expressible self to become one infinite subjectivity. In *Sartor Resartus* love is credited with a "discerning of the Infinite within the Finite, of the Idea made Real" (i. 115), and Browning's love poetry characteristically strives for such unity of minds, desirable as the goal of love but also as the goal of any poetry that aspires to full communication. Such perfect union is rarely claimed in Browning's love poetry, which disdains the facile affirmations of conventional love poetry as it disdains conventions. Most conspicuously, in "One Word

More," addressed to Elizabeth Barrett Browning, the poet longs for the ability to speak sincerely, naturally, to speak as a man, not as a poet in the artifice of poetry, "art that's turned his nature" (1.64). Even where the speaker claims moments of perfect communication, as in "By the Fireside," the achievement is seen as a rare exception to the usual melancholy of isolation within the self. By Browning's account, "By the Fireside" was addressed to his wife—his best audience—and it does evidently describe a perfect moment of true union in love as the beloved "spares" the speaker the pain of separation:

> . . . you spared me this, like the heart you are,
>   And filled my empty heart at a word.
> If two lives join, there is oft a scar,
>   They are one and one, with a shadowy third;
> One near one is too far.
>
> A moment after, and hands unseen
>   Were hanging the night around us fast;
> But we knew that a bar was broken between
>   Life and life: we were mixed at last
> In spite of the mortal screen. (ll.226–35)

The problem with this rare, perfect moment is that it is so displaced in time that it can hardly be said to have happened at all. The speaker is describing what he "mean[s] to" remember in the "long dark autumn-evenings" (ll.1–2) of the future, and the distant, twilit, autumnal setting already introduces a note of melancholy, but more than this, the peculiar strategy of speaking of the future when a past event will be recalled structures the whole event as nostalgia, a form of melancholy, since the past will already have slipped away. Were it possible, the Coleridgean symbol would be the way to represent an infinite moment, but Browning's conspicuously temporal account undermines the potential of the symbol, replacing it with a souvenir.

The poem's affirmation of the perfected "moment, one and infinite" (1.181) would seem to indicate that Browning has here achieved his poetic goal of fitting the infinite into the finite, but if such an epiphany has occurred in the speaker's subjectivity, it is not achieved in the poem's form. The poem could only express the perfect and infinite union of souls beyond the barrier of the mortal screen if it could find what Donald Hair has called the idealist goal of language (142–68), the Coleridgean language that echoes and shares in the "ineffable Name." Hair points out that this would be a language that "repairs the divisions brought about by the fall, and makes sign and signifier, soul and speech, one" (143). In "With Christopher Smart," from *Parleyings with Certain People of Importance in Their Day* (1887), Browning very likely remembered "By the Fireside" as he described Smart's achievement of such a language:

>   Such success
> Befell Smart only out of throngs between
> Milton and Keats that donned the singing-dress—
> Smart, solely of such songmen, pierced the screen
> 'Twixt thing and word, lit language straight from soul—(ll.110–14)

In "By the Fireside," however, Browning does not find the idealist Word that would capture the infinite in the material of language, but ostentatiously puts off the possibility of achieving an adequately spiritual language until after death, in heaven:

> Think, when our one soul understands
>   The great Word which makes all things new,
> When earth breaks up and heaven expands,
>   How will the change strike me and you
> In the house not made with hands? (ll.131–35)

As later in "Abt Vogler," the Pauline allusion in the phrase "house not made with hands" (see 2 Corinthians 5:1) puts off perfect expression until heaven. Unable to transcend the fallen temporal language, Browning emphasized the transience of the moment as always already over, consigned to the ruins of history and recoverable only in melancholy, nostalgic contemplation. The poem, moreover, recovers the moment by way of an allegorical quest in which the speaker "tread[s] / This path back" (121–22) to a "ruined chapel" (31) "in the heart of *things*" (36, my emphasis). Most of the poem, in fact, consists of a brooding on the enigmatic mystery of things, from the ruined chapel to the stone bridge to the scattered homes, and especially to the natural growths, described in Browning's finest grotesque style:

> Oh the sense of the yellow mountain-flowers,
>   And thorny balls, each three in one,
> The chestnuts throw in our path in showers!
>   For the drop of the woodland fruit's begun,
> These early November hours,
>
> That crimson the creeper's leaf across
>   Like a splash of blood, intense, abrupt,

> O'er a shield else gold from rim to boss,
>   And lay it for show on the fairy-cupped
> Elf-needled mat of moss,
>
> By the rose-flesh mushrooms, undivulged
>   Last evening—nay, in today's first dew
> Yon sudden coral nipple bulged,
>   Where a freaked fawn-coloured flaky crew
> Of toadstools peep indulged. (ll.51–65)

The extended syntax of the fifteen-line sentence emphasizes the temporal mode of fallen language and also crams the language full of material things. The simile comparing the autumnal colors to a splash of blood on a shield even suggests the grotesque in Bagehot's sense, seeing through the historical residue of a "cumbrous mass of barbarism and cruelty," and suggests Benjamin's sense of melancholy's focus on the ruins of history. Further, the mountain flowers "each three in one" may be a deliberate allusion to D. G. Rossetti's "The Woodspurge," which describes the tendency of deep grief to fixate on the enigmatic nature of things (or things of nature):

> From perfect grief there need not be
> Wisdom or even memory;
> One thing then learned remains to me—
> The woodspurge has a cup of three. (ll.13–16)

Whether or not Browning had "The Woodspurge" in mind, his stress on "the sense of" the flower and his grotesquely erotic account of the mushrooms reveals a melancholy concentration on the material "thingness" of things, so that the poem's apparent celebration of the "one and infinite" moment paradoxically takes the form of melancholy allegory as described by Benjamin: "Mourning is the state of mind in which feeling revives the empty world in the form of a mask, and derives an enigmatic satisfaction in contemplating it . . . in the description of that world which is revealed under the gaze of the melancholy man . . . feeling . . . is released from any empirical subject and is intimately bound to the fullness of an object" (*Origin,* 139). The subjectivity of the subject, the infinite soul, is represented not only in "the heart of things" but as an allegorical path through the emotional resonances of material things. Somewhat surprisingly, the melancholy underlying the apparent optimism of "By the Fireside" is a reversal of the problem encountered in such programmatically optimistic poems as the end of *Paracelsus,* "Rabbi

Ben Ezra," and "Saul": in those poems the optimism was achieved only at the level of the signifier rather than the subject, whereas in "By the Fireside" the subject is said to achieve transcendence, but the signifier, language, remains immersed in matter.

Browning's strongest statement about the inability of even love to transcend the finite condition of mortal existence is found in "Two in the Campagna," where the speaker denies the possibility of transcendence altogether. As in "Master Hugues," the speaker of "Two in the Campagna" likens the intricacies of thought to a spider's web and wonders if his beloved is thinking along the same exceedingly unlikely lines. Once again the thoughts of the speaker are represented through the enigmatic and idiosyncratic representation of things, specifically ruins and grotesque natural objects:

> For me, I touched a thought, I know,
>   Has tantalized me many times,
> (Like turns of thread the spiders throw
>   Mocking across our path) for rhymes
> To catch at and let go.
>
> Help me to hold it! First it left
>   The yellowing fennel, run to seed
> There, branching from the brickwork's cleft,
>   Some old tomb's ruin: yonder weed
> Took up the floating weft,
>
> Where one small orange cup amassed
>   Five beetles,—blind and green they grope
> Among the honey-meal: and last,
>   Everywhere on the grassy slope
> I traced it. Hold it fast! (ll.6–20)

Even though the speaker wants to stress the passion and life of "primal naked forms" (1.28) for the purposes of his seduction, the campagna, with its ancient ruins, is awash with death: "An everlasting wash of air—/ Rome's ghost since her decease" (ll.24–25). David Shaw, commenting on the "teeming promiscuity" of the beetles, also suggests that "the speaker is a victim of his own analogies" who "does not 'come out' where he planned to" (*Dialectical Temper*, 121). Certainly the analogical or allegorical language does not arrive at transcendence. In a poem remarkable for its apparently blighting sincerity, the speaker acknowledges the failure of love to unite two souls:

> No. I yearn upward, touch you close,
>   Then stand away. I kiss your cheek,
> Catch your soul's warmth,—I pluck the rose
>   And love it more than tongue can speak—
> Then the good minute goes. (ll.46–50)

For Browning, love, like poetry, is an attempt to put the infinite into the finite, and "Two in the Campagna" acknowledges the pain that comes out of the inevitable failure of mortal aspiration: "Infinite passion, and the pain / Of finite hearts that yearn" (ll.59–60). Shaw argues that the poem is a dialectic enabling the growth of the speaker's soul from the aesthetic to the ethical stage, but he does full justice to the melancholy of the aesthetic stage: "[T]he truth to which the poem points has a nostalgic quality, a depth of brooding introspection, that cannot be reached, and perhaps could not have been borne by Browning if it were. The speaker loves the woman 'more than tongue can speak.' But he also feels a pang of the soul's incurable loneliness" (122). This is very well put, and Shaw may well be right that the speaker, abandoning seduction for candor, is growing toward an ethical stage, but the phrase "more than tongue can speak" characterizes not only the speaker's difficulty but the poet's inability to achieve the immediacy in writing of what "tongue can speak" or of achieving the infinite in any form of language. Finally, however the speaker may grow, the poet can hardly hope to grow beyond the aesthetic and yet remain a poet.

As has perhaps become evident, one could survey Browning's multitudes of men and women indefinitely to illustrate his unrealizable desire in the dramatic monologues to enter into the infinite soul or consciousness of another person, to know that person from the inside, as the speaker of "Two in the Campagna" wishes to enter into the soul of his lover: "I would I could adopt your will, / See with your eyes" (ll.41–42). In the sense that Browning's poems were attempts to create "persons," the impossibility of putting the infinite soul into the finite discourse of the poem necessitated ultimate "failure"—the poet can never fully "represent" the infinite and can never fully enter into the mind of either his character or his readers. Browning was, of course, fully aware of this: quite obviously, the poet cannot create other subjectivities, but only puppets, as Browning very clearly saw in his climactic and most ambitious work with dramatic monologues, *The Ring and the Book*.

IV. Filthy Rags of Speech

The Ring and the Book was far from Browning's last poem, but it does climax his experimentation with genre and a poetics of melancholy. *The Ring and the Book* has been often and rightly called Browning's masterpiece, but not, as Browning believed, by virtue of finally comprising "R.B.—a poem," the pure white light, as opposed to the prismatic hues of the dramatic monologues (David Shaw, *Dialectical Temper,* 235). Browning cannot be said to have succeeded, as Shaw suggests, in his effort "to blend [the poem's] dizzying play of color back into the 'pure white light,' the divine truth that swirls through its masks in a succession of temporary incarnations" (238). Rather than blending the refracted lights of fallen human truth into the pure white of God's truth, the kaleidoscopic effect is, perhaps, suggestive of the melancholic anomie described by Durkheim as "mind endlessly moving, a veritable kaleidoscope that changes from one moment to the next" (see above, p. 141).

Shaw is closer to describing the real achievement of *The Ring and the Book* as "a kind of overgrown morality play" casting Caponsacchi as the "dashing deliverer," Pompilia as the spotlessly innocent, saintly heroine, and Guido as the absolute, satanic villain (236): the work is clearly an allegory, perhaps even, as Shaw suggests, an allegory of Browning's rescue of Elizabeth Barrett from the clutches of her tyrannical father, but surely an allegory, as DeVane argued, of "the Perseus-Andromeda myth and its cognate legend of St. George slaying the dragon" (345). Browning even changed the date of Pompilia's rescue from April 29, as recorded in the old yellow book, to April 23, St. George's Day (DeVane, 339), and the various characters allude to the legend, by DeVane's count, no fewer than thirty times. *The Ring and the Book* almost parodies the allegorical mode, presenting both the tale and its explication in a frame narrative spoken in books i and xii by a dramatized version of Browning himself. The tale is even presented in the excessively didactic mode of allegory rejected in *Sordello,* where "the wearer's quality" is in effect "chalk[ed] broadly on each vesture's hem" by the dramatized poet "in motley, pointing pole in hand" to "Show man, on evil or on good lay stress" and reveal "which sinner is, which saint" (see above, pp. 151–52). Other than the poet of the frame, the most authoritative interpreter of events is undoubtedly Pope Innocent in book x, and the pope, speaking Browning's nineteenth-century theology rather than thinking and feeling his way through his own seventeenth-century Catholic worldview, is arguably, like David in "Saul" or like Rabbi Ben Ezra, the puppet of an ideology, not dramatizing the development of a soul but ventriloquizing a doctrine. Like David's, the pope's speech is magnificent, but his character is wooden.

The great aesthetic achievement of *The Ring and the Book* consists in its incarnation of perspectives in the more fully dramatized narratives, which sufficiently contextualize one another to offer discernible truth in and through fallen human subjectivities, as Kierkegaard said Schleiermacher had done in his work on Schlegel's *Lucinde:*

> He constructs a host of personalities out of the book itself and through them illuminates the work and also illuminates their individuality, so that instead of being faced by the reviewer with various points of view, we get instead many personalities who represent these various points of view. But they are complete beings, so that it is possible to get a glance into the individuality of the single individual and through numerous merely relatively true judgments to draw up our own final judgment. Thus it is a true masterpiece. (*Either/Or, Part One*, 357)

The Ring and the Book is a masterpiece not because it transcends Browning's melancholic allegorical mode, but because it sustains that mode on a massive scale. As often in Browning's poetry, the poem exhibits a clear awareness that fallen language is a tissue of lies, allegorized again as clothing, a vesture that conceals at least as much as it reveals. As the pope, in particular, insists, God's truth cannot be expressed in fallen language but is reserved in heaven:

> This [*sic*] filthy rags of speech, this coil
> Of statement, comment, query and response,
> Tatters all too contaminate for use,
> Have no renewing: He, the Truth, is, too,
> The Word. We men, in our degree, may know
> There, simply, instantaneously, as here
> After long time and amid many lies . . .
> But be man's method for man's life at least! (x. 372–81)

To paraphrase Abt Vogler: on earth the broken lights, in heaven the pure white light. Still, though *The Ring and the Book* relies on the lies of "man's method," the pope does suggest that "long time and many lies" (the 23,000 lines of the poem, perhaps) may show us, if only through a glass darkly, the truth as it will be revealed in heaven. Certainly, at least, the speaker of the last book believes that

> Art,—wherein man nowise speaks to men,
> Only to mankind,—Art may tell a truth
> Obliquely, do the thing shall breed the thought,
> Nor wrong the thought, missing the mediate word. (xii. 854–57)

Browning's image of the poem as a ring, moreover, would seem to suggest that the poem achieves more than a representation of what Abt Vogler calls the "broken arcs" of earthly perception, that the artistry of the poet has fitted them into the "perfect round" of divine truth. Similarly, the pure gold of the ring is an image for the pure gold of the finished poem, as though Browning, like Paracelsus, claimed to transmute the impurities of fallen matter into the purity of true gold and truth itself. The ring, however, is not truth incarnate but, as Browning insists, an allegorical sign: "a figure, a symbol say; / A thing's sign" (i. 31–32). As Donald Hair remarks (169), the poem's opening question, "Do you see this ring?" immediately places the poem within the tradition of emblem poetry that Browning had admired since his childhood love of Francis Quarles's *Emblemes,* and consequently indicates the poem's allegorical mode from the outset.

The "thing signified" by the emblem, the poem distilled from contemplation of the "old yellow book" (i. 33), is distinctly a product of melancholy as an absorbed contemplation of history as a "field of ruins." The dying body of Pompilia and the corpses of the Comparini are directly and indirectly the subjects of meditation for all of the characters, and the pope especially, Browning's surrogate, speaks with relentless melancholy of the fallen and debased nature of humanity. Further, the poem as a whole is a meditation on the dead past, specifically on an artifact that is ostentatiously characterized as a ruin, the detritus of a once living past:

> dwindled into no bigger than a book
>   . . . and that little, left
> By the roadside 'mid the ordure, shards and weeds.
> Until I haply, wandering that way,
> Kicked it up, turned it over, and recognized,
> For all the crumblement, this abacus,
> This square old yellow book. (i. 671–77)

Far more clearly than Galuppi's toccata, the old yellow book is a memento mori meaning "dust and ashes, dead and done with" (see above, p. 173), but more than that, the particular emblems that Browning contemplates in *The Ring and the Book* suggest that his was specifically the melancholy of time confronting eternity. As Hair points out, his purpose remained the impossible one of fitting the infinite into finite forms:

> The book is square . . . and his artistry is circular, so that he is taking a square and making it into a circle. The circle is an ancient picture of heaven and perfection, the square (in so far as it is associated with the four elements) of earth. "Squaring the circle"—strictly speaking it should be "circling the square"—was one concern of the alchemists, who would thereby make heaven and earth one. "Putting the infinite within the finite" (the business of all poetry) is Browning's abstract

> expression of the idea in his 1855 letter to Ruskin. His more concrete aim in making a ring out of a book—to "save the soul"—is imaged in the same fusion of square and circle. (175)

As Hair suggests, Browning is returning to the Faustian figure of Paracelsus, not only attempting to square the circle but to transmute the mere ore of fact into the pure gold of truth.

As if to parody the frame poet's and even the pope's claims to have arrived at a pure truth through interpretation of fallen human language, the manifestly fallible speakers of the other monologues all unconvincingly make the same claim as the poet. Most damningly, the evil Guido presents himself as a textual analyst and even justifies the murder on the grounds that he had authoritatively interpreted the word of the court on an earlier occasion:

> I, being used to serve,
> Have simply . . . what is it they charge me with?
> Blackened again, made legible once more
> Your own decree, not permanently writ,
> Rightly conceived but all too faintly traced. (v. 1995–99)

Guido's metaphor of blackening is more sinister than the introductory speaker's claim to have distilled gold, but the claims are similar in their assertions of being the correct and authoritative readings of the perplexing testimony. But Guido is only doing what all the speakers do. Most obviously, the lawyers are professional "close readers": both of them contrive to interpret the testimony in ways opposed to the poet's reading. The three speakers of public opinion similarly claim to find the authoritative truth beyond the verbal signs of the testimony, and Tertium Quid, certainly the cleverest of these speakers, seems a parody of the poet as he uses his ingenuity to entertain an audience with an objective and accurate reading of the texts. Tertium Quid not only recapitulates the inability of law to sift the evidence and find the truth in the first trial, he also sends a preemptive warning to later textual analysts of the trial (and of *The Ring and the Book*) about the ways in which multifarious texts may be further perplexed by clever reading. By giving each side its due, Tertium Quid only succeeds in casting deeper and deeper shadows on the multitudinous evidence and in compounding the confusion.

Speaker after speaker in the poem emphasizes that even what is clearly understood in the mind is liable to "the blunder incident to words" and the resultant failure of transmission in the "clumsy process" (iv. 512–13) of putting understanding into words. The pope describes at length the impossibility of even the most sincere speaker uttering absolute truth in mortal language: the glorious "robe" of Paracelsus, the "armor" of Sordello, have become for the pope the "filthy rags of speech" (x. 372). Significantly, the character with the surest grasp of absolute truth, Pompilia, can neither read nor write, and when she recognizes the truth of Caponsacchi it is because she is not confused by the signs that conceal as well as reveal "things," by the false words misrepresented as Caponsacchi's by Guido's forgery. Pompilia insists on the impossibility of expressing God's truth in mortal words: "Let us leave God alone! / Why should I doubt He will explain in time / What I feel now, but fail to find the words?" (vii. 1759–61). Unable to communicate the truth in language, Pompilia chooses to "withdraw from earth and man / To my own soul, compose myself for God" (vii. 1769–70).

By a very different route, Robert Browning arrived at a conclusion similar to Elizabeth Barrett's early thought—there could be no authoritative language on earth, no poetic authority prior to a heavenly apotheosis. In almost her final dying words, Pompilia asserts that not even love enables people to speak truly and communicate fully. Like Elizabeth Barrett, Pompilia insists that such communication is reserved for God and his angels, "who, apart, / Know themselves into one" (vii. 1833–34). As Pompilia sees, and presumably as Browning had come to see, any notion of lovers being "mixed at last / In spite of the mortal screen" is wishful thinking.

In *The Ring and the Book* Browning had come full circle, back to the subject of his earliest dramatic monologues, the outrageousness of treating people like objects, particularly the lawful outrage of husbands treating their wives like property. As described by the pope, Guido's crime is to reduce Pompilia to a "pale awe-stricken wife, past hope / Of help i' the world now, mute and motionless, / His slave, his chattel, to use and then destroy" (x. 562–64). Not surprisingly in this context, Browning also reverts to the imagery of puppetry that he had explored in *Pippa Passes* and the early monologues. In fact Tertium Quid, the speaker arguably most like Browning, and even more like the casuist speakers of the late monologues (Mr. Sludge, Don Juan in *Fifine at the Fair,* Prince Hohenstiel-Schwangau), conspicuously compares the whole series of events to a Punch and Judy show in which "the crowd or clap or hiss / Accordingly as disposed for man or wife" (iv. 1284–85).

Elsewhere, also, Browning invites his readers to see the central characters reified in their social roles as puppets, as when Caponsacchi is described in the introduction: "Now heaven, now earth, now heaven and earth at once, / Had plucked at and perplexed their puppet here" (I .1020–21). Like all of

Browning's men and women, the characters are pulled by strings of the poet's devising, sometimes almost comically: "Then up pops Curate Carlo" (ii. 159), just on cue, pat, like the catastrophe in the old comedy. Slinn has pointed out that Caponsacchi is "a puppet of his own masculinity" (*Browning*, 118). If Pippa were right that "God's puppets first and last are we," even Guido's conduct would be explained and justified, for as he says, "I did / God's bidding and man's duty, so breathe free" (v. 1702–3). Similarly, he argues that

> all this trouble has come on me
> Through my persistent treading in the paths
> Where I was trained to go,—wearing that yoke
> My shoulder was predestined to receive,
> Born to the hereditary stoop and crease. (v. 123–27)

As Slinn notes, Guido explicitly represents himself as a puppet and therefore a "victim of society's conflicting requirements": "Guido can be said to exist, as in his second monologue, only as a self-dramatising consciousness, defending himself through transferring responsibility from himself as puppet to social determinism as puppet-master" (*Browning*, 117).

This seems a weak enough defense, but it is precisely the defense made for himself by the infinitely more likable Fra Lippo Lippi. As the example of Caponsacchi indicates, good and bad characters alike are puppets in *The Ring and the Book:* the speaker of the introduction, Browning himself apparently, is conducted like a puppet to the old yellow book: "(Mark the predestination!) when a Hand / Always above my shoulder, pushed me once . . . Across a square in Florence, crammed with booths" (i. 40–43) to the booth selling the book and to the book itself. Even Pompilia, cast in the role of wife and of damsel in distress, has no choice but to play out her role, and at one point she rather pathetically describes herself as a marionette dangling in the void, "held up, amid the nothingness, / By one or two truths only—thence I hang, / And there I live" (vii. 603–5). Though Browning was well aware of his role as puppet-master, his representation of people manipulating others as puppets always implies a moral judgment against such assumptions of mastery. Most conspicuously, Guido is plainly evil when he buys a wife and expects her to sing the song he dictates: "With a wife I look to find all wifeliness? / As when I buy, timber and twig, a tree—/ I buy the song o' the nightingale inside" (v. 604–6). Using a similar analogy, he compares Pompilia to a purchased hawk, for him to "hoodwink, starve and properly train . . . / And should she prove a haggard,—twist her neck!" (v. 709–10). As he sees it, the crime of which he is accused is merely his justifiable effort to be the puppet-master, "To practice mastery, prove my mastership" (v. 717). Further, to produce the false love letters that will be used in evidence against her, Guido actually manipulates Pompilia's hand to form the letters, much as Porphyria's lover manipulated her limbs for his satisfaction.

The manipulation of a person like a meat puppet is far from being an obscure innuendo in the poem. In the poem's most startling resemblance to Benjaminian melancholy as an allegorical brooding on a skull or a corpse, the pope foregrounds the grotesque notion of treating people like meat puppets with his account of the trial of the dead Pope Formosus:

> the great door of the church
> Flew wide, and in they brought Formosus' self,
> The body of him, dead, even as embalmed
> And buried duly in the Vatican
> Eight months before, exhumed thus for the nonce.
> They set it, that dead body of a Pope,
> Clothed in pontific vesture now again,
> Upright on Peter's chair as if alive. (x. 37–44)

The manipulation of a corpse inevitably recalls "Porphyria's Lover," and the final phrase of course recalls the portrait of the Duchess, "looking as if she were alive." This bizarre imagery is not merely incidental to *The Ring and the Book,* but rather seems a deliberate parody of the poetic form and method described in the introduction as a Frankenstein-like attempt to bring the dead to life. The poet cannot repeat "God's process" of creating life from nothing, but "in man's due degree . . . / Creates, no, but resuscitates, perhaps" (i. 717–19):

> although nothing which had never life
> Shall get life from him, be, not having been,
> Yet, something dead may get to live again,
> Something with too much life or not enough,
> Which, either way imperfect, ended once:
> An end whereat man's impulse intervenes,
> Makes new beginning, starts the dead alive . . .
> —Mimic creation, galvanism for life. (i. 727–40)

Browning was sufficiently serious about this account of his poetic process that he took care to disavow the resemblance to Faustian overreaching, and while not going so far as to claim a Christ-like ability to bring the dead to life, he puts his process in the company of Elisha's:

> Oh, Faust, why Faust? Was not Elisha once?—
> Who bade them lay his staff on a corpse-face.
> There was no voice, no hearing: he went in
> Therefore, and shut the door upon them twain,
> And prayed unto the Lord: and he went up
> And lay upon the corpse, dead on the couch,
> And put his mouth upon its mouth, his eyes
> Upon its eyes, his hands upon its hands,
> And stretched him on the flesh; the flesh waxed warm:
> And he returned, walked to and fro the house,
> And went up, stretched him on the flesh again,
> And the eyes opened. 'Tis a credible feat
> With the right man and way. (i. 760–72)

Browning's claim to speak the whole truth in *The Ring and the Book* is simply that he is the right man and knows the right way to bring his long dead characters to life, "have [his] will with" them and so "title . . . the dead alive once more" (i. 778–79). It is an extraordinary claim, but Browning's mention of Faust and his parody of himself with the anecdote about Formosus seem deliberately to undermine and subvert it. Browning had not long ago been outraged by contemporary spiritualist claims to make the dead speak and had satirized them in "Mr. Sludge the Medium," which has long been recognized as a poem in which he put to the test claims for authority much like his own. In addition, in "Mesmerism" he had recently shown the danger of contemporary claims to exercise power over others, to have one's way with them. Far from claiming transcendent truth in *The Ring and the Book,* Browning sums up with one crucial lesson: "This lesson, that our human speech is naught, / Our human testimony false, our fame / And human estimation words and wind" (xii. 834–36).

The Ring and the Book is fittingly seen as the climax of Browning's career by Dorothy Mermin, who quotes these lines and draws the conclusion that "Only the artist can interpret truly, only art can speak truly" (*Audience,* 64), but considering Browning's consistent suspicion of claims for authoritative analysis and speech, it would seem that he was a good deal less inclined than this to make claims for even the artist.

The Ring and the Book is an apotheosis of Browning's poetic process of insinuating himself under other people's skin to render them symbolic counters of psychic states otherwise unrepresentable. It is therefore also the apotheosis of his poetics of melancholy, an "allegory of his own mind" that replaces infinite subjects with finite objects, people with puppets and corpses, and vital language, "brother's speech," with the empty clothes of thought, even the cerements of thought, mere filthy rags of speech. Inevitably failing to bring the dead to life, *The Ring and the Book* remains a brilliant testimony to the intensity of melancholic brooding upon death.

CHAPTER FIVE

Edward Fitzgerald: Melancholy, Orientalism, Aestheticism

Edward Fitzgerald was an exact contemporary of Tennyson and the Brownings, as well as a close friend of Thackeray and Carlyle, and he was probably the most melancholy member of this set of marked melancholiacs. Unlike Tennyson and the Brownings, however, Fitzgerald was an agnostic, and consequently he lacked the strong sense of conscience and duty that might have disciplined and given shape to his anomic imagination. As a result, Fitzgerald saw himself as effeminate, as less a potential "masculine" poet than a mere "feminine" man of taste. As a result, his life and poetic career strikingly reflect the gradual transition of Victorian England from a culture of production to a commodity culture: a major element in his melancholy is his own personal abandonment of original poetry and his sad resignation to a life of passive connoisseurship of aesthetic commodities. Fittingly, his greatest poetic production, "The Rubaiyat of Omar Khayyam," became not only one of the great poems of the age, but in its various manifestations in giftbook editions, one of its greatest aesthetic commodities. With absurd appropriateness, my voice-recognition software recognizes "Omar Khayyam" as "Hallmark I am."[1]

Fitzgerald's own scant original poetry, lacking the striving and moral earnestness of his contemporaries, settled into a distinctly minor key of melancholy in insignificant reveries of passive melancholia such as "The Meadows in Spring":

    'Tis a sad sight
      To see the year dying;

When Autumn's last wind
Sets the yellow wood sighing
   Sighing, ah sighing. (*Letters,* 1: 98)

The poem seems to epitomize Fitzgerald's life, as described by A. C. Benson: "a melancholy life it was. 'His life,' said one of his friends, 'is a succession of sighs, each stifled ere half-uttered; for the uselessness of sighing is as evident to him as the reason for it'" (177). Fitzgerald stifled his poetic sighing because, like Arnold, he believed that the melancholy of his age and his own temperament were unpoetic.

Fitzgerald would probably not have diverted his melancholy into more significant works than "The Meadows in Spring" if he had not found himself in sympathy with the Persian texts introduced to him by E. B. Cowell. It was seemingly inevitable that Fitzgerald would be introduced to Orientalism in one form or another: not only Tennyson but also Fitzgerald's other Cambridge contemporaries were all finding relief from the rigor of Victorian masculine earnestness in detours through the supposedly effeminate and lushly sensual East. In a letter to Frederick Tennyson, Fitzgerald noted that the vigorous conservatism of Disraeli's "Young England" was being pushed aside by a glut of Orientalism: Kinglake's *Eothen,* Milnes's *Palm Leaves,* Warburton's *Crescent and the Cross,* and Henry Herbert's *Marmaduke Wyvil.* As Fitzgerald sardonically put it, "Ye Gods! In Shakespeare's day the nuisance was the Monsieur Travellers who had 'swum in a gundello'; but now the bores are those who have smoked *tschibouques* with a *Peshaw!* Deuce take it: I say 'tis better to stick to muddy Suffolk" (*Letters,* 1: 480). Fitzgerald did stick to muddy Suffolk, but touched perhaps with the traditional scholar's melancholy, he could not resist being drawn into the study of Persia by Cowell, and, in particular, into the study of a Persian allegory by Jámí that might almost have been a model for such melancholy allegories as Shelley's *Alastor* and Keats's *Endymion.* According to Fitzgerald, Jámí's "Salámán and Absál" was an allegory of "Persian Mysticism—perhaps the grand Mystery of all Religions" (*Letters,* 2: 219). Like *Alastor* and *Endymion,* Jámí's poem, or at least Fitzgerald's translation of it, is an allegory of the growth of the protagonist's mind spurred by erotic desire and pursuit of a lost ego-ideal (Lacan's phallus) in the form of a female beauty who seems an image of his own soul. Inevitably, erotic love "infected all his soul with melancholy" (Arberry, 71). Like Endymion, Salámán finds erotic satisfaction with his beloved, Absál, but unlike Endymion's beloved, Absál is not a goddess, and sexual gratification, as in courtly love, can only short-circuit any quest for full self-realization in wisdom. The meaning of Salámán's plight is provided by a Sage in language suggestive of Shelley's *Alastor* and of Ficino's neo-Platonic model of desire for a phantasmic erotic ideal that is degrading and bestial if the lover settles for a material embodiment, but leads to the highest wisdom if not short-circuited by sexual gratification:

> The Mighty Hand that mix'd thy Dust inscribed
> The Character of Wisdom on thy Heart;
> Oh Cleanse thy Bosom of Material Form,
> And turn the Mirror of the Soul to SPIRIT,
> Until it be with SPIRIT all possest,
> Drown'd in the Light of Intellectual Truth.
> Oh veil thine Eyes from Mortal Paramour,
> And follow not her Step! (76)

Salámán's SPIRIT is willing, but his flesh is weak, and he flees the dictates of conscience as represented by his father "in the Name of God" (75). The resultant conflict between his conscience and his desire is inevitably a will-destroying melancholy:

> Unto the Soul that is confused by Love
> Comes Sorrow after Sorrow—most of all
> To Love whose only Friendship is Reproof,
> And overmuch of Counsel—whereby Love
> Grows stubborn, and increases the Disease.
> Love unreproved is a delicious food;
> Reproved, is Feeding on one's own Heart's Blood. (77–78)

Like Keats's Endymion, Salámán weds himself to Sorrow, flees the dictates of conscience, and once again finds blissful repletion, this time on a paradisial isle. This sensual idyll, of course, is precisely the temptation that lures a prince from his duty or tempts a Victorian poet to "some paradisal isle" as in "Locksley Hall," or a reclusive, melancholy scholar-poet like Fitzgerald to sensual but emasculating Eastern idylls. The temptation is so great that it can be ended only by magic, in this case a supreme act of the father's will:

> To Gracelessness Ungracious he became,
> And, quite to shatter his rebellious Lust,
> Upon Salámán all his WILL discharged.
> And LO! SALÁMÁN to his Mistress turn'd,
> But could not reach her—look'd and look'd again,
> And palpitated tow'rd her—but in Vain!
> Oh Misery! what to the Bankrupt worse

Than Gold he cannot reach! To one Athirst
Than Fountain to the Eye and Lip forbid!—
Or than Heaven opened to the Eyes in Hell! (83)

In the Persian original this telepathy is merely magic, but for the Victorian Fitzgerald, as he explains in a note, it is the newest science: "He Mesmerizes Him!" (83n). The result, in either case, is that Salámán becomes Shelley's Poet seeking his vision of the soul within his soul, or an Endymion seeking the unattainable Cynthia, or more literally the prince seeking the character of Wisdom on his heart, turning the mirror of the soul to SPIRIT. In short, "Salámán and Absál," in Fitzgerald's translation, turns out to be a remarkable reenactment of melancholy Romantic allegories of desire turned to the purposes of Wisdom and, further, of the Victorian exercise of manly self-control, enslaving sensuality to the stern control of "WILL."

"Salámán and Absál," however, does not end with Shelleyan longing for an ideal that cannot be reached because it is already internalized, but rather with a final allegorical movement that, like *Endymion,* allows a magical happiness by wedding the protagonist to an erotic object that is both a beautiful woman and the highest ideal. An allegory of ideology itself, it represents the imaginary solution of an insoluble problem.[2] *Salámán* builds a magic fire and enters it with Absál, but the flame

> passing him, consumed ABSÁL like Straw,
> Died his Divided Self, and there survived
> His Individual; and, like a Body
> From which the Soul is parted, all alone. (86)

Actually, as the poem later makes clear when expounding the allegory, what dies in the flame is not the soul but the body's sensuality; the fire is

> Ascetic Discipline
> That burns away the Animal Alloy,
> Till all the Dross of MATTER be consumed,
> And the Essential Soul, its raiment clean
> Of Mortal Taint, be left. (94–95)

Not surprisingly, the consummation of Absál is a torment to Salámán, who is a wiser but a sadder man. Still, in a deft pre-Freudian turn, this newer melancholy is not only *like* mourning but *is* mourning, so the pathological condition of melancholy without an apparent cause and therefore without limit is replaced by the "normal" condition of grief. Salámán goes from illness to health. Further, the Sage, assuming the role of therapist, is able by an act of will to engender a mourning like melancholia that will lead beyond the phantasm of sensual, erotic love to the better and higher libidinal object of the highest beauty and Wisdom. The Sage repeatedly raises a "Fantom Image" of Absál to pacify Salámán's grief, but then annihilates it and replaces Absál with "a Celestial love; / ZUHRAH . . . the Lustre of the Stars" (89). The allegory hardly needs the explication that Jámí, and Fitzgerald, provide:

> what is ZUHRAH?—that Divine Perfection,
> Wherewith the Soul inspir'd and all array'd
> In Intellectual Light is Royal blest,
> And mounts THE THRONE, and wears THE CROWN, and reigns
> Lord of the Empire of Humanity. (95)

Fitzgerald's "Salámán and Absál" is not a great poem, and it certainly cannot compete with his "Rubaiyat," but it is nevertheless a remarkable documentation of the intersection of late Romantic, early Victorian melancholy with a languorous desire for sensual pleasure and beauty best explored by an Oriental detour that subjects both effeminate longing and the East to the mastery of conscience. In an overtly allegorical form it represents both the erotic quests of *Alastor* and *Endymion* and also the major concerns of *Pauline, Paracelsus, Maud,* and *Sonnets from the Portuguese*: brooding on erotic desire that is ultimately a yearning for wholeness of being and that, barring magic or divine intervention, is sustainable only as the melancholy of "Infinite passion, and the pain / of finite hearts that yearn."

Fitzgerald was one of Tennyson's few friends who disagreed with Trench's dictum "Tennyson, we cannot live in art!" Rather, like Tennyson's soul in "The Palace of Art," he attempted to remove himself from the demands of Victorian life and live in a quiet aesthetic reverie—if not in a palace of art, at least in a suburban grange akin to Tennyson's "cottage in the vale" ("Palace of Art," 291). He was, however, troubled in conscience by this withdrawal from an active to a contemplative life, viewing it at times as effeminate self-indulgence and casting himself into a chaste and ascetically disciplined life of melancholy contemplation. He was troubled even that his poetic and scholarly Orientalism was mere sensual self-indulgence since he saw "effeminate Persian" as antithetical to vigorously English "masculine thought" (*Letters,* 2: 190), and he even had reservations about appropriating the exotic East as a kind of aesthetic courtesan: "there's all Turkey, Greece, and the East to be prostituted . . . ; and I fear we shan't hear the end of it in our lifetimes. Suffolk turnips seem to be so classical compared to all that sort of thing" (*Letters*, 1: 550). Consequently, it is entirely appropriate that he was attracted to Jámí's allegory with its magical cure for melancholy and surprising kinship with the Keatsian, Shelleyan poetry of sensation celebrated by Hallam.

Fitzgerald's poetry of sensation provides a clear link between the Victorianism of Hallam and Tennyson and the later Victorian aestheticism and decadence primarily through the publication and reception of "The Rubaiyat of Omar Khayyam," but both Tennyson and Fitzgerald saw art for art's sake as a kind of unmanly hedonism, and Fitzgerald worried that the "Rubaiyat" might be self-indulgent in this way. His sense of the moral value of "Salámán and Absál" and of the possibly corrupting effect of the "Rubaiyat" are both implied in his agreement to publish a fourth edition only on condition that it be bound with "Salámán and Absál," perhaps as an allegorical corrective pointing from sensual pleasure to Wisdom—or at least, in a Keatsian way, to a beauty that is not valued for its own sake, but because, in the vision of Zuhrah, beauty is truth. To the extent that he could control publication of the "Rubaiyat," Fitzgerald eventually stipulated that it not be published except "in more reputable Company," with "Salámán by way of Chaperon" (*Letters*, 4: 73).

"Salámán and Absál" may be seen as an allegorical justification of strenuous melancholy as a path to Wisdom, but Fitzgerald wrote the "Rubaiyat" in what he called a mood of "self-contented indolence" (*Letters*, 2: 50), more like sloth than like the heroic action that he believed necessary to the poet who would write a great poem. His advice to Tennyson had been to overcome the hypochondriacal melancholy indolence of an exhausted civilization, to "fly from England and go among savages" (*Letters*, 1: 623). Only in that way could he reinvigorate the poetic tradition with fresh blood—just what Lady Ellerton had told the poet to do in Kingsley's *Alton Locke*,[3] but he himself turned rather guiltily to the exhausted vein of a great civilization that he believed had been in decline for many centuries. Thinking himself incapable of writing a great original poem, he tried to assuage his melancholy by immersing himself in the languorous, sensual mood of poetic melancholia, dealing in his own susceptibilities by reading and translating the works of kindred spirits. His first exercise in translation, in fact, was with Lucretius, and he found solace for his sadness in other melancholy Epicureans as well, particularly Omar Khayyam: "Omar breathes a sort of Consolation to me! Poor Fellow; I think of him, and Olivier Basselin, and Anacreon; lighter Shadows among the Shades, perhaps, over which Lucretius presides so grimly" (*Letters*, 2: 273).

Fitzgerald was at the most melancholy period in his life when he began to read Omar Khayyam. As a letter to Thackeray indicates, his indolence was anything but self-contented: "Life every day seems a more total failure and mess to me: but it is yet bearable: and I am become a sad Epicurean—just desirous to keep on the windy side of bother and pain" (*Letters,* 2: 75). The tradition of melancholy as a self-indulgently indolent luxury was consolation, but like Arnold, Fitzgerald saw it as unpoetic.

Just as Arnold said of "The Scholar Gypsy" that "Homer *animates*—Shakespeare *animates*—the Gipsy Scholar at best awakens a pleasing melancholy," Fitzgerald also believed that poetry should animate, or should at the very least be vigorous. As he frequently repeated, in poetry "all is got if '*go*' is got" (*Letters,* 2: 74), and he had lost what little "go" he had ever had. Unlike Arnold, who blamed the unpoetic age for his inability to write animating poetry, Fitzgerald blamed himself—he could have gone among savages or at least struggled on in the "vigorous North," but he chose instead to "go on puddling away faintly at Persian" and luxuriating in "the Sweetmeat, Childish Oriental World" (*Letters,* 2: 184). For this reason the resultant poem, the "Rubaiyat," is, as Christopher Decker has said,

> one of the best poems ever written about the condition of not being a great poet. . . . It praises humility not because it is Christian to do so, but because the humble life is one in which disappointment is so reduced as to assume the features of contentment. For Fitzgerald, rhyme's vexation was less a dull narcotic, numbing pain than a way of taming the fierceness of boredom and loss. (*Rubaiyat,* xx)

Unlike Browning, Fitzgerald seemed content with being a failure like Andrea del Sarto, but ironically, his retreat into melancholy produced a great poem after all. He had given up the idea of writing a great original poem, but his translation of Omar Khayyam is itself an original poem, inspired by Khayyam but recreating the Persian in his own image and producing a single unified English poem out of Khayyam's disconnected Persian quatrains. Scholars have disagreed about the extent to which Omar Khayyam was a religious poet or was indeed the sad Epicurean that Fitzgerald thought him, but Fitzgerald himself was sure that, as Iago said of Desdemona, the wine he drank was made of grapes, that he wrote "without any Pretense at divine Allegory: his wine is the veritable juice of the grape" (*Rubaiyat,* 6). In any case, Fitzgerald was not concerned to make an accurate translation but to "tesselate" the "scattered" Persian quatrains into a "very pretty *Eclogue,*" though one with an un-Christian and un-Victorian moral (*Letters,* 2: 294), and "As to my making Omar worse than he is in that Stanza about Forgiveness—you [Cowell] know I have translated none [of the quatrains] literally, and have generally mashed up two—or more—into one" (*Letters*, 3: 68). What Fitzgerald saw in Omar Khayyam was his own nineteenth-century skepticism, melancholia, and Epicureanism, and he therefore appropriated it as not only a kindred spirit but even as an intellectual property; writing to Cowell, he asserted that "in truth I take old Omar rather more as my property than yours: he and I are more akin, are we not? You see all [his] Beauty, but you can't feel *with* him in some respects as I do" (*Letters*, 2: 305). Strikingly, in a letter to Cowell, Fitzgerald, the Victorian "Hamlet of literature" (Benson, 188), expressed his own immoral skepticism not only behind the mask of Omar Khayyam but also behind the mask of Hamlet's melancholy madness: "I think you would almost feel obliged to leave out the part of Hamlet in representing him to your Audience: for fear of Mischief. Now I do not wish to show Hamlet at his maddest but mad he must be shown, or he is no Hamlet at all" (*Letters*, 2: 305).

The reference to Hamlet is especially important because it indicates how Fitzgerald was not, as he thought, disabled by unpoetic melancholy but empowered by the "imagination penetrative" of melancholy, epitomized by Hamlet's apostrophe to Yorick's skull. That Fitzgerald had precisely this apostrophe in mind is evident when he alludes to it in describing his "Epicurean Infidel" as a "poor little Persian Epicurean, who sings the old standing Religion of the World. 'Let us make the best of To-day,—who can answer for To-morrow!' To this complexion does one come at last?" (*Letters*, 2: 277).

The dominant theme of Fitzgerald's "Rubaiyat" is not Omar Khayyam's but is the theme of Hamlet's graveyard musings—that human life is returned to dust for any base use: "Imperious Caesar, dead and turned to clay / Might stop a hole to keep the wind away" (V.i.213–14). The "Rubaiyat" finds a better use for Caesar's clay, though life's insignificance and transience is no less sharply felt:

> I sometimes think that never blows so red
> The Rose as where some buried Caesar bled;
>   That every Hyacinth the Garden wears
> Dropt in its Lap from some once lovely Head. (xviii)

Like Ruskin, Fitzgerald broods most particularly on a Hamlet-like consideration of the lips that once had kissed:

> And this delightful Herb whose tender Green
> Fledges the River's Lip on which we lean—
>   Ah, lean upon it lightly! For who knows
> From what once lovely Lip it springs unseen! (xix)

The most insistent image of the "Rubaiyat" ineluctably summons Yorick's lips in tracing the clay lips of the wine cup to clay lips that once had laughed and kissed in life:

> Then to this earthen Bowl did I adjourn
> My Lip the secret Well of Life to learn:
>   And Lip to Lip it murmur'd—"While you live
> Drink!—for once dead you never shall return."
>
> I think the Vessel, that with fugitive
> Articulation answer'd, once did live,
>   And merry-make; and the cold Lip I kiss'd
> How many Kisses might it take—and give!
>
> For in the Market-place, one Dusk of Day,
> I watch'd the Potter thumping his wet Clay
>   And with its all obliterated Tongue
> It murmur'd—"Gently, Brother, gently, pray!" (xxxiv–xxxvi)

The melancholy lesson taught by the lip of the wine cup is entirely orthodox, merely that the body is dust and will to dust return, but Fitzgerald's agnosticism is suggested in a nihilism that also seems to doubt the immortality of the soul: "Thou art but what / Thou Shalt be—Nothing" (xlvii). Also, the still more subversive moral is that God wickedly made life in order to damn it. The stanza in which Fitzgerald may have made Omar "worse than he is" expresses this conviction:

> Oh, Thou, who Man of baser Earth didst make,
> And who with Eden didst devise the snake;
>   For all the Sins wherewith the Face of Man
> Is blackened, Man's Forgiveness give—and take! (lviii)

The close ties of the "Rubaiyat" to Hamlet enable us to see it as an example of melancholic allegory. Seeing the clay lips of the wine bowl as signs of living lips and their dissolution into dust, Omar Khayyam sees as the Benjaminian allegorist to whom nature appears "not in bud and bloom but in the overripeness and decay of its creation . . . As eternal transience."[4] The ultimate melancholy emblem is Yorick's skull or, in Benjamin's term, a "death's head . . . The figure of man's most extreme subjection to nature" (*Origin*, 166). Further, regarded as a translation, Fitzgerald's poem is implicitly allegorical in the sense that it uses language in which the words are at a double remove, at least, from the things signified. Fitzgerald's comments on his mode of translation emphasize the removal of signifier from signified in a striking way; other translators, he remarked, "try to render [elegant Persian] into *Elegant* English; but I think it should be translated *something* as the Bible is translated, preserving the Oriental Idiom. It should be kept as Oriental as possible, only using the most idiomatic Saxon *words* to convey the Eastern metaphor" (*Letters*, 2: 119). The reference to the Bible is to the most authoritative of English texts, but it subverts the authority of even the Bible with the reminder that the vigorous English words are already at a remove from the Oriental idiom, let alone the signified Truth. Further, it undermines the authority of Fitzgerald's English appropriation of Persian thought by stressing, first, the metaphoric character of the Eastern text and thus the originary separation of signifier from signified in the substitutions of emblem for identification, and second, the separation of Saxon words from Oriental idiom. All in all Fitzgerald's theory of translation emphasizes the Benjaminian or deManian sense of the ghostly emptiness of all language in which the sign can only be "*repetition* . . . of a previous sign with which it can never coincide, since it is the essence of this previous sign to be pure anteriority" (de Man, *Blindness*, 207).

Clearly the "Rubaiyat" epitomizes many of the various implications of poetic melancholy in the Victorian age. In the first place, it is bred in the Victorian sense of identification with the melancholy Hamlet, and it represents the "imagination penetrative" identified with Hamlet. Beyond this, it seeks poetic authority through an Oriental detour that will imitate the Bible's cultural authority as it subverts the Bible and even the logos underpinning Western thought by its anticipation, like Browning's, of the poststructuralist theory of language as an allegorical chain of signifiers forever removing itself further from lost and unrecoverable origins.

The great cultural importance of Fitzgerald's "Rubaiyat" is not merely in its exemplification of the Victorian age's melancholy agnosticism but in its exemplary severing of poetic beauty from any kind of Christian duty: it demonstrates that skepticism and pessimism were not poetically disabling but could be the very stuff of poetic beauty. The story of the Victorian reception of the "Rubaiyat" has been often told, but a brief review of it here will help to establish the transition from Tennysonian melancholy to the art-for-art's-sake aestheticism of Swinburne and the Pre-Raphaelites and finally to the "New Hedonism" of Pater's aestheticism and Wilde's decadence. Not expecting much, if anything, in the way of sales, Fitzgerald anonymously printed 250 copies of the "Rubaiyat" at his own expense with the antiquarian bookseller Bernard Quaritch, and after taking a few copies for distribution to friends he left the bulk of the edition with Quaritch.[5] The demand was nil, and the pamphlets languished in

Quaritch's shop until the poem was "discovered" by the Pre-Raphaelites. Swinburne's account of this discovery cannot be regarded as gospel truth, but it will do to summon the spirit of the Pre-Raphaelite enthusiasm:

> Two friends of Rossetti's—Mr. Whitley Stokes and Mr. Ormsby—told him (he told me) of this wonderful little pamphlet for sale on a stall . . . to which Mr. Quaritch, finding that the British public unanimously declined to give a shilling for it, had relegated it to be disposed of for a penny. Having read it, Rossetti and I invested upwards of sixpence apiece—or possibly threepence—I would not wish to exaggerate our extravagance—in copies at that not exorbitant price. Next day we thought we might get some more for presents among friends—but the man at the stall asked twopence! Rossetti expostulated with him in terms of such humorously indignant remonstrance as none but he could ever have commanded. We took a few, and left him. In a week or two, if I'm not mistaken, the remaining copies were sold at a guinea; I have since—as I dare say you have—seen copies offered for a still more extravagant price. (*Letters*, 6: 188)

Swinburne, Rossetti, and others paid tribute to the "Rubaiyat" by raising its commodity value but more significantly by raising its cultural value. Swinburne paid the even greater compliment of imitation, using the stanza form of the "Rubaiyat" for one of his most important poems, "Laus Veneris," the title poem of the first edition of *Poems and Ballads*,[6] the book that outraged Victorian morality and contributed importantly to the aestheticist and decadent late Victorian reevaluation of the relation of the arts to morality and to the social order. Like the "Rubaiyat," "Laus Veneris" represents an embrace of languorous beauty at the expense of moral striving. "Laus Veneris" is Swinburne's version of the Tannhäuser legend and recounts the knight's deliberate choice of the pagan Venus and sensual mortality over the Christian religion, asceticism, and the empty promise of immortal, if ethereal, life. Swinburne's poem, with its explicitly sensual refusal of Christ, is far more shocking than Fitzgerald's "sad Epicureanism":

> Alas, Lord, surely thou art great and fair.
> But, lo, her wonderfully woven hair!
>   And thou didst heal us with thy piteous kiss;
> But see now, Lord, her mouth is lovelier. (ll.17–20)

The moral difference between Fitzgerald's and Swinburne's poems may be most clearly seen in the moral connotations of the technically synonymous terms Epicureanism and hedonism. Walter Pater famously remarked that the word "hedonism" should be avoided around those who do not know Greek because its connotations are so emphatically of immoral sensuality as opposed to the Greek ideal of calm and avoidance of pain. Fitzgerald's poem is sensual with the melancholy dignity of Epicurean Stoicism; Swinburne's poem, on the other hand, courts the moral notoriety of hedonism, and because it vigorously pits the strictures of conscience against sensual indulgence, its sadomasochism represents a far more intense, pathological melancholy:

> Alas thy beauty! for thy mouth's sweet sake
> My soul is bitter to me, my limbs quake
> As water, as the flesh of men that weep
> As their heart's vein whose heart goes nigh to break. (ll.145–48)

A full discussion of Pre-Raphaelitism and aestheticism is beyond the scope of the present study, but it is very much to the point to note that Fitzgerald, far from being the end of a line of melancholy poetics, clearly connects Tennyson's early Victorian poetry of sensation to the sensualism of late Victorian poetry and poetics. Fitzgerald's and Tennyson's commitment to early and mid-Victorian ideals of masculine vigor made them ambivalent about indulgence in the lassitude of melancholia, but for the Pre-Raphaelites and aestheticists, the commitment to art, and particularly to sensual beauty as an aesthetic ideal, led to a positive celebration of melancholy even as a pathological condition, a disease. "Laus Veneris," like William Morris's "The Defence of Guenevere," very specifically represents what Pater described as the defining characteristic of aesthetic poetry: "the deliberate choice between Christ and a rival lover" (191). In his much quieter, more decorous way, Fitzgerald made the same choice through Omar Khayyam's call for "a Flask of Wine, a Book of Verse—and thou" rather than the promise of Paradise (xi). It is no wonder that the aesthetic school admired Fitzgerald, whose life and poetry seem defined in Pater's definition of aesthetic poetry as melancholy: "it is that inversion of homesickness known to some, that incurable thirst for the sense of escape, which no actual form of life satisfies" (190). Oddly, and no doubt coincidentally, Pater's language echoes Paracelsus's longing for a "form of life unknown." In lines that seem to sum up the "Rubaiyat," Pater further characterized aesthetic poetry as the "continual suggestion, pensive or passionate, of the shortness of life. This is contrasted with the bloom of the world, and gives new seduction to it—the sense of death and the desire of beauty: the desire of beauty quickened by the sense of death" (198). Pater's most notorious exposition of aesthetic Epicureanism brings us full circle back to melancholy as "the emotion of the trapped," the emotion of Mariana or of the Soul in "The Palace of Art." Unlike the melancholy of high Victorianism, however, the late-century melancholy of "art for art's sake," intimated in Fitzgerald's translations and explicit in the work of Pater, Swinburne, Rossetti, and Wilde, has more or less resolved the dialectic of social conscience and Romantic self by adopting a late Romanticism that sets aside conscience, as it sets aside social purpose, as irrelevant to the purposes of art. Pater's prescription for the aesthetic life, for "success in life," entirely sets aside all that lies outside the "abysmal deeps of personality" as it prescribes hedonistic immersion in solipsistic reverie: "to burn always" with a hard, gemlike flame in the ecstatic reception of the "impressions, images, sensations" that constitute all experience:

> [E]xperience, already reduced to a swarm of impressions, is ringed round for each of us by that thick wall of personality through which no real voice has ever pierced on its way to us, or from us to that which we can only conjecture to be without. Every one of those impressions is the impression of the individual in his isolation, each mind keeping as a solitary prisoner its own dream of a world. (160)

The emotion of the trapped carried to its utmost pitch of intensity, a kind of acute melancholia, is an exaggerated version of sad Epicureanism: it is what Dorian Gray called the "new hedonism," and it is a condition explicitly characterized elsewhere in Pater's work as a disease, the "malady of reverie." By century's end the Wordsworthian, Coleridgean paradigm of a healthy imagination has been transformed through various stages of melancholia to the notion of poetic imagination as morbidly diseased.

Pater's definition of aesthetic poetry, in fact, is a fair definition of melancholy itself as the emotion of the trapped: "a passion of which the outlets are sealed, begets a tension of nerve, in which the sensible world comes to one with a reinforced brilliancy and relief—" (193). This passion, a strong narcotic, like a poison in the blood, obviously heightens Fitzgerald's melancholy reverie, or even Mariana's, to a pitch approaching insanity, like a "beautiful disease or disorder of the senses" (192), but it originates in a Keatsian as well as Fitzgeraldian and profoundly Swinburnean sense that awareness of the finality of death intensifies the sense of beauty. In Wallace Stevens's phrase, "Death is the mother of beauty" ("Sunday Morning") or in Fitzgerald's, "never blows so red / the rose as where some buried Caesar bled" (xviii).

Finally, seeing the nineteenth-century poetic tradition as it passes from Tennyson's generation through Fitzgerald and into the aestheticism of Pater and Wilde clarifies the often-noted gender transgressiveness in late-century aestheticism. From Tennyson's association of melancholy sensibility with women and Hallam's sense of the transgressive nature of indulgence in melancholy, poetic sensibility had been figured as potentially unmanly, a loss of vigor and self-control in exchange for appropriating a female or even Oriental erotic reverie. As Fitzgerald saw it, such effeminate melancholy was disabling to masculine, poetic creativity and led him to a resigned acceptance of the devolution of the poet to the mere aesthete, the womanly man of taste: "I pretend to no Genius, but to Taste: which, according to my aphorism, is the feminine of Genius" (*Letters*, 1: 669). The resolution of the gender ambiguities attending melancholy and genius may, perhaps, be glimpsed in the deliberate assumption by the homoerotic Pater, Wilde, and others, of the highest aesthetic sensibility in a disease, a disorder of the senses, as late-century science constructed the discourse of homosexuality, and of a homosexual identity. This is not the place to discuss the late Victorian imbrication of the discourse of melancholia and sexology, but only to note that the disengagement of poetry from the severe moralism of the Victorian age in "art for art's sake" and decadence results in a lassitude commonly regarded as melancholy, but much diminished from the fierce dialectic of conscience and mutinous feeling that I have been exploring. The disengagement, moreover, is also a disengagement from the central moral, ethical, and ideological values of the age, and it marks the marginalization of poetry from public discourse that remains with us over a century later.

Notes

Chapter One

1. The phrase "the eternal I AM" is from Coleridge's definition of the imagination in chapter 13 of *Biographia Literaria,* and "Nature's holy plan" is a late variant from Wordsworth's "Lines Written in Early Spring" *(Lyrical Ballads,* 76n*).* See also Coleridge's discussion of "The Poet, described in ideal perfection" in chapter 14 of *Biographia Literaria.* For a full discussion of the development of poetic authority in Wordsworth and Coleridge, see Riede, *Oracles.*

2. T. S. Eliot may well have been thinking of Arnold's rejection of *Empedocles* when he described the problem of Hamlet as "an emotion which can find no outlet in action. . . . The intense feeling, ecstatic and terrible, without an object or exceeding its object, is something which every person of sensibility has known" ("Hamlet," 102).

3. A critical element in the discourse about melancholy from the time of the ancient Greeks, of course, had been the notion that melancholy is the disease of scholars and poets and, in general, that it is the distinctive mark of men of genius. As Klibansky, Panofsky, and Saxl discuss at length in their classic *Saturn and Melancholy,* the belief that melancholy is the invariable condition of exceptional men had its origins in Aristotle's "Problem XXX.I," which began with the simple question "Why is it that all those who have become eminent in philosophy or politics or poetry or the arts are clearly melancholics?" (18). With the beginnings of humanism in the early Renaissance, Marsilio Ficino and other neo-Platonists definitively established the modern idea of "genius" based on the melancholy humor, particularly describing the "self-sufficient 'homo literatus'" as "torn between the extremes of self-affirmation, sometimes rising to hubris, and self-doubt sometimes sinking to despair; and the experience of this dualism roused him to discover the new intellectual pattern, which was a reflection of this tragic and heroic disunity—the intellectual pattern of 'modern genius'" (247).

4. James's comments notwithstanding, however, psychology never entirely displaced spiritual concerns with materialism. Jenny Bourne Taylor has pointed out that "'Psychology' was firstly understood as the 'study of the soul' and although by mid-century the emphasis had shifted to the mind and the brain, this centrality of the soul, underpinned by many of the assumptions of natural theology, remained essentially intact" (197).

5. In *The Physiology and Pathology of the Mind* (1867), Maudsley did

momentarily entertain the notion that insanity and genius might be related, but he quickly rejected the notion that "a morbid state of nervous element is the condition of genius" with the observation that "any one so constituted is nowise an example of the highest genius; for he lacks, by reason of his great sensibility, the power of calm, steady, and complete mental assimilation, and must fall short of the highest intellectual development" (quoted in Radden, *Nature,* 243).

6. The idea that the Victorians were troubled by a sense of the mind divided against itself is not a new one, of course. See Miyoshi's important overview of the topic.

7. As Christopher Herbert has compellingly demonstrated, a sense of fragmented or fractured consciousness, which he describes as anomie, is endemic in Victorian thought. My point in suggesting that this Victorian state of mind be recognized as melancholia rather than (or in addition to) anomie is not simply to provide an alternative label, but rather to provide an analytic structure in the polarization of self and character, and to suggest a psychological and cultural discourse that enables us better to see how the loss of a sense of unity with oneself could be seen not only by Victorians like Arnold and Carlyle as a disabling pathology but simultaneously by Victorians like Browning, Hallam, and Tennyson as a source of poetic meaning.

8. David Adams links Freud, Nietzsche, and Benjamin in a tradition of melancholy:

> Nietsche's Übermensch belongs to a long line of belated figures characterized by the inhuman demands placed upon them. The *Übermensch,* like Freud's *Über-ich* burdened ego and Walter Benjamin's angel of history carry within their names an indication of the exta-human nature of their desire to exercise a redemptive memory. The melancholy and horror to which each succumbs is a symptom of the human will divided against itself, unable to make whole the accumulating wreakage of history. (85)

For a discussion of the guilt associated with melancholy, see Benjamin, *Origin,* 224–25.

9. See Rowlinson, "Lyric," for a discussion of the effects of commodity culture on lyric poetry in the nineteenth century.

10. Wordsworth did not specifically mention modern journalism, but he was evidently describing it when he argued that the "most effective" causes of the "savage torpor" were "the great national events which are daily taking place, and the encreasing [*sic*] accumulation of men in cities, where the uniformity of their occupations produces a craving for extraordinary incident which the rapid communication of intelligence hourly gratifies" (*Prose Works,* 1: 128).

11. For a powerful reading of Kant's *Critique of Judgment* in these terms see Davis, 59–97.

12. For a full discussion of Arnold's thwarted attempt to represent inwardness fully in this poem, see Riede, *Matthew Arnold,* 175–95.

13. See Bronfen for a full discussion of this image and related issues.

14. For a pertinent discussion of the relation of sound in poetry to inwardness, see Ong.

15. "The Topography of Reality: Sketching a Metapsychology of Secrets," in

The Shell and the Kernel, 158. For Abraham and Torok, Reality, with a capital R, is "defined as what is rejected, masked, denied precisely as 'reality'; it's that which *is*, all the more so since it cannot be known; in short, reality is defined as a secret" (157).

16. See Benjamin's comment that allegory corresponds "perfectly to the commodity fetish" (*Arcades*, 368).

17. Carlyle characteristically berates surface "truths" as superficial "formulas" and "hearsays," and he argues that heroic minds pierce to the "mystic deeps of man's soul" (*Works*, 27: 30). See, for example, the argument in "Characteristics" that "of our thinking, we might say, it is but the mere upper surface that we shape into articulate Thoughts; underneath the region of argument and conscious discourse, lies the region of meditation; here in its quite mysterious depths, dwells what vital force is in us; here, if aught is to be created, and not merely manufactured and communicated, must the work go on" (*Works*, 28: 4–5).

18. Demogorgon in *Prometheus Unbound* speaks of the impossibility of expressing the secrets beneath the veil of life: "If the Abysm / Could vomit forth its secrets: but a voice / Is wanting, the deep truth is imageless" (iv. 114–16). Shelley anticipated a Nietzschean view of the symbolic order as the human construction of what we call empirical reality—the veil that those who live call life does not correspond to the deep truth of the *ding an sich*.

19. Despite his usual dismissals of Shelley, Carlyle here combines his allusion to *Hamlet* with an allusion to Shelley's account of melancholy in modern poetry in "To a Sky-Lark": "We look before and after, / And pine for what is not—/ Our sincerest laughter / With some pain is fraught—/ Our sweetest songs are those that tell of saddest thought."

20. Benjamin is seemingly inconsistent about the relation of allegory to the veil or the vesture of deep truth. Usually he regards the veil of representation as mere semblance, as in his comment that "allegory, as the sign that is pointedly set off against its meaning, has its place in art as the antithesis to the beautiful appearance (*Schein*) in which signifier and signified flow into each other" (*Arcades*, 374). In this view allegory is a destructive, even deconstructive, mode. As Stanley Corngold has shown, however, Paul de Man recognized in Benjamin's work a sense that allegory may also incarnate an outward appearance that effectively communicates the deep truths of the inner self. Corngold notes that in *Blindness and Insight*, "de Man composes an unacknowledged paraphrase of Benjamin's thesis on obscurity: "'[The] outward appearance [of the *schöne seele*],' he writes, 'receives its beauty from an inner glow (or *feu sacré*) to which it is so finely attuned that, far from hiding it from sight, it gives it just the right balance of opacity and transparency, thus allowing the holy fire to shine without burning' (158). See W. David Shaw, *The Lucid Veil*, for a thorough analysis of the ubiquitous imagery of the veil to represent mystery in Victorian literature.

21. The painted veil is of course most famously Shelley's image, but Carlyle used it as well: "only on a canvas of Darkness, such is man's way of being, could the many-coloured picture of our Life paint itself and shine" (*Works*, 28: 26).

22. See Benjamin, *Origin*, 175–76, on the dialectic of sound and content in poetry.

23. In *Allegories of Reading* de Man, fortuitously echoing Adorno, claims that Benjamin's *Origin of German Tragic Drama* fails to produce the "truly dialectical"

history of Romanticism that de Man evidently saw himself writing because, like Hegel, Benjamin bypasses the Romantic moment.

24. In *Arcades* Benjamin quotes this phrase from *Origin* to elucidate the meaning of Baudelaire's nineteenth-century allegory (324).

25. *Letters*, 1: 35. The editors of the letters point out that this is partly a recollection of Sir Thomas Browne's remark in *Christian Morals* that "The created world is but a small parenthesis in eternity," and that the specifics of the "shelf" are apparently recollected from reading Lyell.

26. For Benjamin's arguments about redemptive language, see Pensky, 122–23. For a compelling argument that Benjamin's redemption of ruins in allegory follows a strict secular, even Marxist, logic, see Buck-Morss, 115–24.

Chapter Two

1. The bride abandoned by her lover is also one of Freud's examples of the inferior female melancholic.

2. Christ's *The Finer Optic* discusses the significance of a heightened attention to detail across a broad spectrum of Victorian works, conspicuously including the poetry of Tennyson and Rossetti and the discussion of pathetic fallacy in Ruskin's *Modern Painters*.

3. For a fascinating discussion of the afterlives of words in Tennyson's poetry, see Douglas-Fairhurst, 182–269.

4. For an excellent discussion of Tennyson's contribution to the conception of Englishness, see Lucas, chapter 8.

5. See the editorial comments in Tennyson, *Poems*, 1: 148n.

6. Tennyson's focus on commodity culture is also representative of nineteenth-century allegory as Benjamin understood it. Benjamin's emphasis on allegory as a record of ruin and decay is even intensified in his shift from German baroque drama to the modern world. As Kelley puts it, "whereas decay was [in German baroque culture] a melancholy, plodding affair, in [the "commodified world"] it is very nearly instantaneous and, as such, a shocking sign that decay and ruin, not continuity, make history" (253).

7. For a discussion of Arthur as conscience see Reynolds, 246–47.

Chapter Three

1. Citations of contemporary reviews refer to the convenient reprinting in *Correspondence*.

2. In a lucid discussion that I need not rehearse here, Schiesari analyzes feminist versions of the psychoanalytic tradition from Luce Irigaray's denial of female melancholia to Kaja Silverman's argument that melancholy is an especially female "pathology"—"a psychic condition which is somehow endemic to the female version of the positive Oedipus complex" (69)—and to Julia Kristeva's assigning of an "asymbolic" depression to most women, while attributing the powerful symbol-making capacity of melancholia primarily to male genius (78–95).

3. According to Gerard Manley Hopkins, "The Lake School expires in Keble and Faber and Cardinal Newman" (quoted in Fraser, 12).

4. The attempt to reconcile admiration for Byron with a belief in the intrinsic morality of poetry is evident in a letter of 1828: "I think that, humanly speaking, Lord Byron's extraordinary sensibility of heart & mind was his bane. He could not stand unhurt in that burning fiery furnace—for 'the likeness of the Son of God' was not in the fire! Religious knowledge he had none; but every real poet must have *natural devotion*—& *he* was a real poet! . . . A relation of mine was in St Peters at Rome as Byron entered it,—& saw him throw himself in a transport of enthusiasm, on the earth before a cross, & kiss the feet of the Crucified. You see—the *knowledge* was not there—but the *feeling* was there!" (*Correspondence*, 2: 139).

5. Barrett wrote that "Through the whole course of my childhood, I had a steady indignation against Nature who made me a woman, and a determinate resolution to dress up in men's clothes . . . & go into the world to 'seek my fortune.' '*How*' was not decided; but I rather leant towards being poor Lord Byron's PAGE" (*Correspondence*, 6: 42).

6. For a discussion of the poem as subversive of "the acquiescent female tradition" (79), see Cooper, 73–79.

7. A whimsico-serious letter to Mary Mitford about her dog Dash makes it clear that the poem's moral brought Coleridge to mind. She advised Mitford not to "let the Cynics laugh at the dog-lovers—seeing that philo-dogism (if the dog may stand as a representative of all other 'blessed living' soulless things—) is far better & higher & holier than their philosophy. Do not men dishonour their own natures in casting scorn upon the creatures of their Creator?" (*Correspondence*, 3: 240).

8. Helen Cooper has pointed out the likeness to Tennyson's subjects, and she has also pointed out that Barrett had apparently not read Tennyson's poetry at this point. Much to Barrett's annoyance, contemporary reviewers also noted the resemblance to Tennyson and pointed out the evident "influence." Immediately after reading "The Poet's Vow," Mary Mitford wrote to Barrett, saying, "Do read Tennyson's 'Ladye of Shalot'" (*Correspondence*, 3: 195).

9. Her main criticism of Letitia Landon (L. E. L.), her only real rival as a woman poet, was that she lacked sincerity, that she failed to express her genuine individuality and fell into mere "convention," that "Her genius was not strong enough to assert itself in truth": "She was the actress and not Juliet" (*Correspondence*, 5: 72). Both as a poet and as a woman, sincerity—*truth*—was a moral imperative. L. E. L. "believed that great lie, *that poetry is fiction*—and it was fatal to her not merely as a poet but as a woman. It is a creed desecrative of the soul, & of nature, & of 'supernal spirits.' The ruin of it, extends beyond literature" (*Correspondence*, 5: 97). Because of the Victorian belief that women were closer to God than men in the simplicity and openness of their nature, anything other than fully sincere self-expression smacked of artifice, a sin against nature and against God. Presumably it was not by self-assertion but by fictionalizing oneself, by playing a role, that the poet might set herself in opposition to God's creation.

10. Helen Cooper, similarly, argues that by adopting the voice of Eve, Barrett "first challenged" the Romantic disenfranchisement of women poets by treating women as "the Other in male poetics" (6).

11. The desire to return to Eden is the theme of such poems as "The Deserted Garden," "The Lost Bower," and "Hector in the Garden."

12. Writing about mesmerism to Mary Russell Mitford, Barrett said, "I would give a great deal, *not to believe a word of it:* & I do believe, in spite of my repulsion. Some people say . . . 'If there's anything in it, the devil is in it'—and my

feeling is something approaching to *that*. If I believe, I tremble. Not that, in so many words, I set it down for Satanic influence—do not mistake me—: but that there is something horrible & cold to me in the whole matter & mystery—like the undressing of the soul from its familiar conventions & plunging of it, shiveringly, into a new element. In fact the whole Temple of Human nature seems rent from the top to the bottom, & to tremble before the flood of the agency. They may well call it,—as some mesmerists do,—a *modification of death*" (*Correspondence*, 9: 283). Here and elsewhere, Barrett's comments on mesmerism indicate a mixture of awe and horror at the possibility of an agency that could actually and literally provide the kind of absolute spiritual apocalypse for which she saw poetry striving but never fully achieving under the existing conditions of mortal existence.

13. See introduction, 32–33.

14. Looking at Barrett's specific allusions to the beloved Caterina of the Portuguese poet Camoens and at a 1678 translation of five letters written by a Portuguese nun, Leighton makes this point generally about the sonnets:

> Thus the title, *Sonnets from the Portuguese*, is one that teases with a wealth of literary connotations. It proposes a translation; it remembers another poem; it echoes, perhaps, the highly literary disposition of the Portuguese nun herself. However, the sense of derivativeness—the sense of a text remembering some other original—is a connotation which finds support, not only in these specific references, but also in a recurring anxiety about the language of feeling, expressed in the letters of both poets. The "dust of figures stirring" in the title of *Sonnets from the Portuguese* is not just a dust flung in the eyes of "Peeping Tom" readers. It is not just a decoy. It is also a quiet revelation. The idea of translation—of mediating what is remote and foreign—of writing at a distance from the original—is an idea that finds considerable support in certain preoccupations of both Robert's and Elizabeth's letters. ("Stirring," 229)

15. An almost identical moment occurs in Arnold's "Switzerland" series, which also exhibits the melancholy of love in a belated tradition. See Riede, *Matthew Arnold*, 163–80.

Chapter 4

1. For excellent readings along these lines, see Tucker, *Browning's Beginnings*, 30–52, and Armstrong, *Victorian Poetry*, 112–26.

2. Shaw explores Kierkegaardian elements in Browning's work at length throughout his *The Dialectical Temper* (1968).

3. Bagehot notes that he is quoting from "Locke on the Human Understanding," book iv, Chap. iii. i.2.

4. As various critics have discussed extensively, *Pippa Passes* constitutes a complete analysis of the human condition if, as Pippa says, "God's puppets, best and worst / Are we" ("Introduction," 195–96). See Tucker, *Browning's Beginnings*, 122–31; Slinn, *Browning;* and Riede, "Genre and Poetic Authority."

Chapter 5

1. A proof of artificial intelligence seems to be the mean-spirited critic in the software who also, ludicrously, calls the wine-bibbing "Rubaiyat" the "liver biopsy" and hears "Keatsian" as "cutesy."

2. See Jameson's definition of ideology as "the function of inventing imaginary or formal 'resolutions' to unresolvable social contradictions" (79). The unresolvable contradiction in this case is the impossibility of reconciling the erotic poetic imagination with the requirements of chaste, manly self-control.

3. See James Eli Adams, 120–21.

4. See chapter 1, 29.

5. See Decker for the full printing and publishing history, 30–45.

6. Due to his difficulty getting the volume published in England, the first edition was published in America under the title *Laus Veneris and Other Poems and Ballads*. The English edition was more simply called *Poems and Ballads*.

Works Cited

Abraham, Nicholas, and Maria Torok. *The Shell and the Kernel: Renewals of Psychoanalysis,* ed. and trans. Nicholas T. Rand. Chicago: University of Chicago Press, 1994.

———. *The Wolf Man's Magic Word: A Cryptonomy,* trans. Nicholas Rand, with a foreword by Jacques Derrida. Minneapolis: University of Minnesota Press, 1986.

Adams, David. *Colonial Odysseys.* Ithaca, N.Y.: Cornell University Press.

Adams, James Eli. *Dandies and Desert Saints: Styles of Victorian Manhood.* Ithaca, N.Y.: Cornell University Press, 1995.

Adorno, Theodor. *Aesthetic Theory,* ed. Gretel Adorno and Rolf Tiedemann, trans. Robert Hullot-Kentor. Minneapolis: University of Minnesota Press, 1997.

Agamben, Giorgio. *Stanzas: Word and Phantasm in Western Culture,* trans. Ronald L. Martinez. Minneapolis: University of Minnesota Press, 1993.

Albright, Daniel. *Tennyson: The Muses' Tug-of-War.* Charlottesville: University Press of Virginia, 1986.

Alexander, Edward. *Matthew Arnold, John Ruskin, and the Modern Temper.* Columbus: The Ohio State University Press, 1973.

Arata, Stephen. *Fictions of Loss in the Victorian Fin de Siècle: Identity and Empire.* Cambridge: Cambridge University Press, 1996.

Arberry, A. J. *Fitzgerald's Salaman and Absal: A Study.* Cambridge: Cambridge University Press, 1956.

Armstrong, Isobel. "Msrepresentation: Codes of Affect and Politics in Nineteenth-Century Women's Poetry." In *Women's Poetry, Late Romantic to Late Victorian: Gender and Genre,* ed. Isobel Armstrong and Virginia Blain. London: Macmillan, 1999, 3–32.

———. *Victorian Poetry, Poetics, and Politics.* London/New York: Routledge, 1993.

Arnold, Matthew. *The Complete Prose Works,* ed. R. H. Super. 11 vols. Ann Arbor: The University of Michigan Press, 1960–1977.

———. *The Letters of Matthew Arnold,* ed. Cecil Y. Lang. 6 vols. Charlottesville: University of Virginia Press, 1996–2001.

———. *The Poems of Matthew Arnold,* ed. Kenneth Allott, 2nd ed., Miriam Allott. New York: Longman, 1979.

Austin, Linda. "Reading Depression in Hardy's 'Poems of 1912–13.'" *Victorian Poetry* 36 (1998): 1–15.

Bagehot, Walter. "Wordsworth, Tennyson, and Browning, Or, Pure, Ornate, and Grotesque Art in English Poetry." In *Victorian Literature: Prose,* ed. G. B. Tennyson and Donald J. Gray. New York: Macmillan, 1976, 1025–34.

Barrett, Elizabeth. *Greek Christian Poets and the English Poets.* London: Chapman and Hall, 1863.

Batten, Guinn. *The Orphaned Imagination: Melancholy and Commodity Culture in English Romanticism.* Durham, N.C.: Duke University Press, 1998.

Benjamin, Walter. *The Arcades Project,* trans. Howard Eiland and Kevin McLaughlin. Cambridge, Mass.: Harvard University Press, 1999.

———. *Illuminations,* trans. Harry Zohn, ed. Hannah Arendt. New York: Schocken Books, 1969.

———. "On Language as Such, and on the Language of Man." In *One Way Street and Other Writings,* trans. Edmund Jephcott and Kingsley Shorter. London: Verso, 1985.

———. *The Origin of German Tragic Drama,* trans. John Osborne. London: NLB, 1977.

———. *Reflections: Essays, Aphorisms, Autobiographical Writings,* trans. Edmund Jephcott. New York: Harcourt, Brace, Jovanovich, 1978.

Benson, A. C. *Edward Fitzgerald.* New York: Macmillan, 1905.

Bloom, Harold. *The Anxiety of Influence: A Theory of Poetry.* London: Oxford University Press, 1973.

———. *The Ringers in the Tower: Studies in Romantic Tradition.* Chicago: The University of Chicago Press, 1971.

Bradley, A. C. *Shakespearean Tragedy.* Cleveland: Meridian Books, 1962.

Bronfen, Elisabeth. *Over Her Dead Body: Death, Femininity, and the Aesthetic.* New York: Routledge, 1992.

Brontë, Charlotte. Editor's Preface to the New 1850 Edition of *Wuthering Heights.* Reprint London: Penguin, 1965.

Browning, Elizabeth Barrett. *The Complete Works of Elizabeth Barrett Browning,* ed. Charlotte Porter and Helen A. Clarke. 6 vols. New York: Thomas Y. Crowell, 1900.

———, and Robert Browning. *The Brownings' Correspondence,* ed. Philip Kelley, Ronald Hudson, and Scott Lewis. 14 vols. to date. Winfield, Kan.: Wedgestone Press, 1984–.

Browning, Robert. *The Poems,* ed. John Pettigrew and Thomas J. Collins. 2 vols. New Haven, Conn.: Yale University Press, 1981.

———. *The Ring and the Book,* ed. Richard D. Altick. New Haven, Conn.: Yale University Press, 1971.

Buckley, Jerome Hamilton. *Tennyson: The Growth of a Poet.* Cambridge, Mass.: Harvard University Press, 1974.

Buck-Morss, Susan. *The Dialectics of Seeing: Walter Benjamin and the Arcades Project.* Cambridge, Mass.: The MIT Press, 1989.

Burke, Kenneth. *The Philosophy of Literary Form: Studies in Symbolic Action.* 3rd ed. rev. Berkeley: University of California Press, 1973.

Butler, Judith. *The Psychic Life of Power: Theories in Subjection.* Stanford: Stanford University Press, 1997.

Campbell, Matthew. *Rhythm and Will in Victorian Poetry.* Cambridge: Cambridge University Press, 1999.

Carlyle, Thomas. *The Collected Letters of Thomas and Jane Welsh Carlyle*, ed. Clyde de L. Ryals et al. 32 vols. to date. Durham, N.C.: Duke University Press, 1970–.

———. *The Works of Thomas Carlyle*. 30 vols. London: Chapman and Hall, 1896.

Chesterton, G. K. *Robert Browning*. London: Macmillan, 1922.

Christ, Carol. *The Finer Optic: The Aesthetic of Particularity in Victorian Poetry*. New Haven, Conn.: Yale University Press, 1975.

Coleridge, Samuel Taylor. *A Critical Edition of the Major Works*, ed. H. J. Jackson. Oxford: Oxford University Press, 1985.

———. *Lectures and Notes on Shakespeare and Other English Poets*. London: G. Bell and Sons, Ltd., 1814.

———. *The Statesman's Manual*. In *The Collected Works of Samuel Taylor Colderidge*, ed. R. J. White. London: Routledge & Kegan Paul, 1972), 3–114.

Colley, Ann. *Tennyson and Madness*. Athens: The University of Georgia Press, 1983.

Cooper, Helen. *Elizabeth Barrett Browning, Woman and Artist*. Chapel Hill: University of North Carolina Press, 1988.

Corngold, Stanley. "Genuine Obscurity Shadows the Semblance Whose Obliteration Promises Redemption: Reflections on Benjamin's 'Goethe's Elective Affinities.'" In *Ghosts: Interventions in Contemporary Literacy and Cultural Theory*, ed. Gerhard Richter. Stanford, Calif.: Stanford University Press, 2002.

Cosslett, Tess, ed. *Victorian Women Poets*. London: Longman, 1996.

Croker, John Wilson. "Poems by Alfred Tennyson." In *Tennyson's Poetry*, ed. Robert Hill Jr. New York: W. W. Norton & Co., 1999.

Culler, A. Dwight. *The Poetry of Tennyson*. New Haven, Conn.: Yale University Press, 1977.

David, Deirdre. *Intellectual Women and Victorian Patriarchy: Harriet Martineau, Elizabeth Barrett Browning, George Eliot*. Ithaca, N.Y.: Cornell University Press, 1987.

Davis, Walter A. *Deracination: Historicity, Hiroshima, and the Tragic Imperative*. Albany: State University of New York Press, 2000.

deGroot, Joanna. "'Sex' and 'Race': The Construction of Language and Image in the Nineteenth Century." In *Sexuality and Subordination*, ed. Susan Mendus and Jane Rendall. London/New York: Routledge, 1989, 89–138.

de Man, Paul. *Allegories of Reading: Figural Language in Rousseau, Nietzsche, Rilke, and Proust*. New Haven, Conn.: Yale University Press, 1979.

———. *Blindness and Insight: Essays on the Rhetoric of Contemporary Criticism*. 2nd ed. Minneapolis: University of Minnesota Press, 1983.

DeVane, William Clyde. *A Browning Handbook*. New York: Appleton-Century-Crofts, 1955.

Douglas-Fairhurst, Robert. *Victorian Afterlives: The Shaping of Influence in Nineteenth-Century Literature*. Oxford: Oxford University Press, 2002.

Drew, Philip, ed. *Robert Browning: A Collection of Critical Essays*. Boston: Houghton Mifflin, 1966.

Duttman, Alexander Garcia. *The Gift of Language: Memory and Promise in Benjamin, Heidegger, and Rosenzweig*, trans. Arline Lyons. Syracuse, N.Y.: Syracuse University Press, 2000.

Eliot, George. *Adam Bede*. London: Penguin, 1985.
Eliot, T. S. "Hamlet and His Problems." In *The Sacred Wood*. London: Butler and Tanner Ltd., 1928, 95–103.
———. "*In Memoriam*." Reprinted in *Tennyson's Poetry*, ed. Robert W. Hill, Jr. New York: W. W. Norton, 1971, 613–20.
Erickson, Lee. *The Economy of Literary Form: English Literature and the Industrialization of Publishing, 1800–1850*. Baltimore, Md.: The Johns Hopkins University Press, 1996.
———. *Robert Browning: His Poetry and His Audiences*. Ithaca, N.Y.: Cornell University Press, 1984.
Ferguson, Harvie. *Melancholy and the Critique of Modernism: Søren Kierkegaard's Religious Psychology*. London: Routledge, 1995.
Ficino, Marsilio. *Commentary on Plato's Symposium on Love*, trans. Sears Jayne. Dallas, Tex.: Springs Publications, 1985.
Finn, Mary E. *Writing the Incommensurable: Kierkegaard, Rossetti, and Hopkins*. University Park, Pa.: The Pennsylvania State University Press, 1992.
Fitzgerald, Edward. *The Letters of Edward Fitzgerald*, ed. Albert McKinley Terhune and Annabelle Burdick Terhune. 4 vols. Princeton, N.J.: Princeton University Press, 1980.
———. *"The Rubaiyat of Omar Khayyam": A Critical Edition*, ed. Christopher Decker. Charlottesville: University Press of Virginia, 1997.
Fletcher, Angus. *Allegory: The Theory of a Symbolic Mode*. Ithaca, N.Y.: Cornell University Press, 1964.
Foucault, Michel. *The Order of Things: An Archaeology of the Human Sciences*. London: Tavistock, 1974.
Fraser, Hilary. *Beauty and Belief: Aesthetics and Religion in Victorian Literature*. Cambridge: Cambridge University Press, 1986.
Freud, Sigmund. *The Standard Edition of the Complete Psychological Works of Sigmund Freud*, ed. and trans. James Strachey. London: Hogarth Press, 1966–1974.
Gaskell, Elizabeth. *The Life of Charlotte Brontë*. London: J. M. Dent, 1971.
Gilbert, Sandra M., and Susan Gubar. *The Madwoman in the Attic: The Woman Artist and the Nineteenth-Century Literary Imagination*. New Haven, Conn.: Yale University Press, 1979.
Gottfried, Leon. *Matthew Arnold and the Romantics*. Lincoln: University of Nebraska Press, 1963.
Greenblatt, Stephen. *Shakespearean Negotiations: The Circulation of Social Energy in Renaissance England*. Berkeley: University of California Press, 1988.
Hair, Donald S. *Robert Browning's Language*. Toronto: University of Toronto Press, 1999.
Hallam, Arthur Henry. *The Writings of Arthur Hallam*, ed. T. H. Vail Motter. New York: Modern Language Association of America, 1943.
Hanssen, Beatrice. *Walter Benjamin's Other History*. Berkeley: University of California Press, 1998.
Harrison, Antony. *Victorian Poets and the Politics of Culture*. Charlottesville: University Press of Virginia, 1998.
Hazlitt, William. *The Complete Works of William Hazlitt*, ed. P. P. Howe. 21 vols. London: J. M. Dent, 1930–1934.

Herbert, Christopher. *Culture and Anomie: Ethnographic Imagination in the Nineteenth Century.* Chicago: The University of Chicago Press, 1991.

Homans, Margaret. *Royal Representations: Queen Victoria and British Culture, 1837–1876.* Chicago: The University of Chicago Press, 1998.

Hopkins, Gerard Manley. *Poems of Gerard Manley Hopkins,* ed. with notes by Robert Bridges. London: Oxford University Press, 1937.

———. *Selected Letters,* ed. Catherine Phillips. Oxford University Press, 1990.

Horne, R. H. *A New Spirit of the Age.* 1844; rpt. New York: Garland, 1986.

———. *The Sermons and Devotional Writings of Gerard Manley Hopkins,* ed. Christopher Devlin, S.J. London: Oxford University Press, 1959.

Irvine, William, and Park Honan. *The Book, the Ring, and the Poet.* New York: McGraw Hill, 1974.

Irving, Washington. *The Life and Voyages of Christopher Columbus,* ed. John Harmon McElroy. Boston: Twayne Publishers, 1981.

Jaffe, Audrey. *Scenes of Sympathy: Identity and Representation in Victorian Fiction.* Ithaca, N.Y.: Cornell University Press, 2000.

James, William. *The Varieties of Religious Experience: A Study in Human Nature.* London: Longmans, Green, and Co., 1906.

Jameson, Frederic. *The Political Unconscious: Narrative as Socially Symbolic Act.* Ithaca, N.Y.: Cornell University Press, 1981.

Jones, Sir William. *L'Histoire de Nader Chah.* In *The Works of Sir William Jones.* 13 vols. London: Stockdale, 1807, vol. 11.

Kaplan, Cora. "Introduction to *Aurora Leigh.*" In Cosslett, 69–82.

Keats, John. *The Poems of John Keats,* ed. Jack Stillinger. Cambridge, Mass.: Harvard University Press, 1978.

Kelley, Theresa. *Reinventing Allegory.* Cambridge: Cambridge University Press, 1997.

Kierkegaard, Søren. *The Concept of Dread,* trans. Walter Lowrie. Princeton, N.J.: Princeton University Press, 1957.

———. *Either/Or, Part One,* trans. Howard V. Hong and Edna H. Hong. Princeton, N.J.: Princeton University Press, 1988.

———. *Either/Or, Volume Two,* trans. Walter Lowrie, revised by Howard A. Johnson. Princeton, N.J.: Princeton University Press, 1972.

Klibansky, Raymond, Erwin Panofsky, and Fritz Saxl. *Saturn and Melancholy: Studies in the History of Natural Philosophy, Religion and Art.* London: Nelson, 1964.

Knoepflmacher, U. C. "Dover Revisited: The Wordsworthian Matrix in the Poetry of Matthew Arnold." *Victorian Poetry* 1 (1963): 17–26.

Knowles, James. "A Personal Reminiscence." Reprinted in *Tennyson's Poetry,* ed. Robert W. Hill, Jr. New York: W. W. Norton, 1971, 573–82.

Korg, Jacob. "A Reading of *Pippa Passes.*" *Victorian Poetry* 6 (1968): 5–19.

Kristeva, Julia. *Black Sun: Depression and Melancholia,* trans. Leon S. Roudiez. New York: Columbia University Press, 1989.

———. *Desire in Language: A Semiotic Appoach to Literature and Art,* ed. Leon S. Roudiez, trans. Thomas Gora, Alice Jardine, and Leon S. Roudiez. New York: Columbia University Press, 1980.

Lacan, Jacques. "Desire and the Interpretation of Desire in *Hamlet,*" trans. James Hulbert. *Yale French Studies* 55/56 (1977): 11–52.

Landon, Letitia. *The Golden Violet.* London: Fischer, Son & Co., 1837.

Landow, George. *Victorian Types: Victorian Shadows: Biblical Typology in Victorian Art, Literature, and Thought.* Boston: Routledge & Kegan Paul, 1980.

Langbaum, Robert. *The Poetry of Experience: The Dramatic Monologue in Modern Literary Tradition.* New York: W. W. Norton, 1957.

Leighton, Angela. "'Stirring a Dust of Figures': Elizabeth Barrett Browning and Love." In *Critical Essays on Elizabeth Barrett Browning,* ed. Sandra Donaldson. New York: G. K. Hall, 1999, 71–101.

———. *Victorian Women Poets: Writing against the Heart.* Charlottesville: University Press of Virginia, 1992.

Lepenies, Wolf. *Melancholy and Society,* trans. Jeremy Gaines and Doris Jones. Cambridge, Mass.: Harvard University Press, 1992.

Lewis, Linda M. *Elizabeth Barrett Browning's Spiritual Progress: Face to Face with God.* Columbia: University of Missouri Press, 1998.

———. "'Schooled by Sin': Reclaiming Eve in Elizabeth Barrett Browning's *A Drama of Exile.*" *Victorians Institute Journal* 22 (1994): 1–14.

Lootens, Tricia. *Lost Saints: Silence, Gender, and Victorian Literary Canonization.* Charlottesville: University Press of Virginia, 1996.

Lucas, John. *England and Englishness.* Iowa City: University of Iowa Press, 1990.

Ludlow, J. M. "Theories of Poetry and a New Poet." *North British Review, American Edition* 19 (180, August 1853): 296–344.

Macaulay, Thomas Babington. *Critical and Miscellaneous Essays.* 4 vols. New York: D. Appleton, 1880.

Martin, Loy D. *Browning's Dramatic Monologues and the Post-Romantic Subject.* Baltimore, Md.: The Johns Hopkins University Press, 1985.

Maudsley, Henry. *Heredity, Variation and Genius.* London: John Bale, Sons & Danielsson, 1908.

McCole, John. *Walter Benjamin and the Antinomies of Tradition.* Ithaca, N.Y.: Cornell University Press, 1993.

McGann, Jerome. "Dante Gabriel Rossetti and the Betrayal of Truth." *Victorian Poetry* 26 (1988): 339–61.

———. *The Poetics of Sensibility: A Revolution in Literary Style.* Oxford: Oxford University Press, 1996.

———. "Rossetti's Significant Details." *Victorian Poetry* 7 (1969): 41–54.

Mermin, Dorothy. *The Audience in the Poem: Five Victorian Poets.* New Brunswick, N.J.: Rutgers University Press, 1983.

———. *Elizabeth Barrett Browning: The Origins of a New Poetry.* Chicago: University of Chicago Press, 1989.

Mill, John Stuart. "Pauline." In Drew, 176–77.

———. "Tennyson's Poems" (1835). Reprinted in *Tennyson's Poetry,* ed. Robert W. Hill. New York: W. W. Norton, 1971.

———. "Thoughts on Poetry and Its Varieties." In *Victorian Literature: Prose,* ed. G. B. Tennyson and Donald J. Gray. New York: Macmillan, 1976.

Miller, J. Hillis. *The Disappearance of God: Five Nineteenth-Century Writers.* Cambridge, Mass.: Harvard University Press, 1963.

Miyoshi, Masao. *The Divided Self: A Perspective on the Literature of the Victorians.* New York: New York University Press, 1969.

Moretti, Franco. *Modern Epic: The World System from Goethe to García Márquez,* trans. Quintin Hoare. London: Verso, 1996.

Nicolson, Harold. *Tennyson: Aspects of His Life, Character, and Poetry.* Boston and New York: Houghton Mifflin, 1925.

Nietzsche, Friedrich. *The Birth of Tragedy* and *The Genealogy of Morals,* trans. Francis Golffing. New York: Doubleday, 1956.

Ong, Walter. *Orality and Literacy; The Technologizing of the Word.* New York: Methuen, 1982.

Paden, W. D. *Tennyson in Egypt: A Study of the Imagery in His Earlier Work.* Lawrence: University of Kansas Publications, 1942.

Pater, Walter. *Selected Writings of Walter Pater,* ed. Harold Bloom. New York: Signet, 1974.

Peacock, Thomas Love. *The Works of Thomas Love Peacock,* ed. H. F. B. Brett-Smith and C. E. Jones. 10 vols. New York: G. Wells, 1924–1934.

Pensky, Max. *Melancholy Dialectics.* Amherst: University of Massachusetts Press, 1993.

Poe, Edgar Allan. "The Philosophy of Composition." In *Complete Poems and Selected Essays,* ed. Richard Gray. London: J. M. Dent, 1993, 105–14.

Pound, Ezra. *The Cantos of Ezra Pound.* London: Faber and Faber, 1964.

Preyer, Robert. "Robert Browning: A Reading of the Early Narratives." In Drew, 157–76.

Radden, Jennifer. "Love and Loss in Freud's *Mourning and Melancholia:* A Rereading." In *The Analytic Freud: Philosophy and Psychoanalysis,* ed. Michael P. Levine. London: Routledge, 2000, 211–30.

———. *The Nature of Melancholy: From Aristotle to Kristeva.* Oxford: Oxford University Press, 2000.

Raymond, William O. *The Infinite Moment and Other Essays in Robert Browning.* Toronto: University of Toronto Press, 1950.

Reynolds, Matthew. *The Realms of Gold, 1830–1870: English Poetry in a Time of Nation Building.* Oxford: Oxford University Press, 2001.

Richardson, James. *Vanishing Lives: Style and Self in Tennyson, D. G. Rossetti, Swinburne, and Yeats.* Charlottesville: University Press of Virginia, 1988.

Ricks, Christopher. *Tennyson.* 2nd ed. London: Macmillan, 1989.

Riede, David G. *Dante Gabriel Rossetti and the Limits of Victorian Vision.* Ithaca, N.Y.: Cornell University Press, 1983.

———. *Dante Gabriel Rossetti Revisited.* New York: Twayne, 1992.

———. "Elizabeth Barrett: The Poet as Angel." *Victorian Poetry* 1994: 121–30.

———. "Elizabeth Barrett's Poetry of Exile." *Victorians Institute Journal* 27 (1999): 91–112.

———. "Genre and Poetic Authority in *Pippa Passes.*" In *Critical Essays on Robert Browning,* ed. Mary Ellis Gibson. New York: G. K. Hall, 1992, 186–201.

———. *Matthew Arnold and the Betrayal of Language.* Charlottesville: University Press of Virginia, 1988.

———. *Oracles and Hierophants: Constructions of Romantic Authority.* Ithaca, N.Y.: Cornell University Press, 1991.

Rossetti, Christina. *The Works of Christina Rossetti,* ed. Martin Corner. Ware, Hertfordshire: Wordsworth Editions, 1995.

Rossetti, Dante Gabriel. *Poems,* ed. Oswald Doughty. New York: Dutton, 1961.

Rowlinson, Matthew. "The Ideological Moment of Tennyson's 'Ulysses.'" *Victorian Poetry* 30 (1992): 265–76.

———. "Lyric." In *A Companion to Victorian Poetry*, ed. Richard Cronin, Alison Chapman, and Antony H. Harrison. Oxford: Blackwell, 2002, 59–79.

———. *Tennyson's Fixations: Psychoanalysis and the Topics of the Early Poetry*. Charlottesville: University of Virginia Press, 1994.

Ruskin, John. *The Works of John Ruskin*, ed. E. T. Cook and Alexander Wedderburn. 39 vols. London: George Allen, 1904.

Ryals, Clyde de L. *Becoming Browning: The Poems and Plays of Robert Browning, 1833–1846*. Columbus: The Ohio State University Press, 1983.

Rylance, Rick. *Victorian Psychology and British Culture, 1850–1880*. Oxford: Oxford University Press, 2000.

Said, Edward. *Culture and Imperialism*. New York: Random House, 1994.

———. *Orientalism*. New York: Random House, 1979.

Sandison, Alan. *The Wheel of Empire: A Study of the Imperial Ideal in Some Late Nineteenth- and Early Twentieth-Century Fiction*. London: Macmillan, 1967.

Schiesari, Juliana. *The Gendering of Melancholia: Feminism, Psychoanalysis, and the Symbolics of Loss in Renaissance Literature*. Ithaca, N.Y.: Cornell University Press, 1992.

Schiller, Friedrich. *On the Naïve and Sentimental in Literature*, trans. Helen Watanabe-O'Kelly. Manchester, UK: Carcanet Press, 1981.

Sedgwick, Eve. *Between Men: English Literature and Male Homosocial Desire*. New York: Columbia University Press, 1985.

Shaw, Marion. *Alfred Lord Tennyson*. New York: Simon and Schuster, 1988.

Shaw, W. David. *The Dialectical Temper: The Rhetorical Art of Robert Browning*. Ithaca, N.Y.: Cornell University Press, 1968.

———. *The Lucid Veil: Poetic Truth in the Victorian Age*. London: Athlone, 1987.

Shelley, Percy Bysshe. *Shelley's Poetry and Prose*, ed. Donald H. Reiman and Sharon Powers. New York: W. W. Norton, 1977.

Sheridan, Frances. *The History of Nourjahar*. Reprinted in *Oriental Tales*, ed. Robert L. Mack. Oxford: Oxford University Press, 1992.

Sinfield, Alan. *Alfred Tennyson*. London: Basil Blackwell, 1986.

Slinn, E. Warwick. *Browning and the Fictions of Identity*. Totowa, N.J.: Barnes and Noble, 1982.

———. *The Discourse of Self in Victorian Poetry*. Charlottesville: University Press of Virginia, 1991.

Stasny, John, ed. *Victorian Poetry: Essays from the Period*. New York: Garland, 1986.

Stein, Richard. *Victoria's Year: English Literature and Culture, 1837–1838*. New York: Oxford University Press, 1987.

Stone, Marjorie. *Elizabeth Barrett Browning*. New York: St. Martin's Press, 1995.

Sussman, Herbert. *Victorian Masculinities: Manhood and Masculine Poetics in Early Victorian Literature and Art*. Cambridge: Cambridge University Press, 1995.

Swinburne, Algernon. *The Swinburne Letters*, ed. Cecil Y. Lang. 6 vols. New Haven, Conn.: Yale University Press, 1959–1962.

Taylor, Charles. *Sources of the Self: The Making of the Modern Identity*. Cambridge, Mass.: Harvard University Press, 1989.

Taylor, Jenny Bourne. Review of *Victorian Psychology and British Culture* by Rick Rylance. *Victorian Studies* 45 (2003): 196–98.

Tennyson, Alfred. *The Letters of Alfred Lord Tennyson*, ed. Cecil Y. Lang and Edgar F. Shannon, Jr. 3 vols. Cambridge, Mass.: Harvard University Press, 1981–.
———. *The Poems of Tennyson*, ed. Christopher Ricks. 3 vols. Berkeley: University of California Press, 1987.
Tennyson, Hallam. *Alfred Lord Tennyson: A Memoir by His Son*. 2 vols. 1897; rpt. New York: Greenwood Press, 1969.
Thomas, Ronald R. *Dreams of Authority: Freud and the Fictions of the Unconscious*. Ithaca, N.Y.: Cornell University Press, 1990.
Thomson, James. "The City of Dreadful Night." In *Poetry of the Victorian Period*, ed. Jerome Hamilton Buckley. Glenview, Ill.: Scott, Foresman and Company, 1965: 585–99.
Tucker, Herbert F. *Browning's Beginnings: The Art of Disclosure*. Minneapolis: University of Minnesota Press, 1980.
———. *Tennyson and the Doom of Romanticism*. Cambridge, Mass.: Harvard University Press, 1988.
Wordsworth, William. Lyrical Ballads *and Other Poems*, ed. James Butler and Karen Green. Ithaca, N.Y.: Cornell University Press, 1992.
———. *The Prose Works*. 3 vols., ed. W. J. B. Owen and Jane Worthington Smyser. Oxford: Oxford University Press, 1974.

Index

Abraham, Nicholas, 20–21
Adams, James Eli, 209
Adams, David, 204
Adorno, Theodor, 10, 13–14, 24, 27–28, 34, 41, 45, 49, 205–6
Aeschylus, 111
Agamben, Giorgio, 31, 122
Alexander, Edward, 16
Althusser, Louis, 7
Anacreon, 193,
Arata, Stephen, 12
Aristotle, 91, 122, 203
Armstrong, Isobel, 17, 44, 53, 57, 70, 75–76, 93, 97–98, 208
Arnold, Matthew, 1, 2, 6, 13, 16, 21, 33, 34, 76, 139, 150, 155, 189, 194, 204; "The Buried Life," 14–15, 20, 33, 153; *Empedocles on "Etna*, 2–3, 33, 83, 142, 203; "Memorial Verses," 2, 17; "Preface" to *Poems*, 2, 33; "The Scholar Gypsy," 33, 194; "Stanzas from the Grande Chartreuse," 2–3, 33, 139; "Stanzas in Memory of the Author of Obermann," 2; "Switzerland," 208; "Thyrsis," 33
Aytoun, W. E., 119

Bagehot, Walter, 11, 85, 153–54, 176, 208
Baring, Rosa, 76
Barthes, Roland, 125
Basselin, Olivier, 193
Batten, Guinn, 88

Baudelaire, Charles, 13, 18, 145; *Les Fleurs du Mal*, 11
Beethoven, Ludwig, 19
Benjamin, Walter, 22–27, 29–35, 37, 40, 46, 48, 76, 83, 89, 145, 164, 185; *Arcades*, 11, 27, 205, 206; "On Language as Such and on the Language of Man," 86; "On Some Motifs in Baudelaire," 13; *The Origin of German Tragic Drama*, 11, 29, 153, 156–57, 176, 196–197, 204
Benson, A. C., 189
Bloom, Harold, 113, 155–56
Bradley, A. C., 15–16, 82–83
Bronfen, Elizabeth, 53–54, 102, 204
Brontë, Charlotte, 119; *Villette*, 20
Brontë, Emily, *Wuthering Heights*, 20, 52
Browne, Sir Thomas, 206
Browning, Elizabeth Barrett, 1, 11, 24, 34, 38, 91–133, 145, 147, 150, 167, 174, 179, 183, 188, 207; *Aurora Leigh*, 81, 120, 131–33; *Casa Guidi Windows*, 120; "The Cry of the Children," 123; "The Dead Pan," 109; "The Deserted Garden," 207; "A Drama of Exile," 112–19; *The English Poets*, 106–7; *An Essay on Mind*, 103–4; "Felicia Hemans," 104–5; *The Greek Christian Poets*, 106–8; "Grief," 110; "Hector in the Garden," 207; "Insufficiency,"

110–11; *Last Poems,* 131; "The Lost Bower," 207; "Perplexed Music," 110; *Poems* (1844), 107–9, 112, 120; *Poems before Congress,* 119–20, 131; "The Poet's Vow," 99–102; "The Romaunt of the Page," 99; *The Seraphim,* 102–3, 107, 117; *The Seraphim and Other Poems,* 106, 110; *Sonnets from the Portuguese,* 40, 120–31, 192, 208, "The Soul's Expression," 110, 130; "To George Sand: A Desire," 120, "To George Sand: A Recognition," 120; "A Vision of Poets," 111; "Victoria's Tears," 98–99; "The Young Queen," 98

Browning, Robert, 1, 2, 10, 12, 16, 33, 34, 38, 88, 92, 124, 129, 131, 134–87, 188; "Abt Vogler," 146, 171–72, 175, 180; "Andrea del Sarto," 135, 165, 168–71, 194; *Bells and Pomegranates,* 12; "The Bishop Orders His Tomb at St. Praxed's Church," 163; "Bishop Blougram's Apology," 154; *A Blot in the Scutcheon,* 154; "By the Fireside," 174–77; "Childe Roland to the Dark Tower Came," 142, 155–57, 169; "A Death in the Desert," 146; *Dramatic Lyrics,* 157, 158, 163; *Dramatic Romances and Lyrics,* 157, 163; *Dramatis Personae,* 157, 171; *Fifine at the Fair,* 154, 183; "Fra Lippo Lippi," 105, 184; "House," 147; "How It Strikes a Contemporary," 154; "Johannes Agricola in Meditation," 157–60, 170; "The Last Ride Together," 134; "The Lost leader," 163; "Master Hugues of Saxe-Gotha," 172–73; "Mesmerism," 186; "Mr. Sludge, the Medium," 154, 183, 186; "My Last Duchess," 163–64, 185; "One Word More," 173; *Paracelsus,* 40, 138–46, 148, 151, 155, 171, 176, 181–83, 192, 199; *Parleyings with Certain People of Importance in Their Day,* 175; *Pauline,* 2, 40, 135–39, 155, 192; "Pictor Ignotus," 163, 165; "The Pied Piper of Hamelin," 163; *Pippa Passes,* 146, 148, 159, 183, 208; "Porphyria's Lover," 157–62, 164, 195; *Prince Hohenstiel-Schwangau,* 183; "Rabbi Ben Ezra," 146, 170, 176–77; *The Ring and the Book,* 154, 178–87; "Saul," 147, 151, 167, 171; *Sordello,* 146, 148–53, 162, 183; "A Toccatta of Galuppi," 134, 173, 181; "Two in the Campagna," 177–78, 192

Buckley, Jerome Hamilton, 63
Buck-Morss, Susan, 206
Burke, Edmund, 64, 97
Burton, Robert, *The Anatomy of Melancholy,* 4, 61
Butler, Judith, 7, 9–10, 13, 160
Byron, George Gordon, Lord, 2, 10, 18, 25, 35, 93, 94, 96, 97, 99–101, 108, 111, 114, 131, 145, 207; *Cain,* 118; *Childe Harold's Pilgrimage,* 3, 37, 38, 65; *Manfred,* 3, 34, 38, 83, 100, 118, 140; "Prometheus," 115

Campbell, Matthew, 44, 51, 53, 58
Carlyle, Thomas, 2, 3, 6, 8, 11–12, 22, 24, 30, 34, 42, 58, 63, 108, 131, 135, 171, 188, 205; on "cash nexus," 88, 169; on "piercing imagination," 25–27, 43, 78, 141, 153, 204; *Sartor Resartus,* 2, 11, 26, 138–39, 143, 173
character, 6–9, 16, 42, 43, 44, 61, 69, 76
Chaucer, Geoffrey, *The Legend of Good Women,* 72
Chesterton, G. K., 134, 136, 139, 154, 168
Chorley, Henry, 120
Christ, Carol, 51–52, 86
Clough, Arthur Hugh, 16
Coleridge, Samuel Taylor, 1, 5, 11, 82, 95–96, 108, 111, 117, 174, 200; *Biographia Literaria,* 1, 203;

Index

"Dejection: An Ode," 1; "The Eolian Harp," 24; "Kubla Khan," 34–37, 45, 54, 73, 156, 172; "The Rime of the Ancient Mariner," 100; *The Statesman's Manual*," 21–24, 166–67
commodity culture, 10–13, 82, 87–88, 94, 99, 128–29, 157, 162–65, 169, 188
Cooper, Helen, 98, 128, 204
Corngold, Stanley, 33, 205
courtly love, 82, 86, 121–31, 189–90
Cowell, E. B., 189
Croker, John Wilson, 57
Culler, A. Dwight, 63, 70, 75, 85, 87

Dante Alighieri, 61, 152
David, Deirdre, 94–95, 116
Davis, Walter, 204
Decker, Christopher, 194, 209
DeMan, Paul, 13, 27–29, 32–33, 34, 125, 197, 205
Derrida, Jacques, 20–21
Descartes, René, 147
Devane, William Clyde, 142, 179
Dickens, Charles: "A Christmas Carol," 4; *Our Mutual Friend*, 22, 23, 31; *A Tale of Two Cities*, 20
Dilthey, Wilhelm, 140
Disraeli, Benjamin, 189
Dürer, Albrecht, 21
Durkheim, Emile, 141, 179
Douglas-Fairhurst, Robert, 206
Duttman, Alexander, Garcia, 30

Eliot, George, *Adam Bede*, 20
Eliot, T. S., 41–43, 45, 203
Erickson, Lee, 11, 164

Faber, Frederick William, 207
Ferguson, Harvie, 78
Ferrier, J. F., 53
Ficino, Marsilius, 38, 122–23, 126, 127, 137, 141
Finden's Tableaux of the Affections, 99
Fitzgerald, Edward, 30, 88, 188–202; "The Meadows in Spring," 188; *Sálámán and Absál*, 40, 189–93;

The Rubaiyat of Omar Khayyam, 53, 188, 193–98
Fliess, Wilhelm, 5
Foucault, Michel, 9, 158
Freud, Sigmund, 4–5, 7, 9, 20, 34, 52, 85, 91–92, 93, 132, 204, 206; *Civilization and its Discontents*, 7, 90; "Mourning and Melancholia," 5–6, 14, 15, 35, 191
Gladstone, William Ewart, 90
Goethe, Johann Wolfgang von, 2, 22, 33, 131; *Faust*, 3, 15–16, 22, 83, 139–40
Greenblatt, Stephen, 70, 164

Hair, Donald, 143, 174–75, 181–82
Hallam, Arthur Henry, 3, 6, 9, 46–48, 52, 59, 70, 78, 92, 193; "On Some of the Characteristics of Modern Poetry," 10, 17–20, 28, 41–42, 45, 62–64; "On Sympathy," 63, 136, 144
Hanssen, Beatrice, 10, 58
Harrison, Antony, 93
Hegel, Georg Wilhelm Friedrich, 6, 36, 141, 160, 206
Hemans, Felicia, 94, 104
Herbert, Christopher, 141, 204
Herbert, Henry, *Marmaduke Wyvil*, 189
higher criticism, 5
Homer, 57, 61, 111
Hopkins, Gerard Manley, 21, 134, 207; "No Worst There Is None," 14–15
Horne, Richard Hengist, *Orion*, 12

Irving, Washington, *Life and Voyages of Christopher Columbus*, 65–66, 69

Jaffe, Audrey, 18
James, William, 4, 21, 23, 31
Jameson, Fredric, 209
Jámí, 189
Jones, Sir William, 66, 71, 72
journalism, 11–13

Kant, Immanuel, 6, 14, 204

Kaplan, Cora, 123
Keble, John, 95–96, 207
Keats, John, 2, 18, 25, 35, 41, 64, 65, 193, 200; *Endymion,* 34, 37, 46, 76, 79, 80, 122, 189–92; "The Eve of St. Agnes," 75; "The Fall of Hyperion," 111; "Ode on Melancholy," 4, 19; "Ode to a Nightingale," 110; "On First Looking into Chapman's Homer," 63, 65–66; "To Autumn," 50
Kelley, Teresa, 22, 36, 153, 206
Kenyon, John, 119
Kierkegaard, Søren, 13, 27, 33, 139, 144, 147, 156; *The Concept of Dread,* 138, 154; *Either/Or,* 49, 138, 179–80; *The Sickness unto Death,* 135, 136
Killham, John, 75
Kinglake, Alexander, *Eothen,* 189
Kingsley, Charles, *Alton Locke,* 193
Klibansky, Raymond, 16
Kofman, Sarah, 53
Kristeva, Julia, 3, 42–43, 45, 206

Lacan, Jacques, 3, 35, 40, 53, 85, 92, 93, 97
Langbaum, Robert, 58, 60, 146, 155, 158, 171
Landon, Letitia (L. E. L), 105, 207; "The Golden Violet," 91
Leighton, Angela, 96, 123–25, 128
Lepenies, Wolf, 140
Locke, John, 146–48
Lootens, Tricia, 120–21, 123
Lowrie, Walter, 135, 144
Lucas, John, 82, 206
Lucretius, 193
Ludlow, J. M., 33, 76, 142
Lukacs, Georg, 10
Lyell, Charles, 206
Lyotard, Jean François, 3

McGann, Jerome, 12, 94
Martin, Loy, 134, 173
Marx, Karl, 4, 8, 22, 58, 88, 169
Maudsley, Henry, 4–5, 7, 14, 204
Meredith, William, 139

Mermin, Dorothy, 95, 97, 113, 121, 128, 186
Mill, John Stuart, 2, 19, 50, 92, 136
Milnes, Monckton, 189
Milton, John, 61, 64; "Il Penseroso," 4; *Paradise Lost,* 113
Mitford, Mary Russell, 207
Miyoshi, Masao, 16, 39
Morchen, Hermann, 28
Moretti, Franco, 22
Morris, William, 12, 19, 89; "The Defence of Guenevere," 199; "Concerning Geffray Teste Noire," 22, 81
Moxon, Edward, 11

narcissism, 6, 35, 37–38, 122, 123, 142
Newman, John Henry, 95–96, 207
Nicolson, Harold, 41
Nietzsche, Friedrich, 9, 125, 160, 204; *The Genealogy of Morals,* 9, 155
nostalgia, 6, 48, 174–75, 178

Ong, Walter, 204
Orientalism, 46, 65–75, 76–78, 87–90, 143–44, 189, 192, 197, 201

Paden, W. D., 66
Panofsky, Erwin, 16, 203
Pater, Walter, 14, 39, 56, 57, 89, 150, 158, 171, 197, 199–201
Pensky, Max, 134, 164, 206
Plato, 92
Poe, Edgar Allan, 19, 53, 54, 105–6; "The Raven," 19–20
Pound, Ezra, 51, 148
Preyer, Robert, 142
Proust, Marcel, 13

Quaritch, Bernard, 197–98
Quarles, Francis, *Emblemes,* 181

Radden, Jennifer, 5
Reynolds, Matthew, 206
Richardson, James, 50–51

Ricks, Christopher, 42, 63, 73, 80, 84–85
Rilke, Rainer Maria, 28
Rossetti, Christina, "Monna Innominata," 121–22, 135, 172
Rossetti, Dante Gabriel, 12, 19, 39–40, 89, 165, 167, 198, 206; "The Blessed Damozel," 39; *The House of Life*, 40; "My Sister's Sleep," 52; "The Woodspurge," 39–40, 52, 176
Rowlinson, Matthew, 45–46, 61–62, 204
Ruskin, John, 3, 52, 138, 165–66, 168–69; "imagination penetrative," 22–24, 26, 43, 141, 153, 195, 197; *Fors Clavigera*, 12; pathetic fallacy, 85, 156

Said, Edward, 65, 74
Sand, George, 120
Sandys, George, 73
Savary, M., *Letters on Egypt*, 66, 72
Saxl, Fritz, 16, 203
Schiesarii, Juliana, 3–4, 35, 91, 140, 206
Schiller, Friedrich, 2, 8, *On the Naïve and Sentimental in Literature*, 2–3
Schlegel, Friedrich, 179–80
Schleiermacher, Friedrich, 179–80
Sedgwick, Eve, 75
Sennett, Richard, 18
Shakespeare, William, 61, 64, 82; *Antony and Cleopatra*, 72; *Hamlet*, 2, 3, 4, 22–23, 25, 31, 33, 34, 35, 40, 59, 82–83, 86, 108, 140, 195–96, 203; *King Lear*, 156; *Othello*, 127; *The Tempest*, 70
Shaw, W. David, 138, 147, 155, 177–79, 205, 208
Shelley, Percy Bysshe, 2, 18, 19, 25, 35, 41, 64, 92, 93, 111, 193; *Alastor*, 34, 37–38, 76, 78, 80, 122, 136, 137, 142, 145, 155, 189, 191, 192; "Julian and Maddalo," 109; "Lift Not the Painted Veil," 148; *Prometheus Unbound*, 118, 205; "To a Skylark," 205
Shelley, Mary, *Frankenstein*, 139
Silverman, Kaja, 206
Simeon, Sir John, 79
Sinfield, Alan, 65–66, 68
Slinn, E. Warwick, 164, 184, 209
Smiles, Samuel, 7
Smith, Adam, 88
Smith, Alexander, 142
Spenser, Edmund, 106
Stein, Richard, 158
Stevens, Wallace, 200
Stevenson, Robert Louis, 12; "The Strange Case of Dr. Jekyll and Mr. Hyde," 10
Stone, Marjorie, 108, 111
Swinburne, Algernon, 19, 78, 89, 197–98; "Laus Veneris," 198–99; *Poems and Ballads*, 198, 209

Taylor, Charles, 146–48
Taylor, Jenny Bourne, 203
Tennyson, Alfred, 2, 8–9, 10, 11, 12, 18, 19, 28, 34, 38, 41–90, 150, 165, 189, 193, 206; "Akbar's Dream," 75; "Anacaona," 69–70; "Armageddon," 44, 45, 56, 66–67; "A Dream of Fair Women," 65, 72–74; "The Epic," 45; "The Expedition of Nadir Shah into Hindostan," 71; "Fatima," 65, 71–72; "The Hesperides," 68, 70; *Idylls of the King*, 82, 89–90; *In Memoriam*, 46–47, 75–76; "The Lady of Shalott," 14, 20, 49, 53–54, 70, 73, 85, 91, 101; "Locksley Hall," 8, 68–70, 78, 79, 87, 190; "The Lotos-Eaters," 54–58, 60, 61, 68, 70, 71, 134; "Mariana," 14, 24, 49–52, 54, 55, 56, 63, 65, 72, 85, 91, 92, 93, 101, 123–24, 134, 141, 200; *Maud*, 16, 33, 52, 75–90, 142, 145, 156, 192; "On Sublimity," 66; "Oriana," 20; "The Palace of Art," 14, 45, 49, 52–54, 65, 66, 72–73, 85, 150, 192, 200; "Persia," 70; *The Princess*, 46, 75; "Recollections of the

Arabian Nights," 74–75, 80–81; "Supposed Confessions of a Second-Rate Sensitive Mind," 6, 54; "Tears, Idle Tears," 46–49, 59; "Timbuctoo," 67; "Tithonus," 54; "Ulysses," 8, 54, 58–62, 68, 70
Tennyson, Frederick, 189
Thackeray, William Makepeace, 189, 193
Theocritus, 125
Thomas, Ronald, 10
Thomson, James, "The City of Dreadful Night," 4, 17–18, 21, 23, 42
Torok, Maria, 20–21, 205
Trench, Richard Chenevix, 192
Tucker, Herbert, 43–44, 51, 57, 80, 84, 87, 135, 139, 148, 170, 173, 208, 209

Ulloa, Antonio de, *A Voyage to South America*, 66
Vasari, Giorgio, 168
Warburton, Eliot, *The Crescent and the Cross*, 189
Whitman, Walt, 86
Wilde, Oscar, 200–201; *The Picture of Dorian Gray*, 200
Wilson, John, 57
Winter, Peter, 19
Woolf, Virginia, 103
Wordsworth, William, 1, 2, 5, 6, 13, 14, 17, 18, 22, 29, 35, 63, 95–96, 108, 109, 111, 137; "Elegiac Stanzas," 34, 47; "Lines Written in Early Spring," 1, 203; "Ode: Intimations of Immortality," 20; *The Recluse*, 25; "Tintern Abbey," 48

www.ingramcontent.com/pod-product-compliance
Lightning Source LLC
Chambersburg PA
CBHW030136240426
43672CB00005B/143